MARRANO POETS OF THE SEVENTEENTH CENTURY

T0313402

THE LITTMAN LIBRARY OF
JEWISH CIVILIZATION

Dedicated to the memory of
LOUIS THOMAS SIDNEY LITTMAN
*who founded the Littman Library for the love of God
and as an act of charity in memory of his father*
JOSEPH AARON LITTMAN
and to the memory of
ROBERT JOSEPH LITTMAN
who continued what his father Louis had begun

יהא זכרם ברוך

'*Get wisdom, get understanding:
Forsake her not and she shall preserve thee*'

PROV. 4: 5

*The Littman Library of Jewish Civilization is a registered UK charity
Registered charity no.* 1000784

Marrano Poets of the Seventeenth Century

◆

An Anthology of the Poetry of
João Pinto Delgado, Antonio Enríquez Gómez
and
Miguel de Barrios

◆

Edited and translated by
TIMOTHY OELMAN

London
The Littman Library of Jewish Civilization
in association with Liverpool University Press

The Littman Library of Jewish Civilization
Registered office: 4th floor, 7–10 Chandos Street, London W1G 9DQ

in association with Liverpool University Press
4 Cambridge Street, Liverpool L69 7ZU, UK
www.liverpooluniversitypress.co.uk/littman

Managing Editor: Connie Webber

Distributed in North America by
Oxford University Press Inc., 198 Madison Avenue,
New York, NY 10016, USA

First published 1982 by Associated University Presses, Inc.,
on behalf of the Littman Library of Jewish Civilization
First issued in paperback 2007

Catalogue records for this book are available from the
British Library and the Library of Congress

ISBN 978–1–904113–69–0

Printed and bound in Great Britain by
CPI Group (UK) Ltd., Croydon, CR0 4YY

For Lynne

Contents

List of Illustrations

All plates reproduced by permission of the British Library, London.

Acknowledgments

I would like to thank the following for their help in the preparation of this volume, without which it would not have been possible: Dr. A. D. H. Fishlock of London (concerning João Pinto Delgado), Señor A. M. García of University College, London (Miguel de Barrios); the directors and staffs of the Bodleian Library, Oxford, the British Library Reference Division, London, the Portugees Israelitisch Seminarium *Etz Haim*, Amsterdam, and the University of London Library, Senate House, London. I should also like to thank Mrs. María S. Elliott for her help in checking the Spanish texts, and especially my wife concerning the translations.

Introduction

The story of the Marranos, the crypto-Jews of the Iberian Penin-
sula, with its drama and its heroism, has long been a source of
fascination for Jews interested in their heritage and for all those
concerned with the struggle for freedom of conscience against
authoritarianism. The historical, religious, and even sociological
aspects of the phenomenon of Marranism have been the object
of extensive and authoritative studies in the past. One thinks of
Cecil Roth's classic *A History of the Marranos* and more re-
cently Julio Caro Baroja's *Los Judíos en la España moderna y
contemporánea*. The literary aspects have received relatively
little serious attention or if they have been treated, have been the
subject of contentious theorizing, as in the case of Américo
Castro's *La realidad histórica de España*. Academic research
has now expanded greatly, but little of its findings has reached
the general reader. Above all, there has been a need to develop a
balanced, overall view of Marrano literature in both its
Spanish-Christian and Jewish contexts.[1]

The purpose of this volume is therefore twofold: to present the
works of three poets of Marrano origin, João Pinto Delgado,
Antonio Enríquez Gómez, and Miguel de Barrios, together with
translations into English, and secondly, in the introductory
essay and in the notes to the poems, to attempt to outline and
correlate both the Hispanic and the Jewish cultural elements at
play in the works of poets who, though diverse in temperament,
in style, and in personal history, all share a Spanish Christian
upbringing with Jewish beliefs, identity, and aspirations.

In undertaking this twofold task questions of terminology and
definition immediately arise. The first essential is to be clear as
to who it is that we are concerned with. Generally, of course, it
will be understood that we are talking about Jewish converts to
Christianity in Spain (and Portugal) and their descendants.
However, the most common term for them, *Marrano*, presents
problems, not least because in Modern Castilian it has the
meaning of "pig." The origin of the word is itself somewhat

13

obscure: it has been variously derived from the anathema of the New Testament (1 Corinthians 16:22), "Maran atha"; the Arabic *máhram*, "something forbidden," hence pork and by inversion those that refuse it; or *marrar*, a Castilian word meaning "to default."[2] Whatever the truth of the matter, its predominantly pejorative connotations have led some scholars in recent times to replace the term with the word *converso*.[3] But the word *converso* simply means "convert," usually to Christianity from Judaism, and by extension the descendants of such a convert. The use of *converso* for *marrano* is thus open to the serious objection that it does not and, strictly, cannot indicate the actual religious commitment of the individual or individuals concerned, and this is an essential requirement in any study where it is necessary to distinguish between different religious attitudes or degrees of commitment. To be sure, in the sixteenth and seventeenth centuries *converso*, like *cristiano nuevo* ("New Christian") and later *portugués* ("Portuguese"), tended to be used by the Christian population for "Jew," but it would seem unwise to follow usage which was inspired by malice, if not by outright anti-Semitism. It therefore seems best to reserve the term *converso* for the generality of converts from Judaism to Christianity and their descendants.[4] On the other hand, despite the problems of its associations, *marrano* can be justifiably maintained to indicate the committed judaizer or crypto-Jew. If we make the distinction, then we shall be clear in our discussions as to whether in a given instance the reference is to the general social group or to the particular judaizing minority among it.[5]

This is important for another reason, namely that in presenting the Marrano poets and their works, we have not included poets who, though they may have been of *converso* stock, did not consider themselves Jewish in any way. One may point to the example of Saint Teresa of Ávila, whose paternal grandfather was condemned by the Inquisition to do public penance for relapsing into Judaism. Her mysticism may in some indirect way be attributable to her *converso* origins (as escapism from the harassed life of the New Christian?), but such theories are highly speculative and there is no evidence in her literary work or other expressions of opinion which would justify her inclusion among crypto-Jewish poets.[6] The same applies to other poets, such as Jorge de Montemayor and Fray Luis de León, whose poetry would splendidly grace any anthology but who cannot be regarded as Jewish or Marrano in our definition.

Finally, we may note that our attention in this work is focused on the seventeenth century. The reason for this is as follows. Firstly and quite simply, the best poets are to be found in this latter period, in which Spain's Golden Age of literature and art was at its height and which coincided with the apogee of her imperial and economic power. This was the era of Lope de Vega and Pedro Calderón de la Barca, of El Greco and Velázquez. It is not surprising therefore to find Marrano poets taking their place in the literary splendor of the period. Secondly, the character of the Marrano takes on a special quality in this period which is of especial significance. If we consider the early generations of *conversos* as relatively well informed in matters of Judaism and those crypto-Jews among them (the majority at that stage) as practitioners of authentic Judaism, one may draw a distinction between them and later generations whose knowledge was less exact and their practice less normative. The religion of the latter, influenced by Christianity and ignorance, may be truly dubbed "Marranism," rather than Judaism, and a Marrano defined as one who practices this debased form of the faith. Theologically, the phenomenon of Marranism can be dated from the middle of the sixteenth century forward. With it comes the emergence of what we may now call the archetypal Marrano poet—we cannot call him Jewish or strictly a convert—who is in all other respects Spanish but who is feeling his way towards Judaism and his Jewish roots and covertly or overtly expressing his Jewish identification in his verse. It is this situation and experience which lends an added dimension to the poetic literature of the Marranos and renders it worthy of our attention.

The Origins of the Marranos

The history of the Marranos begins in 1391 with the forcible conversion of the Jews in Seville and the anti-Jewish riots which accompanied them, instigated by the Archdeacon of Ecija, Ferrán Martínez. What happened in Seville soon found itself repeated all over Spain in almost every town where Jews lived. It has been estimated that approximately one third of the total Jewish population of Spain died at the hands of the mob rather than submit to baptism, while one third converted to Christianity and a third survived as the remnant of the Jewish community.[7] Further conversions were effected as a result of Saint Vicente

Ferrer's campaign of sermon and harangue against the Jews of Castile and as the outcome of the Valladolid Laws of Restriction of 1412 and the Tortosa disputation of 1413–14, in which the apostate Jeronimo de Santa Fe (Joshua de Lorca before his conversion) was appointed by the anti-Pope Benedict XIII to browbeat the leaders of the Jews of Aragon. The resultant situation was one in which there existed within the Christian community a large body of converts (conversos) whose conversion was often merely a bowing to inevitable circumstances and whose allegiance to Christianity was uncertain.

Suspicion that the conversos were indeed secret Jews became rife among both the general populace and the Church, and an extraordinary atmosphere developed in Spanish society of ambivalence and mistrust toward those whom it had willed to join the main body of the society but whom it would neither trust nor leave alone, of discrimination and obsession with ancestral purity that was to cause division and vitiate attitudes and behavior for centuries to come. The prejudice against the conversos, founded no doubt on antipathy towards Jews per se and fueled by jealousy of the positions to which many conversos rose once free of the shackles imposed on Jews, led to the declaration of the first "statutes of blood," the estatutos de limpieza de sangre.[8] These were ordinances designed to exclude conversos from obtaining office in various walks of life. The first of these was the sentencia estatuto (written judgment) issued at the end of the trial of fourteen prominent New Christians in Toledo in 1449 for unlawfully holding offices open only to those of Christian faith. The trial was held against the background of anti-Jewish riots and popular resentment against converso tax-gatherers,[9] and the verdict deprived the accused of the high offices they held. The implication of the judgment that conversos were not proper Christians was uncanonical and was condemned as heretical, not only by such as Alonso de Cartagena in his Defensorium, but by the Pope, Nicholas V, in his Bulls of 1449 and 1451. However, it was the spirit of the heresy rather than that of papal judgment which was to triumph in Spain. In following years the practice of issuing statutes of blood spread to the religious orders (in particular the Hieronymites and Franciscans), the chapters of cathedrals and chapels, the military orders, the universities, the guilds and professions, the government of regions, chartered towns and municipalities, and the tribunals (including eventually those of the Inquisition).[10]

It was an inevitable consequence of the statutes that there should be established a machinery of inquiry which would seek to discover whether a candidate for, or holder of, office was of *converso* origin. Such a machinery of inquiry—that is to say an "inquisition"—was established by Henry IV (of Castile) under the Franciscan Fray Alonso de Oropesa to look into the renewed conflict between Old and New Christians in Toledo in the 1460s, and one may properly regard this as the direct precedent for the institution of the Inquisition itself. The first commission of the Inquisition, composed of two Dominican friars, was established in 1480 (on the authority of a Papal Bull, dated 1 November 1478) to inquire into the charge of blasphemy brought against Marranos and Jews found celebrating Passover together in Seville in 1477 (their celebration was taken to be a conspiracy to defame the Passion of Jesus in what was coincidentally Holy Week). The first *auto de fe* (or public statement of crimes, and punishment after trial by inquisition) followed in February 1481, and a papal brief of 1482 appointed seven other inquisitors to the tribunal of Seville, including the notorious Tomás de Torquemada. Other tribunals were set up shortly in Jaén, Ciudad Real, Córdoba, Segovia, and Toledo (there were eventually to be fifteen tribunals in all) and in 1483 a Supreme Council, the *Suprema,* was created to oversee their activities.

There is little need here to discuss in detail the workings of the Inquisition.[11] However, it is worth reminding ourselves what sort of organism this was. The Inquisition as an institution was not unique to Spain, though it took on a particular character and growth there; it was the traditional means whereby the Church suppressed heresy. It did not pursue Jews, only *conversos* who were suspected of crypto-Jewish practices. It was a legalistic body which was not in purpose anti-Semitic, though it may be suspected that its officers were not immune to the prejudices of society at large. Its victims were not only *conversos,* even if these were the majority. Its purpose was to seek out heresy and punish it wherever it came from. Its methods, however, may be questioned; above all its secrecy, the suppression of names of accusers and even of specific charges, the lack of means for ver ifying evidence or bringing to light false accusation (there was no cross-examination of witnesses, for example), the use of torture to exact confession of guilt. It was a machine which, for all its scrupulous noting of evidence (to which we owe for the most part our knowledge of its methods and of crypto-Jewish life in

Spain), could be set in motion on the merest suspicion or a malicious accusation[12] and could bring about the death or social undoing of the innocent as well as of those Marranos who were true upholders of their faith and seekers after martyrdom.[13] To expect religious toleration or liberal justice at that period in history is unreasonable, but we may criticize the Inquisition finally for being negativistic and divisive, unjust and contrary to the ideals of the Christianity it sought to uphold. It may even be said to have fostered among *conversos* the very heresy of crypto-Judaism which it sought to suppress.

The same atmosphere of anti-*converso* suspicion which brought about the statutes of blood and the establishment of the Inquisition made it inevitable also that the remaining Jews in Spain should be expelled on the grounds that they were an encouragement to the converts to backslide into Judaism. The expulsion took place in the year 1492: the year which marked the culmination of centuries of crusade by the Christian kingdoms of Spain against the Arabs with the fall of Granada. The prime motivation behind the Reconquest was religious, and the founding of the united kingdom of Spain (under Isabel of Castile and Fernando II of Aragon) can be said to have been based on a spirit of militant Christian zeal. The promise of religious toleration held out to the Moslems of Granada by the treaty of surrender could not possibly be kept, and Jews were to share the same fate of expulsion as those other unbelievers.[14] In the case of the Jews the unforeseen consequence of this act was to make the *converso* problem more inextricable: those Jews who did not wish to leave converted, and in doing so accentuated the problem of distinguishing true convert from false. Statutes of blood proliferated, now with papal blessing (following Pope Alexander VI's brief to the Hieronymite Order in 1495) and tacitly agreed to by the Catholic Monarchs. But now, in addition, there was the Inquisition to make inquiry and ruthlessly pursue the heresy of crypto-Judaism.

Crypto-Jews under the Regime of the Inquisition

During the first period of the existence of the Inquisition, up to the middle of the sixteenth century, the judaizing *conversos,* the Marranos, found it difficult to comprehend the change in their situation and to appreciate the ruthlessness of the Inquisition.

This is what Caro Baroja terms the period of *inadaptación,* the inability to adapt which led judaizers to criticize the Inquisition openly and to proclaim aloud their Jewish faith.[15] Not surprisingly, most of the cases of this type which are recorded (in Inquisitional records) concern older people, rather than the young, though there were many examples of the latter living in the past, as it were, denouncing for instance their baptism and declining to have crucifixes in their possession. A common feature of declarations of faith made by accused judaizers is a mocking denunciation of Christianity. Another interpretation or reason for this kind of behavior may be that they were under the illusion that the situation of persecution was temporary, that either freedom to pursue their crypto-Judaism would be restored in Spain or they would as individuals escape to Jewish communities abroad. As for the content of their religion, it may be said that authentic Judaism survived for at least thirty years after the expulsion of the Jews from Spain.

The situation changes in the middle of the century with the sharp decline of trials of judaizers between 1550 and 1560, due to the dying off of those who had been born between 1480 and 1500 (the "unadapted" old) and the aging of the next generation. In addition, the ruthlessness of the Inquisition had done its work. Judaism was on the verge of extinction in Castile, while the New Christian group as a whole was not subject to accusation, as it was to be later, and had merged into the community at large. As against this, one notes cases of cells of judaizers being uncovered in La Mancha as well as in Andalusia, whose members reveal a level of Judaism approaching orthodoxy. One may cite the case of the group surrounding Juan López de Armenia whose uncle, Diego de Mora, acted as a kind of missionary and religious leader to the group and was preparing one of their number to undertake the role of "rabbi." Diego de Mora was also the grandfather of the poet Antonio Enríquez Gómez.

The union of Spain with Portugal in 1580, however, radically altered this picture of the general decline of the Marranos. When, in 1492, the Jews were expelled from Spain, many chose neighboring Portugal, in preference to Italy, North Africa, and places farther east. Despite the General (forced) Conversion of 1497 and various moves to restrict judaizing among the converts, life for the crypto-Jew was relatively more secure in Portugal than in Spain, owing to the late introduction of the Inquisition. The first *auto de fe* took place in 1540, followed by the Papal Bull of 1547 authorizing the establishment of a full Inquisition, but it was not until 1579 (after several ten-year periods of grace) that the power to confiscate property, which had been so destructive a weapon in Spain, was finally granted and an Inquisition on the Spanish model emerged.[16] Following the unification of the two countries, however, many judaizers from Portugal joined a movement in reverse direction, coming to Spain, where paradoxically the activities of the Inquisition against judaizers had practically come to a halt (while the Portuguese Inquisition was exhibiting the brutal enthusiasm of the novice). There was the attraction also of the economic activity which was still at that period at a high level in Castile. This influx belonged to a different class from the old peasant *conversos* of Spain: they were merchants, mobile and adept, and stronger in their religious convictions. If one recalls, it was the orthodox, sincere Jews who were converted by force en masse, not as in Spain the weaker brethren who succumbed, often calculating their survival. So it is that one finds a resurgence after 1580 of the strength of Jewish faith and conviction among judaizers and of the numbers of trials undertaken by the Inquisition.

During the seventeenth century the declining fortunes of the Marranos, which the union of Spain and Portugal had halted, were further strengthened by several factors, one of the most important of which was the family and commerical ties which grew up between crypto-Jews in Spain and Jews abroad. These had been in existence throughout, but the rise of Amsterdam in the seventeenth century as a Jewish center (vernacular prayer books and Bibles were first printed there in 1611)[17] gave new strength to those links. Further, while the numbers of *autos de fe* increased, the Marranos were more mobile, through their trade, less frightened, and above all more circumspect as compared with their unadapted forebears. *Negativos* (those who refused to recant or admit their crimes to the end) were still "relaxed" or handed over to the secular arm for execution, but the Inquisitors seemed less inexorable than before, and if a judaizer adopted a suitable stance of repentance, he stood a good chance of being released with a minor punishment (such as fines or exile to other parts of Spain), even in cases of relapse. It was sometimes possible too to bribe corrupt officials in order to obtain the release of relatives. Thus it is that we find many cases of Marrano merchants living in prosperity and relative security in this period (particularly during the rule of Philip IV's minister, the Conde-duque de Olivares 1621–43, who encouraged the *conversos* for financial resaons) and continuing to observe Judaic practices in spite of periodic arrests and trials. Many traveled freely abroad, especially to Southwest France, where they had relatives who lived practically as open Jews (Antonio Enríquez Gómez is such a case). Some appeared to have dual personalities, being leaders of commerce and outwardly Christian in Spain while active members of the crypto-Jewish community in France.[18]

On the other hand, it would be wrong to underestimate the terrors of the Inquisition: fear of detection was still a constant problem, while even a close family member could denounce one out of religious difference or malice. Even the element of arbitrariness which had entered the Inquisition in its dealings brought its own dangers. And the Inquisition continued to persecute and investigate accusations, to work through whole families, even to pursue those who had appeared as witnesses for the accused, and, moreover, to produce martyrs, such as Isaac de Castro Tartas and Lope de Vera y Alarcón, "Judah the Believer," who was not even of *converso* stock but declared himself a Jew under pressure of Inquisition persecution. Many indeed were brought into the faith or had their faith renewed by the trials they underwent.

The Communities outside Spain

Reference has already been made to the existence of Jewish or *converso* communities outside Spain whose members originated from the Peninsula and who continued to maintain their links with those who had remained behind. The earliest communities of this kind were established after the first exodus following the riots of 1381, in such places as Salonika, Constantinople, and Smyrna in the Ottoman Empire, and Tunis and Algiers in North Africa. The Expulsion of 1492 swelled their numbers, and these communities, orthodox and reproducing the *aljamas* (Jewish quarters) of Moslem Spain, survived until the Second World War.

Although the intention was often to reach these communities, particularly in the Orient, many Marranos left by way of Italy, France, and later the Low Countries, where they established their own centers. These settlements were distinct in character from those of the Orient in that, being established in Christian countries, the Marranos were obliged to maintain the guise of Christianity, even though this was often transparent. Moreover, they were not homogenous or self-contained communities and were made up of, or contained within them, persons of *converso* origin who considered themselves Christian or who professed no particular belief—all being refugees from the indiscriminate terror of the Inquisition. Nonetheless, the judaizers were often the largest and dominant group among them.

In Italy the greatest centers were at Ferrara and Venice. In the first was established the famous press of Abraham Usque, which was responsible for the Ferrara Bible (1553) and the prayer books for daily use and festivals (1553 and 1555 respectively). These reproduced the archaized language which had been used by Jews in Spain for centuries as the medium for Talmudic discussion and had achieved the status of a second Holy Language.[19] These essential works of Jewish religious life were to be reprinted many times in Venice and in Amsterdam in the next century and a half. The community of Ferrara thrived under the benevolent rule of the Dukes of Este until 1581–83, when, under pressure from the Church, action was taken to end the "scandal" of those whom the Inquisition had condemned but who there flaunted their Judaism. After the breakup of the Ferrara community, Venice, where there had been a settlement of Marranos from the earliest period (before 1492), emerged as the principal center of refuge, with Leghorn and Pisa next in importance. The ghetto still survived in Venice and many Marranos took advantage of this fact to return openly to Judaism, with the result that the Jews of Spanish and Portuguese origin (often designated "Portuguese," without distinction)[20] soon dominated Jewish affairs, overriding the numerically stronger Levantine and German groups. On the other hand, some Marranos preferred to hold on to their nominally Christian status so as to participate in the cultural and commercial life of the general community in a way not possible for Jews, since medieval restrictions on what a Jew could do survived. It was to Venice that Immanuel Aboab, author of the erudite defense of Judaism *Nomología* (1629) and great-grandson of the last Sage of Castile, came, as also did the philosopher and Jewish apologist Isaac (formerly Fernando) Cardoso.

By the early seventeenth century important communities of Marranos had grown up in France, particularly, as we have mentioned, in the Southwest, in Peyrehorade, St. Jean-de-Luz, Bayonne, Bordeaux, and Toulouse, places which were of easy access to Spain. However, Rouen in the north (and to a lesser extent Nantes) also had a large Marrano population, being the center of trade with Holland, Germany, and Flanders, as well as Italy.[21] As for the religious life of these communities, though under the cloak of Christianity, it bore many of the features of orthodox Judaism.[22] There were naturally no synagogues as such, but daily prayers were said in private houses and the festivals kept. The Marranos had their own burial grounds in Bayonne, Bordeaux, and probably Rouen, achieved by belonging to one particular church and securing the connivance of the curé concerned.[23] In addition there is evidence that the vernacular prayer books and Bibles printed in Ferrara were in use, contributing to a higher level of Jewish ritual and practice.[24] Besides these sources, the poet João Pinto Delgado (see poetry section), whose father, Gonçalo, was the leader of the Rouen Marranos in the first decades of the seventeenth century, is known to have made use of Louis-Henri D'Aquin's Latin edition of Rashi's commentaries in his poetry. He and his father also knew Hebrew. Despite the periodic protests of French merchants against the "Portuguese," about which the authorities in the interests of trade did little, the Marrano communities in France thrived until the middle of the century, when Amsterdam eclipsed them in importance.

This brings us, finally, to the Low Countries, where Antwerp was first to receive the fugitives from the Inquisition. It was the greatest port in Europe in the sixteenth century and from 1512 became an important staging post for Marranos on their way to the Jewish communities of the Orient. New Christians were granted the right to settle there in 1537, though immigration was prohibited in the 1540s, to be followed by edicts of expulsion for residents of less than five years standing in 1549 and 1550. Nonetheless, there was a new influx after the union of Spain and Portugal in 1580. Since Antwerp was in the Spanish Netherlands, that is to say under Spanish rule, judaizers were still subject to pursuit by the Inquisition. This fact made life for the would-be Jew unsatisfactory in the Low Countries, although a covert community did grow up. The prospect of greater freedom came with the establishment of the independent United Provinces in the north in 1579, which led to the growth of Amsterdam as a city-state where Jews (no longer in Christian guise) were to attain a peculiar status of religious toleration. The Treaty of Westphalia in 1648, which brought to an end the Thirty Years' War in Northern Europe, resulted in the decline of Antwerp by closing the River Scheldt and lent impetus to the ascendance of Amsterdam politically and commercially and as a center of Jewish life—an ascendance which was to end only with the decline of Dutch power in the eighteenth century.

The growth of the Amsterdam community was swift, and dates from the very end of the sixteenth century with the granting of informal authorization to live as Jews in 1597. Soon there were three synagogues: the *Beth Ya'acob*, the earliest, dating from the turn of the century; the *Neve shalom*, established by North African Jews in 1608; and the *Beth Israel*, founded by dissenters from *Neve shalom* in 1619. These were eventually to settle their differences and combine into the *Kahal Kadosh Talmud Torah* in 1638, a new synagogue being completed in 1675. Cemeteries were at Groede (1602) and Ouderkerk (1616). In 1615 the freedom of Jews in Amsterdam to profess their faith was formally granted by the civil authorities. By the middle of the century there were four hundred families in the community, and Jews, participating in the great commercial activity of the city, controlled a large part of business and new industry, including 25 percent of the shares of the East India Company. Within the community, the full multiplicity of social and cultural organization was represented, from the elected government of the *Parnasim* (wardens), the rabbinic academy *Etz Haim*, and the *Yeshiva de los Pintos*, through the charities established on behalf of widows and orphans, to the secular literary circles and the like. Paradoxically, this was not a community in which freedom of thought was acceptable, and the rulers of the Synagogue appeared to have learned something of the approach of the Inquisition in their dealings with such as the skeptic Uriel da Costa and the philosopher Spinoza.

This, then, is the historical background to the poets we present: persecution within Spain and Portugal but the survival of Judaistic faith and practice through to the seventeenth century, indeed undergoing a resurgence from 1580; cities of refuge outside the Peninsula where communities lived in various degrees of religious freedom, from mere absence of Inquisition to full liberty to be a Jew.[25] Let us now turn to the cultural inheritance which the seventeenth-century Marrano poet shared.

The dedication of the new Synagogue of the Spanish and Portuguese Jews *(K. K. Talmud Torah)*, Amsterdam, 1675; engraving by Bernard Picart from *Cérémonies et Coutumes de tous les peuples du monde* (Amsterdam, 1723)

The Tradition of Language

Wherever the Jews of the Peninsula went they took with them their language, which in the first instance, following the exoduses of 1381 and 1492, means Spanish (Portuguese does not enter the picture really until 1580 and even then, as we shall see, Spanish predominates). It is a matter of debate as to how much the normal language of the Jew in Spain differed from that of his compatriots; what is certain is that within about a hundred years of the Expulsion (1492) a distinct dialect, Judeo-Spanish or Ladino, had evolved, brought about by the isolation of the communities from linguistic developments in Spain, containing many borrowings from Hebrew and Arabic, and influenced by the archaized language of the *meldares* or *yeshivoth*.[26] From this point Ladino, with its own linguistic traditions and culture, takes off on its own: the language and culture of the Marranos are no part of it, since they follow the direct line of development in the Peninsula. At the same time, the language of the *meldares*, which had evolved out of a tradition of oral translation and discussion of Talmud and Torah into a highly hebraicized Spanish which goes back at least to the fourteenth century, had come through into print and achieved its most popular form, as we have seen, in the Ferrara Bible and prayer books of the 1550s. With the reprinting of these works the position of this language was reinforced and remained unchanged over the centuries as the language of the liturgy, alongside Hebrew, but frequently replacing it.[27]

Later emigrants from Spain and Portugal brought with them the language of their country of origin, by now indistinguishable through their integration into Christian society from that of their countrymen. Spanish and Portuguese continued to be the languages of the Sephardi communities for centuries in Amsterdam and later in London, and were employed in all activities, whether commercial or literary, and in the management of the synagogue. In general, however, it would appear to be the case in Amsterdam that Portuguese was preferred as the "vernacular" for sermons and treatises and the like and Spanish as the language of "culture" for poetry and serious literature, not forgetting the special Spanish of the liturgy.[28] The division holds good irrespective of the linguistic origin of the individual, who would be conversant with both. The dominance of Spanish in the cultural field, of course, reflects the situation in the Peninsula where

Spanish literature was enjoying its Golden Age and leading Portuguese writers would employ Castilian in preference to their own language.[29] A further reflection is seen in the (Spanish) literary "academies" or salons founded in Amsterdam by Baron Manuel de Belmonte, the Spanish Resident in the Low Countries. These were the *Academia de los sitibundos* ("Academy of the Thirsty") in 1676 and the *Academia de los floridos* in 1685, at which, in imitation of such gatherings in Madrid, poets and litterateurs of varying abilities staged discussions and literary jousts.[30]

The New Christian who came to Amsterdam, as to Venice for that matter, to take up a Jewish identity in the seventeenth century would have felt very much at home linguistically and found the transition smoothed by the wide use of the vernacular to which he was accustomed. Moreover, religion apart, the cultural environment to which he was used had been largely transferred to this new soil, that is to say the cultural environment of Spain. The Marrano immigrant, unlike his "medieval" coreligionists of the Orient, was a Renaissance man, a "modern."[31] Linguistically and culturally, writers like Menasseh ben Israel and Isaac Cardoso (for all their great Jewish culture), Miguel de Barrios and Antonio Enríquez Gómez are indistinguishable from Lope de Vega and Calderón de la Barca. This fact is important and we must turn now to this Hispanic cultural background.

The Literary Tradition of Spain

Clearly, it would not be possible in so short a study to detail all the literary ideas which flourished and fused together in the two centuries of the Spanish Golden Age. However, the essential traits which come through from the sixteenth to the seventeenth century are as follows.[32]

At the beginning of the sixteenth century, Juan Boscán Almogáver (b. 1487–92, d. 1542) and Garcilaso de la Vega (c. 1501–36) had been instrumental in introducing into Spain the influences of Italian poetry, that is to say Petrarch, the revivified classical authors, particularly Vergil and Horace, and Italian meters, the most important of which was the hendecasyllable. In this way, Spanish poetry can be said to have emerged from the Middle Ages and the somewhat claustrophobic hold of the *cancionero* tradition of stylized courtly-love lyrics.[33] Boscán was the first to imitate the Italian hendecasyllabic meter in Spanish, in poetry which he wrote in 1526 at the suggestion of the Venetian Ambassador to Spain, Andrea Navagero. In addition, at the urging of Garcilaso, who spent several years in Naples, the then flourishing center of Italian humanism and literature, he translated Baldassare Castiglione's *Il libro del Cortegiano* (1528), a discourse on the ideal courtier which was an important medium for the transmission to Spain of Neoplatonic ideas. However, it was Garcilaso who (in poems published posthumously in 1543) demonstrated how the "new" meters could be used to great effect, in poetry which develops the expression and analysis of emotion (generally wordly love) against the Petrarchan natural backdrop of woods, stream, and warbling nightingales, where shepherds come to water their flocks and lament of love. The best examples of this are to be seen in Garcilaso's *Elegies* and *Eclogues*. Greater subtlety in the exploration of states of mind became possible with Garcilaso's poetry, together with a more sensitive awareness of the outside world. Nature becomes the source for imagery, often (as in Garcilaso) in a Neoplatonic framework of nature as a spectacle of love and harmony, in which love properly directed may find a place. (The pastoral novel was to develop these ideas further, but the basic situation outlined remains a constant of both secular and religious poetry in the Golden Age.)

Following Garcilaso, Fernando de Herrera (1534–97) did more than perhaps any other Spanish poet to naturalize the Italian influences: his poetic language is tauter than Garcilaso's, less melodic or Italian-sounding (Garcilaso's often appears over-Italian), and he introduces a conceptual or spiritual dimension into his love poetry. The loved one becomes less of a person than a Platonic "idea." In this connection, Herrera developed the Petrarchan stereotype of the loved one with skin whiter than snow, eyes brighter than the sun, teeth like pearls, and hair of gold, by calling her by the more general and abstract term *Luz* ("light") and opening up the way to complex interplay between the associations of light-sun-white-fire, as well as the standard antitheses of ice-fire, hope-despair and the like. At the same time, in his commentary on Garcilaso's poetry, the so-called *Anotaciones* of 1580, Herrera expounded his own influential literary theories: he declared the main aim of poetry to be *claridad*, that is to say free-flowing, gentle, clear language, rather than overelaborate and obscure—a language conveying precisely the meaning intended.[34] On the other hand, the language of poetry was to be lofty and removed from ordinary diction, and he advocated the invention of words to express exactly an idea for which no words already existed. In this way, while codifying and assimilating Italian influences for general consumption, Herrera was also laying the foundations of the developments of the seventeenth century, which ultimately created a new style distinct from its origins. The developments in question were *culteranismo* and *conceptismo,* which together may broadly be said to constitute the "baroque" in terms of Spanish Golden Age literature.

Culteranismo can be defined as "a style of extreme artificiality, which in practice meant Latinization of syntax and vocabulary, constant use of classical allusion, and the creation of a distinctive poetic diction as far removed as possible from the language of every day discourse."[35] To elaborate further, hyperbaton (the separation of related parts of speech) became the dominant feature of language, undoing the normal structures and displacing key words (or ideas) in order to throw them into relief. Classical allusions were of course not new in poetry, but they were now used with a density and obliqueness that made them original: an allusion expressed in a single phrase could throw into relief a whole image or series of images.[36] In a similar questing beyond the obvious, second-stage imagery was developed in which metaphor was built on metaphor or simile. For example, fair skin (or anything white) is no longer compared with snow, it is said to be snow, giving rise in turn to imagistic development on its own in which the source of the original image in nature is left behind: a white tablecloth becomes *nieve hilada,* "spun snow"; a white bird *nieve volante,* "flying snow"; and through the translation of *nieve* into *espuma* ("foam") transference can be made to the range of crystal-water images. The chief exponent of this style was Luis de Góngora y Argote (1561–1627), in whose hands it rises beyond pedantry to great heights, of which the *Soledades* (*Solitudes,* 1613) are the supreme example. In this unfinished work, the poet weaves a succession of complex structures and images, expounding the theme of the transience of human affairs in the face of the permanence of nature.

Conceptismo can be compared with the ideas of the Metaphysical Poets in England.[37] Rather than evoking and communicating sense impressions, the aim was to establish conceptual relationships between ideas or objects which were in ways alike but also unalike: great delight was taken in exploiting simultaneously the facets which linked, and those which differentiated, the subjects for comparison. It can be said that the pursuit of this type of wit, or *agudeza*,[38] springs from the essentially analytical and metaphorical cast of medieval thought which drew on a world-picture (still prevalent in the seventeenth century) in which the universe was seen as a book or series of signs revealing the greatness of God. Conceit could, through the analogies it exploited, give expression to the hidden affinities which permeate the universe and thus provide an insight into the underlying plan of things. (Another manifestation of this in the seventeenth century was the emblem-books, which presented allegorical pictures with expanded captions designed to teach moral truth, as a kind of visual conceit.) Francisco Gómez de Quevedo y Villegas (1580–1645) was the outstanding writer in this genre, both in his poetry and in his prose (for example, his picaresque novel *La vida del buscón*, 1626). In all his writings, Quevedo delights in depicting life shorn of its enchantments and shows none of the delight in pleasures of the senses that Góngora displays.

This aspect of Quevedo's writing also reminds us that an important aspect of seventeenth-century poetry was the manifestation of the idea of *desengaño*, that is to say disillusionment with all aspects of life, which appears to be a sham, a façade, whereas, on the contrary, reality is to be found beyond life, after death. This essentially Christian perspective lends itself to conceptual play on the theme of life as spiritual death and death as truly life. A supreme example of this view is seen in the major plays of Pedro Calderón de la Barca (1600–1681), one of which is *La vida es sueño (Life Is a Dream)*, whose very title suggests disillusion with this world and anticipation of the next. *Desengaño*, as may be readily imagined, was a natural subject for *conceptismo*.

From what has been said, it can be seen that Quevedo was temperamentally, intellectually, and poetically disposed to being the archenemy of Góngora and *culteranismo*. This might suggest a complete schism or division between the two literary streams; however, this is not so. Many other poets, while they might in their public pronouncements of *ars poetica* favor one camp or the other, often display the influence of each style. Lope de Vega (1562–1635), for example was highly hostile to *culteranismo*, being a partisan of the *claros* (those who favored clarity—compare Herrera) against the *oscuros* (or lovers of obscurity), yet he wrote poems in both the *culto* and the *conceptista* manner. We shall find the same to be typical of the poets in this collection.

The Jewish Inheritance of the Marranos

The literary culture of the Peninsula, as we have outlined it—the subsumed echoes of Garcilaso, the baroque conventions of conceit and ornamentation, etc.—was of course the dominant cultural background of the Marrano poets of the seventeenth century. Whatever the exact degree of their Judaic faith or knowledge, they were culturally more Spanish than Jews. If we consider the Marranos—as one tends to, given their dramatic place in Jewish history—from the point of view of being primarily Jews, we will misunderstand the nature of the problem for the Marrano: at this period the principal question for him was not how to pass as a conforming Catholic Spaniard, but how to become a Jew, how to acquire the Jewish knowledge which would fill out the bare bones of "Jewish feeling" and rudimentary notions of what he felt to be his ancestral religion.

By the middle of the sixteenth century, those notions had indeed become rudimentary. The direct acquaintance with authentic Judaism had died out with the older generation of *conversos* and a different kind of Judaistic religion, Marranism, had emerged.[39] This had as its principal feature reliance on the Old Testament as the source of Jewish Law, without, in general, benefit of post-Biblical Rabbinic exegeses—a reliance which led to an element of fundamentalism in belief. The Apocryphal Books were also given high status as an available source, being contained integrally in the Latin Bible and in the Protestant Spanish translation of Cassiodoro de Reyna (1569), which may have been available. The story of the Maccabees, for instance, enjoyed much popularity among Marranos, while from the canonical Old Testament, the Book of Psalms (if in the Vulgate version, omitting the *Gloria Patri*) assumed great importance both for the general consolation it offered and for use in clandestine services. Other features of Jewish ritual survived erratically: the use of *tallith* is recorded in the seventeenth century, as also of *tephillin* (Inquisitional records refer to "relics" being worn), while covering the head fell into disuse, and kneeling in the Christian manner was introduced. Hebrew drops out except for odd words such as *Adonay*, though in view of the vernacular tradition in Spanish Jewry this is not surprising.[40] Circumcision was clearly too risky a practice in these clandestine circumstances, and in general it was only those who escaped abroad who underwent this rite. *Kashrut* was followed only in so far as it was possible; for example, chickens were slaughtered by cutting the neck instead of wringing. Abstention from eating pork could arouse suspicion, but attempts to do so on Holy Days were made. Similarly with the observation of the Sabbath and festivals, it was a case of making significant gestures, such as wearing clean clothes, avoiding work, engaging in Pentateuchal or other suitable readings.[41] Candles were lit on the Sabbath, often hidden in a pitcher to avoid the necessity of extinguishing them in case of temporary danger. Of the major festivals, Passover and Yom Kippur tended to be observed, while Tabernacles and the New Year were largely neglected. Purim, with its story of Queen Esther who maintained her faith in secret, understandably attained great significance as a festival.

Inevitably, however, as time went on, the influence of the environment came to compound the divergences from normative Judaism brought about by ignorance. Thus, among the group founded by Antonio Homem in Coimbra (Portugal) at the beginning of the seventeenth century, while on the one hand *tephillin* and *tallith* were worn and stress was laid in the sermons on strict adherence to the Law, especially the prohibition against the worship of images, on the other hand, Homem and his followers organized themselves into a *cofradía* (chapter) on the Spanish Catholic model, in honor of Frey Diego da Assumpção (an Old Christian convert to Judaism, burned in 1603). A retable was set up to commemorate his martyrdom, images of Moses and the like were venerated, and Homem, in the discharge of his "rabbinical" duties, wore a miter.

In matters of theology also, the influence of the environment can be seen. The belief in the One God remains central and the profession of it recurs in testimony before the Inquisition. At the same time, the religion tends to be defined in terms of the negation of Christianity: thus the One God is opposed to the Trinity. An example of this can be seen in Antonio Enríquez Gómez's *Romance al divín mártir* (see poetry section), where much is made of the argument that the concept of the Trinity conflicts with the First Commandment of the Decalogue. Many of the anti-Christian polemics of the period, written by ex-Marranos in Amsterdam and elsewhere, expend most of their energies in denial of Christian tenets, rather than in the positive arguing of Jewish beliefs.[42] Further, there emerges the christianized concept of salvation as the prime object of religion, with the Law as the means of achieving it—this in opposition to the agency of Jesus. Indeed, there is also present the concept of "belief in" the Law, which contrasts with the traditional view of the Law as a code of precepts for action. Evidence for this shift comes in the writings of the otherwise soundly informed Isaac Cardoso (see his *Excelencias de los hebreos*, 1679).[43]

Lastly, the messianic belief assumed a position of great importance (beyond the obvious denial of the Messiahship of Jesus) and Marrano circles gave rise to many pseudo-Messiahs, such as, in the sixteenth century, Luis Dias of Setúbal and the so-called *Judeu do sapato* ("Jew of the Shoe") from Évora.[44] The Marranos also supported and perhaps inspired the political messianism of the Sebastianist movement in Portugal, which evolved around the person of the heir to the Portuguese throne, Dom Sebastian, whose disappearance had led to the union with Spain and who, it was believed, would reappear to restore Portugal's independence. Sebastianism proved in fact the driving force of the nationalism which brought about the break with Spain in 1640. From the Marrano point of view the hope was that independence might bring with it the end of the Inquisition in Portugal, though this was not to be. Not surprisingly, the messianic claims of Sabbatai Zevi also found a great response among the Marranos, and particularly the ex-Marranos of Amsterdam. The messianic belief clearly responded to the need among the Marranos for hope of a deliverer from the tribulations suffered at the hands of the Inquisition, and it was perhaps their isolated situation and secretive lives that bred and fostered fantasies of liberation, and indeed of restoration of those abroad to the Promised Land, not of Israel, but of the Peninsula.

Much of the christianizing influences survived the general improvement of the standard of Jewish knowledge in the seventeenth century, as the example of Isaac Cardoso already quoted shows. Yet this example, to view the problem from completely the opposite position, indicates what heights of Jewish erudition could be reached from the religious background we have described. Cardoso was exceptional, but the impulse towards reeducation had ever been present among Marranos, even at the lowest point of their knowledge, and generation after generation had tried to get back to the sources of their religion. The links with the Jewish communities abroad helped, particularly Amsterdam: often there were direct family ties, and occasionally emissaries were sent to Spain, such as Isaac Farque, who as Antonio de Aguiar went to Madrid to circumcise the sons of rich Marranos there (this was in 1632, and testifies to the confidence of crypto-Jews in the period of Olivares). The journeying of judaizing merchants to France and Italy must also have helped: there are many cases in Inquisition trial records of people returning from places such as Bayonne with sound recollection of prayers from the vernacular liturgy, which attests to the circulation of the Ferrara prayer books (and Bible) in those communities, from at least the 1640s onward. For example, the *Shema* recalled by Diego Núñez Silva in 1661, from experience going back as much as twenty years earlier, is virtually indentical with the version given in the *Orden de Oraciones,* Amsterdam, 1648.[45] Even if the dissemination of this knowledge of the liturgy was confined to the immediate entourage of the individual who traveled, there must have been something of a significant ripple effect. On the other hand, this would have been almost entirely oral, with the attendant uncertainties of misunderstanding and memory failure, since there is scant evidence of copies of the vernacular liturgy appearing in Spain itself, although Menasseh ben Israel is said to have sent copies of his Rabbinic compendium *Conciliador* (1632) there.[46]

However, the subject of the availability of books in Spain brings us to the point that, even without the external factors mentioned, the means of gaining Jewish knowledge inside Spain were restricted but not impossible. The traditional Jewish sources, such as the Talmud and Rabbinic commentaries upon it, had long since been put on the Index—the Toledo and Valladolid Indexes of 1551 banned all books on Jewish ritual and Law. Books in Hebrew were proscribed, and to possess them was to court disaster (unless one had special dispensation). On the other hand, as Y. H. Yerushalmi has demonstrated, a great quantity of authentic Jewish knowledge could be acquired through works that were generally available, usually in Latin, but often in the vernacular.[47] In addition to the Old Testament (both in the Vulgate version or in vernacular translation such as the Alba Bible of the fifteenth century, which even contained

Rabbinic commentaries), Jewish literature of the Hellenistic period—the Apocrypha, the writings of Philo and Josephus—was accessible. If the Talmud was banned, the Targum was available in both Aramaic and Latin in the Complutensian and Regian polyglot Bibles. Patristic literature could also provide much information from its discussion of Jewish religious ideas; for instance, Cecil Roth quotes the case of one Antonio Ribeiro Sánchez who was so deeply affected by a passage on circumcision in Saint Augustine's *City of God* that he became a Jew.[48] Since Hebrew continued as a subject of study in universities throughout Europe, including that of Salamanca in Spain, the writings of Catholic Hebraists were also there to be read. Anti-Jewish tracts could also provide valuable information, since the Marrano bent on self-education had only to take as true that which was ridiculed as false. Lastly, there were many miscellaneous works on scientific, theological, or philosophical matters which, though not primarily concerned with Judaism, could contain comments drawn from Rabbinic sources.[49] A particularly valuable source of knowledge was Génébrard's *Chronologia Hebraeorum*, published as an appendix to his *Chronographia* in Paris in 1600 (also Lyon, 1608). This work contains extracts of, for example, the Tractate *Sanhedrin* (fols. 97 a–b) from the Talmud (concerning the Messiah), part of Maimonides' *Mishneh Torah*, his "Thirteen Principles of Faith" and enumeration of the 613 *mitzvot*, as well as assorted prayers from the Roman *Machzor*. Despite calls for the proscription of this work and the banning of parts of it, it was not until 1640 that all the texts of the appendix were suppressed. Even so, these and other prohibited works continued to be found in private libraries, to reappear when the owners were tried on other charges by the Inquisition or when the collections were sold on the death of the owner.

Consequently, a wealth of Jewish literature and sources of Jewish knowledge was available to those who sought it. In this way (to return to our earlier example), Isaac Cardoso was able to leave Spain well enough equipped to become a sage in the Jewish community of Venice within a relatively short space of time. The poet Antonio Enríquez Gómez also shows signs of having been acquainted through Génébrard with Jewish thinking on the Messiah, as can be seen from his *Romance al divín mártir*. Yerushalmi indeed expresses doubt as to whether Uriel da Costa could really have been so surprised by the divergences he found in Amsterdam between Judaism as practiced and the Judaism of the Bible.[50] Whatever the case, and despite the contrasting examples of Cardoso, the university man, and the self-educated Antonio Enríquez Gómez, it remains true that only a minority was able to benefit from the availability of this knowledge— acquaintance with Latin was after all a prime requisite. For the majority, the aspiration to Jewish orthodoxy and knowledge was a dream not realized. Their religion remained for the most part a curious mixture of fundamentalism, negation of Christianity, and christianized monotheism. Most did not maintain a sustained effort at Judaism even: one notes, with Caro Baroja, the number of instances of New Christians being accused of practicing Jewish rites on occasion only.[51] However, we may perhaps describe their faith in a more positive way (bearing in mind that no religious group is homogeneous in knowledge, understanding, or consistency of observance)[52] by saying that it consisted above all of an attitude, the will to be Jews,[53] despite their ignorance, despite—or, because of—the oppression of the Inquisition. Whatever their knowledge, however close to authentic Judaism they managed or failed to come, it is this will which is a persistent strand in the history of the Marranos, manifesting itself in the whole range of religious expression and gesture, from the knowledgeable to the plainly ignorant.

One must bear in mind this range of individual religious experience in face of the most difficult circumstances, when considering what became of the Marrano outside Spain. More often than not he would pass through the crypto-Jewish communities of France or Italy before reaching the authentic Judaism of Venice or Amsterdam. These communities provided a transition between Marranism and Judaism, reproducing the familiar dualism of Christian conformity–Jewish belief, while providing in more extensive form the organization and practice of Jewish life. Many in fact did not move on from there, while others discovered that they did not wish to forsake Christianity and joined the rather pathetic band of those *converso* exiles who could neither return, for fear of the Inquisition, nor identify with their judaizing fellows. The Marrano who reached the open orthodoxy of Amsterdam (the goal of the majority who did move on) found his task of integration made easier by the dominance of the vernacular in Sephardi culture. He could participate, as we have already seen, in all aspects of Jewish life in his native language (or the sister language of Portuguese). The archaic language of the liturgy presented something of a problem with its peculiar hebraized forms but was still recognizable and by and large comprehensible.[54] In addition, leading figures such as Menasseh ben Israel in his *Thesouro dos Dinim (Treasury of Laws)* and *Conciliador* (which sought to reconcile apparently contradictory Pentateuchal sources) provided compendia of Jewish knowledge in an easily assimilable form. In Venice, Moses Altaras published his *Libro de mantenimiento de la alma (Guide for the Care of the Soul)* in 1609, in the manner of Joseph Caro's *Shulkhan aruch*. Further, much erudite discussion took place in the vernacular, as witnessed by Eliau Montalto's treatise on the subject of chapter 53 of Isaiah[55] or another of Menasseh ben Israel's works, *Piedra gloriosa (Stone of Glory)*, concerning the prophecies of Daniel.

Nonetheless, this great advantage of language could not always compensate for the "cultural shock" suffered by Marranos who entered the orthodox Jewish world of Amsterdam. Of course, most of the leading figures came from the same Hispanic cultural background (Menasseh ben Israel, Orobio de Castro, and Saul Levi Mortera are examples), but, whereas they accepted the new cultural conditions without question, others could not and formed a sizable heterodox minority.[56] The case of Uriel da Costa has been mentioned and is notorious: he denied the doctrine of the immortality of the soul as not being unequivocally stated in the Old Testament. The religious rationalism of Baruch Spinoza brought him into conflict with the leaders of the community, and Juan de Prado engaged in acrimonious debate with Orobio de Castro on the subject of whether Jews as well as non-Jews could be saved by adherence to the Noachide laws alone (Orobio denied this to be the case). There were the lesser-known figures of David Pharar, who, on being dismissed from his post as *shochet* on the not unreasonable grounds that he knew nothing of *shechita* (ritual slaughter), formed a new community with Abraham Espinoza (Spinoza's great-uncle) and others; the Karaite, Joseph Salomon del Mendigo; and Rabbi Isaac Aboab da Fonseca, who argued that punishment after death for grave sinners was not necessarily eternal, that even Jesus would be forgiven.[57] The list does not end there of those who, according to Orobio de Castro, had been tainted in the Peninsula with the false sciences of philosophy, medicine, and metaphysics, but whom we may see as having been affected inevitably by their varied journeys from their known, surrounding culture toward what they took to be their beliefs, toward the Judaism they had adopted or had placed upon them.

The Marrano Poets

Finally in this introduction to the background of the Marrano poets, what can we say about the poetry itself? In the matter of content we have, as have been suggested, three different paths to Judaism. João (or Juan) Pinto Delgado, nurtured in clandestine Judaism from an early age, was soon to leave Portugal for France, though only after choosing to complete his literary education: the deep-seated Jewish culture ensured that he had few traumas in becoming an open Jew. Barrios, too, must have had a good grounding in crypto-Judaism, but he was longer in settling in Jewish Amsterdam and veered off in the end into Christian-inspired messianic byways: a onetime army officer, he was a social being, used to moving in elevated circles and with a ready wit which flows in his verse and serves him well as the chronicler of Jewish community life, while the deeply felt religious feeling is there behind the façade. Antonio Enríquez Gómez's leanings were towards politics and commerce: he saw the ways of the world and was part of it, but could mock it in his verse. The crypto-Jewish background was less pervasive than was the case with the others, and it took a crisis in his life at the age of fifty to bring him to Judaism: even so, though it became a staple element in his life from then on, it was somewhat of a book-learned Judaism, without the benefit of the open Jewish society of Amsterdam. Indeed, it can be said that he remained a Marrano all his life.

All these experiences, of course, affected the tone, as well as the content of the individual poet's work: the gravely learned and well-honed literary style of João Pinto Delgado, the wit and sly mockery as well as lyric sincerity of Antonio Enríquez Gómez, and the combination of verbal play and earnest introspection of Miguel de Barrios. At the same time, as will be clear from what has been said earlier, these are differences which are revealed within a broadly common literary idiom. The inheritance of the Spanish Renaissance and the poetic developments from Garcilaso forward inform them all to greater or lesser degree—the vocabulary of amatory imagery, the pastoral metaphor, conceit, and baroque ornamentation. There is, how-

ever, a clearly perceptible line of stylistic evolution between the
restrained and measured tone of Pinto Delgado, who stands at
the earliest point of seventeenth-century poetic developments,
and the greater baroque extravagances witnessed in Enríquez
Gómez's work and most especially in that of Barrios.

On the other side, the Jewish dimension, they all have re-
course to the Bible as the ready handbook of Jewish experience
and borrow from its style and language as well as its themes: the
feel of Jeremiah's words is there in João Pinto Delgado's, as is
that of *Kohelet* in Enríquez Gómez's. Barrios is less oriented
towards the Bible, save for allusions and themes which he
fashions in totally Golden Age style. All three, however, make
successful attempt to reach beyond the Bible toward the Oral
Tradition embodied in the deliberations of the Rabbis of the
Talmud, working the material which they borrow into the fabric
of their verse to enrich its cultural depth. They nonetheless re-
main haunted by the past, especially the sense of guilt concern-
ing their earlier adherence to Christianity, however formal, and
the inadequacy of their observance of Judaism under those con-
ditions. They could hardly be blamed for that, but their feeling of
guilt persists as a major theme, testifying to their intense desire
to be fully part of Judaism and forming, with the theme of their
past sufferings on the one hand, and the hope for messianic re-
demption on the other, the essential nexus of Marrano thought.

As to the enduring value of their poems, it will be for the
reader of this volume to judge. As items of literary documenta-
tion they will surely be appreciated: three poets bringing to us
their intimate thoughts and reactions to a high drama in which
they were involved and to which they bear witness (perhaps
poetry is uniquely suited to such a task). They can be viewed too
as the expression of each poet's Jewish feelings and identifica-
tion, which behind a formal exterior to which (with the exception
of the manuscript writings) no Christian reader could reasonably
object, the Marrano could see mirrored his own experience and
aspirations and derive hope and solace from it. At the same time,
the modern reader may appreciate the range and subtlety of the
poets' style, albeit not that of our own day, and sense that they
have not betrayed either themselves or their fellow Marranos by
the words they have chosen to use.[58]

Notes

1. In a review article in *Bulletin of Hispanic Studies* 40 (1963): 178–80, E. M. Wilson suggested that there was a need for a book which would deal with the Marrano poets against the background of the Jewish centers outside Spain and the Peninsular tradition of devotional literature and the *romance;* while I do not claim that this is that book, its inspiration derives in part from Professor Wilson's remark.

2. Of these, the last seems the most probable, since it has a sound linguistic basis in Castilian, especially if one accepts David Gonzalo Maeso's view that the sense of "renegade" predates that of "pig": see Damián Alonso García, *Literatura oral del ladino* (Madrid, 1970), pp. 18–19.

3. See, for example, R. D. Barnett, *Sephardi Heritage* (London, 1971), p. 4, where the author states that " 'marranos' are better termed *conversos*," as if the terms were interchangeable. In the same volume, H. Beinart, in two articles on "The *Converso* community in 15th/16th and 17th century Spain" (pp. 425 ff.), uses only the term *converso*, but in a way which indicates that he has judaizers specifically in mind: for example (p. 449): "we find *conversos* doing all in their power to guard this day [Yom Kippur]." In drawing the stated distinction between the terms, I follow Y. H. Yerushalmi, *From Spanish Court to Italian Ghetto, Isaac Cardoso*, New York: Columbia University Press, 1970.

4. Throughout this work the term *New Christian* will be used also as a synonym for *converso*.

5. It is equally important to ensure that the use of *Marrano* does not beg the question as to religious inclination: even Cecil Roth, who is particular about definitions, uses the word where no sense of "judaizer" is intended, as in the reference to "Marrano tax-gatherers," *A History of the Marranos* (London, 1932; new edition, New York, 1966), p. 31.

6. Cf. Américo Castro, *La realidad histórica de España* (Buenos Aires, 1954), for the attempt to show Jewish antecedents and traits in many of Spain's leading literary figures: for example (p. 499), "dom Sem Tob, don Alonso de Cartagena, Juan de Mena, Rodrigo de Ceta, Hernando de Pulgar, Fernando de Rojas, Luis Vives, fray Luis de León, Mateo Alemán, Jorge de Montemayor y Santa Teresa, al anónimo autor del *Lazarillo de Tormes*, entre otros, mostrarán la huella de su ascendencia israelita" (". . . show the imprint of their Jewish descent"). Of these only Luis Vives and Sem Tob (the apostate) can be said to have identifiable and relevant Jewish antecedents.

7. See H. Beinart, "The Converso community in 15th century Spain," in *Sephardi Heritage* (London, 1971), p. 425.

8. See A. Sicroff, *Les controverses des Statuts de "pureté de sang" en Espagne du XVᵉ au XVIIᵉ siècle* (Paris, 1960), passim.

9. The particular cause of resentment was the forced loan of 1 million *marvedís* imposed by Juan II of Castile's minister Alvaro de Luna.

10. According to J. Caro Baroja, *Los judíos en la España moderna y contemporánea* (Madrid, 1961–62) 2: 286, it was the controversy aroused by the issuing of such a statute concerning the presbytery of the Archbishop of Toledo (the premier See of Spain) which had the profoundest effect and did most to establish their validity as a legal principle, while those of the military orders, etc., were of less specific application against *conversos*.

11. Cecil Roth, *History of the Marranos*, chapter 5, provides a clear sum-

mary of procedure, based on H. C. Lea's detailed work *A History of the Inquisition in Spain* (New York, 1906).

12. For the role played by the *malsín* (talebearer) see poetry section, passim.

13. Roth, *Marranos,* pp. 126–27, considers the number of true "martyrs" to have been a minority (citing a figure of 3 out of 40 in Majorca, in 1691): most took the way out of repentance, sincere or otherwise.

14. It must not be forgotten that Muslims shared a fate similar to that of Jews: their *conversos,* called *moriscos,* however, were actually expelled in 1609–12.

15. Caro Baroja, *Los judíos en la España,* 1: 433 ff.

16. See I. S. Révah, "Les Marranes portugais et l'Inquisition au XVI siècle," in *Sephardi Heritage,* p. 514. Révah's statistics (p. 515) show that the Portuguese Inquisition was not inactive before 1579, but it was the power of confiscation which had the most destructive effect on families and economic life.

17. These were essentially reprints of the Bible and prayer books printed in Ferrara (see below). These works on their own could not halt the decline of Jewish knowledge prior to 1580, but were invaluable in combination with the other factors mentioned.

18. One such was Diego Rodríguez Cardoso, whose trial took place in the 1660s: he was engaged in the wool trade in Northern Spain and Castile, with commercial links with Holland, France, and Portugal, while living for much of his life in Bayonne, where he was active in the life of the New Christian community. He was even circumcised.

19. See I. S. Révah, "Histoire des parlers judéo-espagnols," in *Annuaire du Collège de France* (1970): 553–62.

20. Cf. the use of the term in Spain for all New Christians, it being assumed after 1580 that all Portuguese were *conversos,* and judaizers to boot.

21. A document in the Archives Départementales de la Seine-Maritime (Arrêts du Parlement, 1649) refers to the trade of Antonio Enríquez Gómez and his cousin with these places, all of which it may be noted had centers of New Christian population.

22. While the French authorities tolerated New Christians as an economic asset and did not enquire into their beliefs, Judaism was officially proscribed in France.

23. See Caro Baroja, *Los judíos en la España* 1: 425–29, and C. Roth, "Les Marranes à Rouen," *Revue des études juives* 88 (1929): 113–37.

24. For detailed discussion of this point, see my dissertation "Two Poems of Antonio Enríquez Gómez," University of London (Ph.D.), 1976, pp. 110–12.

25. In addition to the European centers, there were places in the Americas to which Marranos escaped. However, since most of the area was under Spanish or Portuguese rule, they could not act as centers of refuge in the same way as Venice or Amsterdam, with the exception of Pernambuco (Brazil) during its period of Dutch occupation (1630–54). With the breakup of that community on return to Portuguese rule, other communities began to be established in areas not under Iberian rule, such as the West Indies and, eventually, the British Colonies in North America. See Roth, *History of the Marranos,* chap. 11.

26. See I. S. Révah, "Histoire des parlers," on the language of the *yeshivah.* See also M. J. Benardete, *The Hispanic Culture of the Sephardic Jew* (New

York, 1953), pp. 57–58. On Ladino, see D. S. Blondheim, *Parlers Judéo-Romans et la vetus latina* (Paris, 1925), and M. L. Wagner, *Caracteres generales del judeo-español de Oriente* (Madrid, 1930). (*Revista filológica española,* Anejo 12.)

27. Of the many editions of the prayer book appearing in Amsterdam from 1612 onward, only one, by Manesseh ben Israel, has the Hebrew text, while in the others only the first lines of prayers are given, transcribed in Latin characters.

28. See J. A. Van Praag, "Almas en litigio," *Clavileño* 1 (1950): 22, and C. Roth, "The Rôle of Spanish in the Marrano Diaspora," in *Studies in Honour of I. González Llubera* (Oxford, 1959) pp. 299–308.

29. João Pinto Delgado (see poetry section) is a case in point. Note also that this was true even in the fifteenth century, as the example of Gil Vicente illustrates: several of his poems appear in the *Oxford Book of Spanish Verse,* 2d ed. (Oxford, 1958), pp. 80–81, 444–45.

30. One of the most famous salons in Madrid was the *Academia imitatoria* of about 1586. Miguel de Barrios and Joseph Penso Vega were the leading lights of the Amsterdam *academias.* As a general illustration of the close ties with Spain, one may point to the presence in libraries in Amsterdam of the works of Quevedo and Fray Luis de Granada; see Van Praag, "Almas en litigio," *Clavileño* 1 (1950): 18–19.

31. The terminology is Benardete's (*Hispanic Culture,* p. 21).

32. For this section, see R. O. Jones, *A Literary History of Spain. The Golden Age: Prose and Poetry* (London, 1971), chaps. 5 and 7.

33. *Cancioneros* were collections of such lyrics (in *romance* or ballad and *letrilla* meters) usually by a variety of poets; the most famous of these was the *Cancionero de Baena* (1445).

34. *Obras de Garcilasso de la Vega con anotaciones de Fernando de Herrera* (Seville, 1580).

35. Jones, *Literary History,* p. 142.

36. Ibid., p. 156, quoting Góngora's *Soledad* 1:481–90, demonstrates how a single-word reference to Actaeon in connection with the virginal scene of the spice islands as viewed by the first Europeans suggests that greed will destroy the discoverers, since the erudite reader will recall that Actaeon was destroyed by his own dogs after spying on Diana, the Virgin Huntress, and her maidens.

37. For a convenient parallel, see John Donne's poem "A Valediction: Forbidding Mourning," with its developed metaphor of the compasses.

38. The term is the subject of a treatise by Baltasar Gracián, *Agudeza y el arte de ingenio* (Huesca, 1648).

39. The information here is drawn from a variety of sources, from the works of Cecil Roth, J. Caro Baroja, and H. Beinart *inter alia,* and is intended to give a general view, which may not be applicable to every community of Marranos at every point in the sixteenth and seventeenth centuries.

40. It may, indeed, be false to talk of Hebrew "dropping out" in view of the strength of this vernacular tradition. Several writers in the field refer to Spanish versions of prayers as indicating of itself a decline of Jewish knowledge, but this may not be so (see Beinart, "Converso Community in 15th Century Spain," pp. 469–70). Note, further, that what is taken as impure Spanish is often directly derived from the Ferrara Bible (see prayers given by Caro Baroja, *Los judíos en la España,* vol. 3, appendix 36, pp. 550–51).

41. Caro Baroja, *Los judíos en la España,* 1: 456, refers to readings being taken from the devotional works of Fray Luis de Granada and a book entitled *Espejo de consolación*—perhaps Salomon Usque's *Consolaçam ás tribulações de Israel (Consolation for the Tribulations of Israel)?*

42. This is true of the many treatises written by the leading polemicists Isaac Orobio de Castro, Saul Levy Mortera, and Eliau Montalto, several of which are to be found in the Bodleian Library, Oxford (Neubauer Catalogue MSS 2471–81).

43. Y. H. Yerushalmi, *From Spanish Court to Italian Ghetto,* p. 402, discusses Cardoso's view that "belief in" the Law achieves salvation; for the proposition that circumcision expunges Original Sin, see ibid., p. 92.

44. Other cases of Messianic claimants may be found in Beinart, "Converso Community in 15th Century Spain," pp. 459–60, and Caro Baroja, *Los judíos en la España,* 1: 405 ff.

45. See above, note 24; the Hebrew of the first lines is somewhat mutilated, though recognizable.

46. C. Roth, *A Life of Manasseh ben Israel* (Philadelphia, 1934), p. 66.

47. Yerushalmi, *From Spanish Court to Italian Ghetto,* chapter 6.

48. Roth, *A History of the Marranos,* p. 311.

49. For example, Augustus Ricius's *De Motu Spherae* (1512) proves to be the source of Isaac Cardoso's knowledge of Abraham Zacuto, Ibn Ezra, and Gersonides.

50. Yerushalmi, *From Spanish Court to Italian Ghetto,* pp. 297–98; Yerushalmi suggests that, rather than the shock of ignorance, it was a question of Da Costa's incapacity to free himself from the Christian view of Jewish tradition as purveyed by anti-Jewish tracts.

51. Caro Baroja, *Los judíos en la España,* 1: 405.

52. Caro Baroja makes the perceptive comment (ibid., 1: 392) that any group of believers will show a large proportion, perhaps a majority, who are uncertain regarding even the basic point of their faith. One should not therefore be too harsh in judging the apparent oddities of Marrano religion.

53. Révah's "judaisme potentiel"; see "Les Marranes," *Revue des études juives* 118 (1960): 55.

54. The use of a present participle ending in -*an* in place of the simple present tense seems to reproduce the adjectival origin of the so-called present tense in Hebrew, but is confusable with the normal third person plural of the present tense, e.g., in the *Shemah:* "que yo te encomendan hoy" ("that I command you this day"). Cf. notes to Barrios, *Acto sexto de Contrición,* p. 287, below.

55. British Library MS. Or. 8698 (in two parts, items 145 and 223). Other items in the same manuscript source include discussions on the Noachide Laws and the teachings of the Rambam. On the subject of Montalto's treatise, compare (in Portuguese) Orobio de Castro's "Explicação paraphrastica sobre o capítulo 53 do profeta Izahias" (Bodleian Library, MS. Op. Add. 4° 148, Neubauer Catalogue no. 2474).

56. See I. S. Révah, *Spinoza et le Dr. Juan de Prado* (Paris, 1959), passim.

57. This view does not run counter to those expressed by the School of Hillel in the Talmud discussion on the subject of external punishment for the wicked (*Rosh Ha-shanah,* fol. 16b ff.) but it was clearly too much for the ex-Marrano leaders of the community to accept.

58. This introduction could not be concluded without some reference at least being made to the Marrano poets whose work has not been included in this collection, such as: Diego Enríquez Basurto, son of Antonio Enríquez Gómez and author of a poem on the theme of Job, very much in the style of his father (*El triumfo de la virtud y paciencia de Job* [Rouen, 1649]); Abenatar Melo, who versified the Ferrara translation of the Psalms, adding occasional digressions, for instance relating his experience at the hands of the Inquisition (*Los CL psalmos de David,* Frankfort [Amsterdam?], 1626); and three writers of biblically inspired epics, Jacob Uziel (*David* [Venice, 1624]), Miguel de Silveira (*El Macabeo* [Naples, 1638]), and Estrella Lusitano (*La Machabea* [León, 1604]). While these works are of considerable interest as manifestations of the Marrano background, they cannot be considered of sufficient literary worth to stand on their own in an anthology of poetry.

*Marrano Poets of the
Seventeenth Century*

The Texts and Translations

The texts of the poems have been taken from various sources, printed and manuscript, as indicated in the accompanying notes; if printed, the first edition has been followed, unless otherwise stated. The language of the texts has been modernized, with the exception of (1) some archaic forms, such as *agora* for *ahora* and *proprio* for *propio;* (2) special poetic spellings, common in *culto* writing, such as the reduction of consonantal groups *(coluna* for *columna, retifica* for *rectifica),* the use of metathesis *(protento* for *portento)* and fusion *(dél* for *de él, della* for *de ella, prendella* for *prenderla);* (3) grammatical features prevalent in the seventeenth century, as in the use of *por* for *para,* singular verb with plural subjects and the feminine article *la* with words of the type *alma, agua,* etc. These should present the reader of Modern Spanish with little difficulty and have not been recorded in the notes. Proper names (including Hebrew) appear in the form given by the individual authors.

The translations of the poems are in no way intended to supersede the originals: they are there as an aid to the reader who knows little or no Spanish and aim to reproduce the poems from which they derive in a manner which is both as faithful as possible and as readable. The notes to the texts should compensate for any inadequacies in the translations, as well as providing additional information of interest to the reader. They refer in each case to the Spanish text, in keeping with the precedence this takes over the English version.

O N E

João Pinto Delgado

João Pinto Delgado is undoubtedly the most important literary talent to have emerged from the Marrano background: a poet of considerable standing, if not of the same rank as Luis de León, Garcilaso de la Vega, and other foremost poets of the Golden Age. He was born in the mid-1580s, the eldest of three sons of Gonçalo Delgado and grandson of a minor litterateur, also João Pinto Delgado (with whom he has sometimes been confused). His early life was spent in Vila Nova de Portimão in the Algarve, with a brief period in Lisbon, when his parents moved there at the turn of the century. His parents soon left for the Spanish Netherlands and subsequently France (prior to 1609) and João went back to Lisbon with the aim of pursuing his education and his literary ambitions. This period was most beneficial to the development of his poetic talents, since it brought him into contact with the works of Jorge Manrique, Garcilaso, and Herrera, and even those of his contemporaries Góngora and Luis de León, which circulated at that time in manuscript.

In 1624–26 João joined his parents in Rouen (they had become naturalized there in 1612) and in 1627 published the collection of poems on which his literary reputation is largely founded: *Poema de la Reyna Ester. Lamentaciones del Propheta Ieremias. Historia de Rut, y varias Poesias* (Rouen: David du Petit Val, 1627). In Rouen, the poet and his father were leading figures in the Marrano community, then at its height. Nominally they belonged to the parish of St. Vincent, but they practiced Judaism at a relatively orthodox level, given the conditions of official proscription. However, this relatively untroubled life was disrupted by the crisis which rent the *converso* community as a whole in 1633. This arose out of the refusal of a Spanish priest in Rouen, Diego de Cisneros, to grant a certificate of orthodoxy to a leading member of the Marrano community, Diego

POEMA
DE LA REYNA ESTER
Lamentaciones del
Propheta Ieremias.
Historia de Rut, y varias Poesias.
POR IOAN PINTO DELGADO
Al ilustrissimo, y Reuerendissimo Cardenal
de Richelieu, Gran Maestre, Supremo
y Superentendiente General
de la Nauegacion,
y Comercio de
Francia.

A ROVEN

Chez, Dauid du
Petit Val, Imprimeur
ordinaire du Roy
M. DC. XXVII.

Title page of João Pinto Delgado's *Poema de la Reyna Ester* . . . (Rouen: David du Petit Val, 1627), with woodcuts depicting scenes from the various poems in the collection

Olivera, in support of his application for naturalization. The background, however, was wider and grew out of the resentment of *conversos* of sincere Christian views who because of their family origins nonetheless fell under the suspicion of the Inquisition, making it impossible for them to remain in Spain. This resentment Cisneros fostered in his own campaign against judaizers, enlisting also the help of a special Inquisitor who had come to Rouen on behalf of a particular case in Spain but who had secret orders to investigate the crypto-Jews in France. Accusation and counteraccusation followed each other between the two sides as the quarrel grew more bitter. It was eventually resolved by the French Crown imposing a fine—or accepting a bribe, depending on interpretation—on the judaizing faction and, in a spirit of some realism, allowing them to carry on in their old ways, to the commercial benefit of the French nation. However, the Marrano community of Rouen had been fundamentally shaken and was soon to go into decline. João Pinto Delgado and his father sought refuge from the crisis in Antwerp, from where they moved on to Amsterdam. João became Mosseh, and in 1636–37 and 1640 he was one of the seven *parnasim* or governors of the Talmud Torah Seminary in Amsterdam. He died on 23 December 1653.

In common with the other Marrano poets, João Pinto Delgado looks frequently to the Bible for his themes: there is an evident attraction in those stories which demonstrate the power of God to effect salvation in times of Israel's sorrow, as in the case of Esther and the Exodus narrative, both of which Pinto Delgado deals with (*Poema de la Reina Ester* and *Canción . . . a la salida de Egipto*). His poetic paraphrase of the Lamentations of Jeremiah *(Lamentaciones del profeta Jeremías)* elaborates on the tragedies of Israel's history, while presenting the view that she is responsible for her travail through having failed to adhere to the Law. This reflects a theme seen elsewhere of the guilt felt by the Marrano regarding the inadequacy of his religious observance (Jewish, that is) while under Christian guise—a guilt which is explored in the unpublished "Autobiographical Poems." Together with the *Lamentaciones,* these poems also express the poet's notion of the Inquisition as God's instrument for bringing the Marranos back to Judaism by awakening them to their racial and religious origins. In *Rut* we see both the theme of the Law and its observance and that of Jewish identity elaborated. Throughout there are echoes of the great Spanish-language poets with whose works the poet became acquainted, as we have seen, in Lisbon: one may mention too Pinto Delgado's imitation of Luis de Granada's style of "progress of the soul" *(camino del alma)* witnessed in *Canción a la salida de Egipto,* which uses the theme of Exodus to recount the poet's own spiritual journey to true religious faith. There may also be observed, particularly in *La Reina Ester, Lamentaciones,* and *Rut,* the poet's use of his not inconsiderable reading of Rabbinic sources in a manner which is not merely of antiquarian interest but which greatly enriches the poetic imagery as a whole.

Accordingly, João Pinto Delgado may be regarded as the most successful of the three Marrano poets in absorbing the influences of the Spanish literary culture, even in its most evidently Christian forms, while at the same time infusing it with a Jewish tone and purpose which is learned, profound, and all-pervading. He is at once the most accomplished by Golden Age standards of the Marrano poets, and the most Jewish.

Three Autobiographical Poems

JOÃO PINTO DELGADO

Tres poemas autobiográficos

1   A la salida de Lisboa

Aquí está la infame puerta,
la del olivo y la espada,
para salir tan cerrada,
y para entrar tan abierta.

5   Si en ti la paz se destierra,
no eres del ramo capaz,
porque uno promete paz
y el otro ejecuta guerra.

Recoge, o nave, a Sodoma;
10   sólo a su cómplice embarca,
que, como no eres el Arca,
no hay que esperar la paloma.

Mancha tu cuchillo fiero
y quede pendiente aquí:
15   quedará la insignia en ti
como blasón verdadero.

Y tú, el más fiero león,
que matas quien no te ofende,
por mano de quien te entiende
20   tendrás la satisfacción.

Y aunque nace tu alegría
viendo a tantos perecer,
si a muchos lo hiciste ver,
también has de ver tu día.

25   Si nuestro pecado obliga
a sufrir tanto rigor,
considera que el Señor,
si disimula, castiga.

Three autobiographical poems

1   On leaving Lisbon

Here stands the infamous portal,
that of the olive and the sword,
for exit so securely shut
and for entrance so wide open.

5   If from in you peace is exiled,
you are not worthy of that branch,
since the one gives promise of peace,
while the other wages war.

Gather in, O ship, all Sodom,
10   take only its inmates aboard,
for, as you are not the famed Ark,
we can expect no dove to come.

Stain your bloodthirsty dagger
and let it go on hanging there:
15   upon you will that badge remain
as your true armorial blazon.

And you, the cruelest of lions,
who kills those who do not harm you,
by the hand of One who knows you
20   will you render satisfaction.

And although your delight is born
of seeing so many perish,
that day which you made others
suffer will also dawn for you.

25   If our sins do oblige us
to undergo such cruelty,
remember that the Lord, though he
cloaks his intent, will punish you.

        Si parece que se olvida
30   de castigar su enemigo,
        es sólo porque el castigo
        ha de ser más que en la vida.

            •   •   •   •   •

        Porque el cielo más se indine,
        fabricaste tu palacio
35   donde diste un breve espacio
        para que el cuerpo se incline.

        La doncella, entre el tormento,
        estando en la vida incierta,
        medio viva y medio muerta,
40   responde a tu pensamiento.

        Y entre penas y entre engaños,
        su temor no perdonó
        al padre que la engendró,
        cuanto y más a los extraños.

45   Niegas la vida a quien niega,
        y el que confiesa y se olvida,
        sin ver remedio, su vida
        entre las llamas entrega.

        No basta ver que sudó
50   el pobre con lo que vives,
        pues lo que ganó recibes
        y coges lo que él sembró.

            •   •   •   •   •

        ¡Ay de ti! fiero Esahú
        de quien la virtud no escapa,
55   ¿cómo has de asirle la capa
        a quien la tomaste tú?

If it seems that he forgets
30   to castigate his enemy,
it is only that his punishment
is to be greater than in life.

   •   •   •   •   •

So heaven would be the more outraged,
you built up high your palace
35   wherein you gave but a short space
for the body to incline in.

The maiden in the torment's midst,
standing uncertain of her life,
half alive and half in death,
40   gives her answer to your thinking.

And amidst pain and confusion
that terror did not leave untouched
the father who begot her,
no less than those not of her kin.

45   To him who denies, you deny life,
and he who confesses, careless,
seeing no means of escape,
gives up his life amid the flames.

Not enough for you to observe
50   the poor man sweat—that makes you thrive—,
for what he earned you now receive
and reap the harvest he did sow.

   •   •   •   •   •

Woe betide you, cruel Esau,
from whom virtue cannot escape,
55   how can you seek to uncloak him
whose very cloak you have stolen?

Ya que con justa razón
a tu padre no heredaste
y por el manjar trocaste
60   del cielo la bendición.

Paja serás aquel día
que la casa de tu hermano
pondrá fuego con su mano
a quien a su sangre ardía.

65   Los desterrados vendrán
al nuevo Templo a vivir,
y a quien hicieron servir
tus reyes le servirán.

Entonces tu confusión,
70   que mal agora lo advierte,
ha de ser tu misma muerte
y muerte sin redención.

Verás como siempre fuiste
a quien sus idolatrías
75   se acrescientan con los días,
y en ellos el sol perdiste.

Tienes ojos y no ves,
sin oír tienes oído,
eres ídolo dormido
80   que no anda y tiene pies.

Aflige al que has afligido,
al que a Dios conoce abrasa,
que de otra más fuerte brasa
será tu reino ofendido.

85   Empieza uno y otro robo
y sigue el mayor rigor,
porque no duerme el Pastor,
aunque va matando el lobo.

Since with good reason you did not
have your father's inheritance
and for a dish you did exchange
60   the blessing that came from heaven.

Straw you shall be in that day
when the house of your brother
shall set fire with his own hand
to him who burnt those of his blood.

65   Those who were dispossessed shall come
to the new Temple to live there,
and him whom they made to serve,
your kings themselves shall serve.

At that moment your confusion,
70   which vainly now he warns you of,
will surely be your very death
and that death without redemption.

You shall see how you always were
to them whose idolatries
75   increased with every passing day
and in those days you lost the sun.

You possess eyes and do not see,
without hearing you have ears,
you are but a sleeping idol
80   which does not walk and yet has feet.

Afflict the one you have afflicted,
the one who knows God, consume,
for by another stronger ember
shall your kingdom be assailed.

85   Undertake more and still more theft
and pursue the greatest rigor,
because the Shepherd does not sleep,
although the wolf is ravaging.

Parécete descuidado
90   en soportar tanta injuria:
¡ay de ti, cuando su furia
muestre cuál es su cayado!

Pedirás socorro en vano
a tus dioses, o gentil:
95   si David mató diez mil,
¿qué hará del Señor la mano?

Y tú, Pueblo que probaste
del Dio la piedosa vara,
vuelve, vuelve a Quien te ampara,
100   pues te escucha y no llamaste.

No mudes el corazón
de tu escudo y de tu Rey;
¡sea tu objecto su Ley
y tu vida su razón!

105   Sigue sus santos precetos,
que en medio los escuadrones
entre rabiosos leones,
has de alcanzar tus efetos.

No te olvides del lugar
110   donde holocausto ofrecías,
lunas y pascuas hacías
y ofrendas en santo altar.

Y, aunque se alejó de nos
por nuestro error, no te asombre,
115   porque los lejos del hombre
muy cerca son para Dios.

¡La diestra se olvida aquel,
Jerusalén, que te olvida!
¡falte a sus años la vida
120   a quien te escoge, o Babel!

He appears to you uncaring
90   in tolerating such affront:
woe betide you when his fury
shows you what his crook is made of!

You will plead in vain for succor
from those gods of yours, O Gentile:
95   if David killed his ten thousand,
what shall the hand of the Lord do?

And you, People who have tasted
the merciful rod of God,
return, return to him who helps you,
100   for he listens and you called not.

Do not move within your heart
away from your shield and your King;
let your purpose be his Law
and your whole life be his reason.

105   Hold fast to his holy precepts,
for amid the hostile squadrons
and the ravening lions,
you are bound to gain your purpose.

Do not forget the holy place
110   where the holocaust you offered
kept New Moon and Festivals,
made offerings on the holy altar.

And though he departed from us
through our sins, do not be surprised,
115   because the distances man makes
are but very close for God.

He loses his right hand's cunning
who forgets you, Jerusalem;
the years of his life are cut short
120   of him who chooses you, O Babel!

Tomando instrumento allí
la voz, entre pena tanta,
¡se le pegue a la garganta,
cuando cantare de ti!

125   Y el justo cielo le ampare
si, movido del dolor,
a tus hijos con rigor
en piedras despedazare.

Sagrada Jerusalén,
130   dulce bien, dulce memoria,
¡viva en nos, si no la gloria,
la memoria de tu bien!

Contemple mi pensamiento
siempre en ti y en tu grandeza,
135   porque la humana riqueza
es hoja que lleva el viento.

Jamás irán mis engaños
tras el día de placer,
que al fin el anochecer
140   cierra la cuenta de los años.

Mil veces dischoso aquel
que, en medio de su aflición,
le ofrece al Dio de Sion
que no desprecia a Israel.

145   Y en este confuso mar,
do tanto bajel se anega,
al puerto dichoso llega
donde se habrá de salvar.

Y de los reyes el Rey
150   sólo teme y sólo adora,
que fue, será y es agora:
un Dios, un Pueblo, una Ley.

As my voice, racked by such great pain,
takes up from there its instrument,
may it stick fast inside my throat
if I should try to sing of you.

125   And may just heaven help it
if, stirred to anguish by the grief,
it should with harshest rigor cleave
like shattered stones your children.

O sacred Jerusalem,
130   sweet blessing, sweet remembrance,
let live in us, if not the glory,
the memory of your blessing.

May my thoughts direct themselves
always to you and to your greatness,
135   because human riches are but
as a leaf which the wind bears off.

Never shall my illusions chase
after the day of pleasure,
for in the end the falling night
140   closes all the years' accounting.

A thousand times happy is he
who, in midst of his affliction,
offers to the God of Zion.
who does not disdain Israel.

145   And on this sea of confusion,
in which many a ship is lost,
he will reach the happy port
where sure salvation he will find.

And he only fears and adores
150   the one who is the King of kings
who was and will be and is now:
one God, one People and one Law.

O dichoso el que confía
y que firmemente espera
155   la palabra verdadera
que está señalando el día.

Que siempre dio su lugar
a la Ley de Dio, su pecho;
que Ley que su dedo ha hecho,
160   ¿qué mano podrá borrar?

¡Acude, o Señor, te ruego,
acude a la pena grave!
Sepa el mundo, si no sabe,
que puedes más que su fuego.

165   No desampare tu mano
quien tu Nombre santo invoca;
quedará como una roca
a las olas del tirano.

Y, en tanto, entre las tinieblas,
170   vea el sol de tu verdad;
que abonde todo es maldad,
¿qué puede haber sino nieblas?

2   A la despedida de un amigo

Oveja que en nuestro error
fuiste olvidando tus años,
vuelve, vuelve a sus rebaños,
porque te llama el Pastor.

5   Deja el común devaneo
entre la humana esperanza,
donde tan poco se alcanza,
aunque se alcance el deseo.

O fortunate is he who trusts
and who waits in steadfastness
155   upon the true word of the Lord
which is pointing towards the day.

For he always gave his time
to the Law of God, his valor;
for the Law his finger wrote,
160   what hand can ever wipe away?

Assist me, O Lord, I beg you,
assist me in my grave suffering!
Let the world know, if it knows not,
that you are mightier than its fire.

165   May your hand not leave abandoned
him who your holy Name invokes;
he will remain just like a rock
against the waves of tyranny.

And, meanwhile, amid the darkness
170   let him see the sun of your Truth;
for where all around is evil,
what can there be but clouding haze?

2   *To a departing friend*

Sheep that in our common error
spent your young years forgetting,
return, return there to his flocks,
because the Shepherd calls you.

5   Leave behind the common madness,
amongst the hopes of human kind,
where so little can be achieved,
though one achieve one's heart's desire.

       Los bienes que, sin razón,
10   el hombre sigue engañado,
       al cierto plazo llegado,
       se vuelven en lo que son.

       Ligero viento es la vida,
       la muerte volando viene;
15   mal hace que se previene
       al punto de la partida.

       Dichoso quien escogió
       de dos el mejor camino
       y el velo del desatino
20   la vista no le cegó.

       Dichoso quien, viendo el mar
       subir las ondas al cielo,
       no le consume el recelo
       de no poderse salvar.

25   Vete al fin y en compañía
       el bien que buscas te siga,
       y tempestad enemiga
       jamás te escurezca el día.

       Parte entre nave contento,
30   sin el temor que desvela,
       y un ángel en cada vela
       te sople suave el viento.

       Siempre seguro el timón
       enfrene con señorío,
35   tan obediente el navío,
       como fuiste a la razón.

       Jamás tu sueño interrompa
       náutica voz vigilante,
       ni viento airado te espante,
40   ni cuerda alguna se rompa.

The good things that without reason
10   man follows in his illusion,
when the certain due date arrives,
will change to what they really are.

Life is an insubstantial wind,
death comes upon us in full flight;
15   he ill prepares himself who acts
at the point of his departure.

Happy the one who has chosen
the better of two pathways
and for whom the veil of folly
20   has not obscured his vision.

Happy the one who, seeing the sea
lift high its waves up to the sky,
is not devoured by the fear
that he cannot save himself.

25   Go at last and for company
may the good you seek go with you,
and may no hostile tempest
ever cloud your day with darkness.

Depart contented on your ship,
30   without the fear that chases sleep,
and may an angel on each sail
gently blow the wind for you.

May the rudder ever constant
with mastery keep to course the ship,
35   which is as ready to respond
as you were to reason's call.

May your sleep never be broken
by a watchful seafaring voice,
nor angry wind cause you to fear,
40   nor any rope be made to rend.

Cuando dichoso pisare
tu planta el amado suelo,
cumplido el deseo, al cielo
pide que el mío me ampare.

45   No me ofendas con tu olvido,
que al fin es término indino
olvidar un peregrino
el que peregrino ha sido.

Que si la noche mortal
50   no cierra a mi vida el día,
la santa luz que te guía
será mi norte y señal.

Al fin, en llegando allí,
con el contento que es justo,
55   salgan lágrimas de gusto,
si no salieren por mí.

Y di: "Señor, pues que yo
en tal libertad me veo,
encamina igual deseo,
60   si tanta ventura no."

•   •   •   •   •

(La nueva vida del amigo imaginada)

El día santificado
en ayuno y oración,
alcanzarás el perdón
que se promete al pecado.

65   La Pascua será alegría,
gusto, bien, placer y gloria,
ofreciendo a la memoria
la memoria de aquel día.

Allí verás del cordero
70   la sangre que fue señal
cuando, puesta en el portal,
saltaba el desnudo acero.

When your happy foot should tread
upon the well-beloved soil,
having accomplished your desire,
pray to heaven that it aid mine.

45   Do not hurt me by forgetting,
for surely it is a vile deed,
for one who was a pilgrim once
to forget a fellow pilgrim.

For if the fatal night of death
50   does not close the day of my life,
the holy light which guided you
shall be for me lodestar and sign.

Finally, when you arrive there,
with contentment which is proper,
55   let tears of joy well up from you,
if they do not well up for me.

And say "Lord, since it is that I
find myself in such great freedom,
guide like desires upon their way,
if not crown them with such fortune."

  •   •   •   •   •

(The friend's new life imagined)

On that day which is sanctified
by fasting and by prayer,
you will achieve the pardon
which has been promised for our sins.

65   Passover shall be joy, content,
blessing, rejoicing and delight,
offering up to memory,
the memory of that day.

There you shall behold the blood
70   of the lamb, which was the signal
smeared upon the doorpost, when
the naked sword sprang to its deed.

El pan que con priesa llevan,
huyendo del enemigo,
75   que, como del bien testigo,
en su memoria renuevan.

Al sabat descansarás,
sólo moviendo las plantas
para oír palabras santas
80   que no enfastidian jamás.

Dices entonces, pues que ya
otro medio no conoces:
"¡Vientos, llevad estas voces
a quien tan lejos está!"

85   Y, viendo que mi fortuna
sólo a mis males me llama,
por mí lágrimas derrama,
ya que me debes alguna.

Que pues me detiene aquí
90   tan forzoso inconveniente,
quien todo tiene presente
no se olvidará de mí.

Que si penetra el abismo
y su ser en todo está,
95   ¿cómo no penetrará
en el centro de mí mismo?

Arme el mundo su rigor,
sus armas vibre en mi pecho,
que en mi bien y en su despecho
100   será mi escudo el Señor.

Mal haya quien se engañare
de mentirosa ilusión
y en la mortal ocasión
entre inmundancias se hallare.

The bread which in haste they take,
fleeing from the enemy,
75   which as witness of the blessing
they bring back to their memory.

On the Sabbath you will rest,
not stirring the soles of your feet,
save to go and hear holy words
80   which will never make you weary.

Then you will say, since now you know
of no other way to do it:
"Winds, stir up your loudest voice
for one who is so far away!"

85   And, seeing that my fortune
only calls me to misfortune,
shed some tears on my behalf,
since there are a few you owe me.

For, since I am detained here by
90   such unyielding obstacles,
he for whom all things are present
will not be unmindful of me.

For, if he penetrates the abyss
and his being is in all things,
95   how can he not penetrate
into the center of my self?

Let the world summon its rigor,
brandish its arms against my breast,
since for my good and for their wrath
100   the Lord shall be a shield to me.

Cursed be the one who deceives
himself with lying illusion
and in the moment of his death
finds himself amid uncleanness.

105   Que aquellos que siempre están
lisonjeando al oído,
desamparan el dormido
entre sus penas y afán.

    ¿Qué vale el arrepentir
110 y el querer volver atrás,
si es acabar por jamás
el empezar a morir?

    Llegando el caso preciso
¿cuál hombre de fiero pecho
115 no deseara haber hecho
lo que, viviendo, no hizo?

    Que, en tan miserable estado,
en aflición se convierte,
más que el dolor de la muerte,
120 el dolor de haber pecado.

    Y cuando un grande dolor
entre temores saltea,
aunque de muerte no sea,
causa la muerte el temor.

125 Si este bien consideramos
y en este mal advertimos,
¿cómo este bien no seguimos?
¿cómo este mal no dejamos?

    O terrible inclinación
130 del hombre que no procura
la senda que es más segura
y sigue a la salvación.

    No más engaño que clama
por rigor del infierno:
135 "¡Acude, o Señor eterno,
y ampara al pobre que llama!"

105   For those who are forever
flattering the sleeper's senses
in the end leave him abandoned
to his sorrow and affliction.

Of what value is repentance
110   and the desire to start anew,
if once one begins to die
one is finishing for ever?

When that ordained event draws nigh,
what man of the utmost valor
115   would not wish that he had done
what he, while living, did not do?

For in such hapless circumstance,
what becomes a sore affliction
is not the pain of death itself,
120   but the pain of having sinned.

And when a great pain assails one,
in the midst of all those terrors,
though it may not be the terror
of death, it is the cause of death.

125   If this good thing we consider
and take warning of this evil,
why do we not pursue the good,
why the evil not abandon?

O terrible inclination
130   of the man who does not attempt
to tread the most secure of paths
that leads to his salvation!

No greater self-deceit than that
which cries out through hell's rigors:
135   "Come to me, O eternal Lord,
and assist this poor man who calls."

3   En alabanza del Señor

Señor, tú que gobiernas cielo y tierra,
a cuya potestad el mar inmenso
no muda el pie del límite que encierra.
Tú que penetras con tu rayo el denso,
5   la claridad apuras con tu fuego,
a quien es nieve opuesto el más intenso.
Ilumina, Señor, deste mi ciego
abismo aquella natural figura
que dio mi ser, porque sin ti le niego.
10   Del arco de tu amor, la que asegura
del contrario, la flecha al alma apunta,
despojo sea, como fue tu hechura.
Unánimes, al fin, conforma y junta
los sentidos que, débiles, caminan
15   tras vanidad a la miseria junta.
Como a su centro el elemento, inclinan
el albedrío a la aparencia vana,
donde se pierden cuando más dominan.
Su luz esparce apenas la mañana,
20   cuando la tarde hace tiniebla al día
que desengaña la esperanza humana.
La majestad que en hombros sostenía
el peso de la tierra se resuelve
en vil materia, si pesada y fría.
25   A lo concavo della a pagar vuelve
lo que sacó la poderosa mano,
y desta obligación ninguno absuelve.
Llegada, pues, al trono soberano
de tu justicia el alma, ¿cuál se atreve
30   al descargo del mal del mundo vano?
Si de tu gracia aquel licor no llueve
que fertiliza el ser con dulce aliento,
como a los campos el rocío y la nieve.
¡O nueva maravilla! ¡o gran protento!
35   ¡o conocida gloria y no buscada,
si niebla encubre al lince más atento!
Firme siempre la vista en la dorada
imagen del tesoro el alma emplea,
buscando mucho donde alcanza nada.

3   In praise of the Lord

        Lord, you who govern the heavens and the earth,
    by whose power the immeasurable sea
    does not overrun the bounds that enclose it;
        You who penetrate with your beam the dense gloom,
5   and distill out the brightness with your fire,
    for which the intensest fire opposed is snow;
        Illuminate, Lord, in this my blind-dark
    abyss that natural countenance which gave
    to me the life which without you I deny.
10   With the bow of your love which protects me
    from enemies, aim your arrow at my soul,
    let it be your spoil, as it was your making.
        At last, conform, join in unanimity
    my feelings which, weak-spirited, take the path
15 after vanity allied to misery.
        As the element is drawn to its center,
    so they incline the free will to vain appearance
    where they are lost when most they dominate.
        The morning has scarcely scattered wide its light
20 than the falling evening turns to dusk the day
    which dashes the illusions of human hope.
        That majesty which on its shoulders sustained
    the whole weight of the earth crumbles and dissolves
    into vile matter, heavy indeed and cold.
25   To its hollowness returns to pay the price
    that which the powerful hand created from it,
    and from that obligation none is absolved.
        When the soul, therefore, arrives at the sovereign throne
    of your justice, whoever shall dare to plead
30 aquittal for the evil of this vain world;
        If that liquid of your Grace does not rain down
    which with sweet breath makes the being spring to life,
    as the dewfall and the snow upon the fields?
        O novel wonder! O great portent of good!
35 O glory known to all and never sought,
    since mist engulfs the eyes of the sharpest lynx!
        The soul directs its vision ever-constant
    towards the golden image of the treasure,
    seeking much where little it can achieve.

40 ¿Cuándo bastó la tierra al que desea?
¿o cuando deseó quien se contenta,
porque la gloria en el descanso vea?
 Ya nueva luz el sol nos apresenta,
huyó la escuridad, descubre el cielo
45 la faz serena, ausente la tormenta.
 Lejos ya, lejos espantoso hielo
huye desenfunado y no despierta
del sueño dulce tímido recelo.
 No mueve el son en la cerrada puerta,
50 en su quietud el alma, porque agora
al cielo vive, como al mundo abierta.
 No da piedad el mísero que llora,
cuando pide socorro a mármol duro,
si a duro corazón refugio implora.
55 En las ciudades vive mal seguro
el inocente con el hombre fiero
y entre las fieras halla ampara y muro.
 Mas quien de su camino verdadero
la senda olvida, su castigo aguarde,
60 si no al presente, al límite postrero.
 Del tiempo mío hice, mi Dios, alarde
y vi en los bosques, sin hallar salida,
temprano el mal, el desengaño tarde.
 Colgó de un hilo breve la homicida
65 espada de la muerte, y con la muerte,
la pena eterna de la inmortal vida.
 Contra el contrario, con tu mano fuerte
vibraste el dardo, y si quedó vencido,
su sinrazón y tu razón lo advierte.
70 De un monte a otro anduve tan perdido,
que de la propria diestra me olvidaba,
que es memoria del mal, del bien olvido.
 A vanas apariencias me humillaba,
árboles que criara el agua y viento,
75 de mi ignorancia siendo el alma esclava.
 Pero si el cielo llama el pensamiento
de lo interior del corazón indicio,
alta deidad en mis objectos siento.
 Trace engañado el mundo sacrificio,
80 siendo el lazo que al mísero condena
de su sudor infausto beneficio.

40   When did the earth suffice to him who desired?
Or when did he who is contented desire
that he in still repose might see the glory?
     Now does the sun present us with a new light,
the darkness has fled, the heavens reveal
45   a face of serenity, the storm has passed.
     Far away, already far the fearful frost
flees shorn of its vanity and does not wake
from gentle sleep timorous anxiety.
     The knock upon the fast-shut door does not stir
50   the soul in its tranquillity, because now
it lives in heaven, as open to the world.
     The wretched man who weeps causes no pity
when he seeks succor of a hard marble stone,
if he now craves refuge with a stone-hard heart.
55   The innocent man lives with little safety
in the city with the man who is a beast
and amid the wild beasts finds help and shelter.
     But he who forgets the pathway of his true
life's journey, let him expect his punishment,
60   if not at present, at life's furthest limit.
     My God, I boasted of the time that was mine
and beheld in the leafy groves, without exit,
evil soon and disenchantment all too late.
     From a brief thread hung above me the murderous
65   sword of death, and with death loomed the eternal
punishment of the everlasting life.
     Against the enemy with your mighty hand
you shook the spear and if he lay there vanquished,
his unreason and your reason do proclaim it.
70   From one mount to another I went, so lost
that I forgot my own right hand, which is the
memory of sin and of good, forgetting.
     I bowed myself down before vain semblances,
trees that the wind and water might create,
75   my soul being a slave to my ignorance.
     But if heaven looks upon the thoughts as signs
revealing what lies deep within the heart,
in my aims I sense a high divinity.
     Let the illusioned world plan a sacrifice,
80   for the bond which leads the wretched man to death
yet brings the profit of his hapless labors.

Lleve arastrando el cepo y la cadena,
y fínjase deidad y al que padece
aflija siempre en desusada pena.

85   Que si a los ojos la pared le ofrece,
el sol le niega y le defiende el día,
la exterior vista sólo le escurece.

De sus gemidos nace su alegría,
su manto adorna con el pobre manto,
90   del pasto ajeno sus ovejas cría.

Al duro mármol enternece el llanto,
y con él se endurece el fiero pecho,
o duro *Oficio*, ¿quién te llama *Santo?*

¿Cuándo se verá el tiempo satisfecho,
95   el tiempo y la mitad, que alegre vea
el esparcido pueblo el patrio lecho;

Cuando Baal, que del valor se arrea
de aquel fino metal debido al Arca,
humilde caiga, y el gentil lo crea;

100   Cuando el de llaves áspero monarca
no trocara por el tesoro infame
el de las tierras, con que el mundo abarca;

Cuando tirano, y no pastor, se llame,
sirviendo aquél que, en tanta servidumbre,
105   la escoria vil de sus reliquias lame?

El afligido, entonces, nueva lumbre
verá en el Valle de la Muerte, a cuantos
la ofensa celestial fue su costumbre.

Enjuga, o hija de Sion, tus llantos;
110   vuelve a abrazar los hijos que lloraste,
perdidos muchos y ganados tantos.

En deliciosos faustos los criaste,
de tu grandeza procedió el olvido,
con que al extraño tu heredad dejaste.

115   ¿Dónde está el holocausto? ¿el encendido
fuego y no apagado? ¿adó la gloria
del Santo Templo poco merecido?

Volvió la culpa humana transitoria
aquella majestad que, casi eterna,
120   apenas hoy conserva la memoria.

Piedad no negará, ni pena interna,
al duro bronce, al alma más terrible,

Let them drag out for him the stocks and chain
and let them think themselves a god and ever
85   afflict the suffering with an outmoded pain.
For if they offer to his eyes the blank wall,
deny him the sun, forbid him light of day,
it is but the outward vision they obscure.
Out of his moanings is born their rejoicing,
90   their cloth they veil with the mantle of the poor,
they feed their sheep on pasture which is not theirs.
Weeping softens the heart of hardest marble,
but with it the cruel beast turns to hardness—
O stone-hard Office, who can call you Holy?
95   When shall we see the fulfillment of the time,
the time and half a time when rejoicingly
the scattered people will see their native land;
When Baal, who takes for his own the value
of that fine metal which to the Ark is due,
100   will be abased and the Gentile accept it;
When the harsh monarch who carries the keys
will not barter for vile ignoble treasure
that King of lands who all the world embraces;
When he will be called tyrant, not a shepherd,
105   serving him who in such great servitude
licked the worthless dross of their holy relics?
Then will the afflicted behold a new light
in the valley of death; for as many
as whose custom was the offense of heaven.
110   Wipe dry, O daughter of Zion, your tears;
return, embrace the children for whom you wept,
many of them lost, so many now refound.
In pageantries of splendor you nurtured them,
from your grandeur arose their forgetfulness,
so your inheritance fell to the stranger.
115   Where is the sacrificial offering, the fire
lit and not extinguished? Whither the glory
of the Holy Temple, scarcely merited?
Transitory human sin overturned
that majesty which, though near to eternal,
120   today is scarcely preserved in memory.
Mercy he will not deny, nor internal grief,
to the hard bronze, to the most froward of souls,

del bien antiguo la pasión moderna.
¿Cómo será, Señor, cómo es posible
125 que no anticipe el término prescrito
el eco de gemidos insufrible?

Mil años para ti, como infinito,
un día son, y son los breves años
un siglo al hombre en pena del delito.

130 Falta el refugio y sobran desengaños,
dicen a voces: "¿Dónde está su guarda?"
y nuestra viña roban los extraños.

Quien tu precepto entre silencio guarda,
ignorante te ofende; al que publica,
135 poco el castigo de los hombres tarda.

Y como nadie en sí se justifica,
siendo común la fuerza del pecado,
vano remedio a la miseria aplica.

Cuando el lagar será de ti pisado,
140 que de los hombres estarán contigo,
mil a tus pies, pero ninguno al lado.

Confuso, entonces, viendo el enemigo
tu diestra airada y tu furor ardiente,
será su muerte de tu voz testigo.

145 Por ti, por ti, con tu rigor se aumente
tu gloria misma, que la ofrece el hombre
a quien no oye, a quien no ve ni siente.

De la memoria es y borrado el Nombre
que adora el serafín más abrasado,
150 de tu divino Ser alto renombre.

Vacila el ignorante, y su cuidado
de un yerro a otro, ciego, le encamina,
al vivo muerto, en muertos confiado.

Su entendimiento y su rodilla inclina
155 a vano objecto, do, si el fuego abrasa,
él será dios de su deidad divina.

En las redes el mísero se enlaza
que, ambicioso, tendió quien abrir quiso
la casa humana y la celeste casa.

160 Y el sucesor, que nuevas redes hizo,
retifica al mayor merecimiento
de fe sobrada ingrato paraíso.

El engañado cetro, que en el viento
firmó sus esperanzas, deseara
165 que, con su ser, muriera su tormento,

the present passion of an ancient blessing.
How can it be, Lord, how is it possible
125 that the determined end is not brought forward
by the unsufferable echo of wailing?

A thousand years for you, being infinite,
are but a day and the, to you, brief years are
a century to man in sorrow for his crime.
130 Refuge is lacking, disillusion abounds,
they shout out, mockingly: "Where is their help?"
and our vineyards are plundered by the stranger.

He who observes in silence your commandments
in ignorance offends you; if publicly,
135 the punishment of men but little tarries.

And as no one on his own vindicates himself,
since the power of sin is universal,
vain is the cure he lays on his wretched state.

When the grapes in the winepress are trodden down
140 by you, you will have men in accompaniment,
a thousand at your feet, but none beside you.

Then, when in confusion the enemy sees
your wrathful right hand and your burning fury,
their deaths shall be the proof your voice has spoken.
145 By you, by you alone with your harsh rule is
your glory increased, for mankind offers it
to those who do not hear, do not see or feel.

Now from memory has been expunged the Name
which the brightly burning seraphim adore,
150 the utmost glory of your divine Being.

The ignorant man wavers and his concerns
blindly lead him on from one sin to another,
dead to the living, trusting in the dead.

His understanding and his knee he bends
155 before a vain object which, if the fire takes,
will make him god in his own divinity.

The wretched man ensnares himself in the nets
schemingly spread by one who wished to open
the House of Mankind and the House of Heaven.
160 And his successor, who prepared new nets,
confirms for those who are most deserving
an unpleasant heaven for their abundant faith.

The deluded scepter, which upon the wind
founded his vain hopes, should dearly wish that,
165 with his being's end, his torturing would cease,

Cuando el humilde, a quien cubrió la cara
el afrentoso velo, en el instante
reciba mucha entre la gloria rara;
Antiguo pacto que al amado amante
170   fue recompensa de su justo celo,
del temor santo, de su fe constante.
Si de metal nos prometiste el cielo,
por nuestro error, olvida nuestro olvido,
y aparte tu piedad nuestro recelo.
175   Al corazón de ti más dividido
recoge a ti, porque apurado quede
más que oro fino de crisol salido:
¡o venturoso a quien tal bien sucede!

Poema de la Reina Ester

El sueño y las lástimas de Mardochay

El fiero son que articuló la fama
de Mardochay hiriendo en el oído,
desciende al centro y la piedosa llama,
si en fuego nace, vive en el gemido;
5   y cubre al punto que su llanto empieza
saco su pecho, polvo su cabeza.

En sueño alcanza que el castigo justo,
contra Israel, del cielo se prepara,
si reinando Nabuc con culto injusto
10   atrevido sus dioses adorara,
y de Asuero fue, por su delicia,
agradable la mesa en su inmundicia.

Vio levantarse tempestad terrible
y el movimiento sacudir la tierra,
15   y en el mundo esparcida voz terrible
causar el miedo al corazón la guerra;
y dos dragones que entre sí reñían,
de quien los hombres, y su silbo, huían.

When the humble man whose face was covered
by the affronting veil, in that moment
receives a goodly portion of rare glory;
An ancient pact which for the loving lover
170   was the recompense for his faithful zeal,
for his saintly fear and for his constant faith.
If you promised us a heaven of metal,
for our sin's sake, forget all our forgetting
and let your mercy cast aside all our fearing.
175   The heart that has been the most cut off from you
gather to yourself, so that it may remain
purer than fine gold drawn from the crucible:
O happy he who can such a blessing gain!

The poem of Queen Esther

The lament of Mordecai

When the harsh report that rumor spreads abroad
strikes the ear of Mordecai, it descends
to his soul's center and the piteous flame,
though born in fire, lives in his lamentation;
5   and the instant he begins his plaint, his breast
is clothed with sackcloth and his head with ashes.

In a dream he sees that this just punishment
upon Israel has been prepared by heaven,
for having in Nabuco's reign in wrongful
10   worship brazenly adored their false gods
and found, for their delight, Ahasuerus'
table agreeable in its uncleanness.

He saw rise up a terrifying tempest
and its motion as it passed shake the whole earth
15   and a voice of terror, spreading through the world,
cause fear to wage war upon the hearts of men,
and two dragons who fought against each other,
with men fleeing from them and the hiss they made.

Allí breve escuadrón de aflicta gente,
20   a quien opuestas las naciones varias,
era su intento, con furor ardiente,
sacar del mundo, como en él contrarias;
triste miraba y tenebroso el día
que pueblo tanto humildes oprimía.

25   Clamando al fin por el sonido horrendo
que en los dragones, fiero, se excitaba,
vía una fuente, entre los dos corriendo,
que el furor de sus golpes apartaba;
y vuelta en río, y río tormentoso,
30   en las ondas crecía un mar furioso.

El sol después con el dorado rayo
henchir la tierra de su claro aspecto,
y gente poca en tímido desmayo
subir gloriosa al más honroso efeto,
35   y la paz y verdad, de amor profundo,
con luces santas ilustrar el mundo.

Con el dolor que sus entrañas rompe,
con la piedad que su dolor le aviva,
la voz, con que el silencio se interrompe,
40   de un alma muerta sube al cielo viva;
y en el estado a que llegó infelice
el pueblo aflicto lamentando dice:

"¡Ah! de Jacob los hijos castigados,
que, en los tormentos del antiguo daño,
45   en vuestro mal envueltos los pecados,
la cerviz humilláis a yugo extraño,
¡mirad agora vueltas las cadenas
en vuestro fin y el fin de vuestras penas!

"Pues de Sión el alto bien perdistes,
50   preparad al cuchillo vuestros cuellos:
será la pena a tanto error, si vistes
el instrumento de soberbia en ellos;
que quien su ley entre su gloria olvida,
poca es la paga, si lo fue la vida.

It was here the intention of the many
20   antagonistic nations, with burning wrath,
to remove from the world as a loathsome thing
the small army of an afflicted people;
sorrowful it was to see and black the day
that so many people should oppress the weak.

25   Wailing finally at the horrendous sound
that rose, blood-chilling, from within the dragons,
he saw a fountain which flowed between the two
and interposed between their furious blows;
and now to river, to raging river turned,
30   from out its waves grew up a furious sea.

Then next he saw the sun with golden ray
fill the whole earth with its brilliant aspect,
and a small nation beset by timid fear
rise up in glory to the most honored state,
35   and peace and truth, issuing from deepest love,
infuse the world with a mass of holy lights.

With the pain that pierces his inner being,
with the pity that inflames his anguish,
his voice, which breaks the silence of the night,
40   rises heavenward, though dead his soul, alive;
and lamenting for a people sore-oppressed
and the state to which they have fallen, he says:

"Oh you, the children of Jacob now chastised,
who in torments arising from an ancient wrong,
45   for your sins were wrapped up in your evil,
bow down your neck beneath a foreign yoke,
look now and behold your chains turned back on you
to seek your end and end all your chastisements!

"Since you lost the exalted gift of Zion,
50   make ready your necks to receive the sword's edge:
it shall be the punishment fit for such sins,
if you see in this the instrument of pride;
for he who neglects the Law when at his height,
pays so small a price if with his life he pays.

55   "Mas ¡ay! que veo el pueblo más amado,
el escogido del Saber eterno,
ramos de aquél que con cuchillo airado
por santo amor trocó su amor interno,
y triste fin su vida condenada,
60   reliquia poca de furiosa espada!

     "De graves canas siento los gemidos,
entre suspiros muertos inocentes,
en llanto siempre y en dolor nacidos,
despojo agora de contrarias gentes,
65   y en sacrificio míseras doncellas,
que su virtud será castigo en ellas.

     "¿Cuál corazón podrá sufrir la pena
que en el discurso engendra la memoria,
viendo en teatro de ciudad ajena
70   viva la infamia y muerta nuestra gloria?
si no castigos a la culpa iguales,
la muerte, al fin, después de tantos males.

     "Dichoso aquél que entre la espada y fuego
dejó la vida, humilde a su enemigo,
75   cuando, llegado al último sosiego,
fue de los males de Sión testigo,
y en las ruinas de su Templo santo
entre la muerte sepultó su llanto.

     "Viendo el lugar que, más oculto al hombre,
80   un hombre solo penetrar podía
y articulando el inefable Nombre,
pedir al cielo su piedad un día,
si el enemigo en él firmó su planta
¿quién negara la vida en pena tanta?

85   "Agora ausente del sagrado muro,
del santo culto, muertos nuestros reyes,
cual hoja al viento el pueblo no seguro,
sujeto al fuero de diversas leyes,
en el profundo de tristeza y miedo,
90   la voz le ofende y le señala el dedo.

55 "But woe is me, for I can see the best-loved
people, the chosen of the eternal Wisdom,
branches of him who with angry blade in hand
exchanged for a holy love the love within,
their lives now condemned to meet a sorry end,
60 these few survivors of the sword of fury!

"I can hear the groaning cries of grave gray age,
amid whimpered sighs the deaths of innocents,
weeping for a lifetime, come to life in pain,
now the spoil of nations hostile to them,
65 and in their sacrifice like wretched maidens,
for their virtue brings on them their punishment.

"What human heart could stand to bear the anguish,
which memory in the course of time engenders,
to see upon that alien city's stage
70 infamy live on and all our glory die,
if not punishment proportioned to the sin,
then death, at last, after so many ills?

"Fortunate was he who between the sword and fire
humbly gave up his life to his enemy,
75 when he, coming to the ultimate repose,
was witness to the sufferings of Zion,
and in the ruins of her holy Temple
amid death interred his lamentation.

"Beholding the place, deepest hidden from men,
80 where one man alone was permitted entry
and uttering there the ineffable Name,
on one day plead to heaven for its mercy,
if the enemy had planted there his foot,
who would have denied his life in such a trial?

85 "Now separated from the sacred Wall,
from the holy Temple rite, our kings all dead,
the imperiled people as leaves upon the wind,
subject to the fief of divers foreign laws
in the depths of affliction and seized by dread,
90 rumor assails and points the finger at them.

"¿Cuál más humilde calla nuestro agravio?
¿quién no se alegra oyendo nuestra pena?
y al inocente ¿cuál compuesto labio
en la opinión del mundo no condena?
95   que en odio tanto, alegre en la mudanza,
de nuestro mal su proprio bien alcanza.

"¿Cómo, Señor, la fuerza del delito
te obliga así, que en nuestro mal te agrades?
siendo la nube a un sol que es infinito,
100   y un monte opuesto al mar de tus piedades;
si nuestro error, aunque major condene,
tu luz no encubre, ni tu mar detiene.

"Mira, Señor, que un breve santuario
al pueblo fuiste, que tu ausencia llora,
105   y aunque ese error se ha vuelto su contrario,
amaste un tiempo y no olvidaste agora;
en tanto mal la voz de sus gemidos
los aires rompa y suba a tus oídos.

"Cuando tu espada desnudar quisiste
110   en la venganza del major pecado,
piedoso el celo de tu siervo oíste,
en su respuesta, por tu honor, fiado;
si parte fue su labio de obligarte,
el todo supla do faltó la parte."

115   Dijo, y llevado del dolor presente,
que en pena tanta su eleción le niega,
llega al palacio, de sí mismo ausente,
y el mal le escusa, si atrevido llega;
porque a sus leyes era intento opuesto
120   entrar en él con hábito funesto.

"Who so humble as keeps silence at our wrong?
Who does not rejoice to hear our suffering?
And what fabricating tongue does not condemn
the innocent before the world's opinion?
95   For in such hatred, rejoicing at our change,
in our ill-fate they find their own well-being.

"How is it, Lord, that the weight of our offense
thus forces you to take pleasure in our ill?
It is a cloud across an infinite sun,
100   and a mountain against your sea of mercies;
unless it be, though others worse condemning,
your light engulf, your sea arrest our error.

"Behold, Lord, you were a brief sanctuary
for the people that now bewails your absence,
105   and though their sin has become a stumbling block,
you once loved and have not now forgotten them;
in such dire straits may the sound of their lament
break through the skies and rise to reach your hearing.

"Whenever you desired to unsheathe your sword
110   to exact vengeance for the greatest sin,
you in mercy hearkened to your servant's zeal,
he trusting for your honor in that reply;
if it was required his tongue should entreat you,
then complete the whole, supply the missing part."

115   He spoke and transported by the present grief,
which in such pain withholds his power of choice,
he arrives at the palace beside himself,
and if he dares come, his plight excuses him;
because it is to contravene their laws
120   to enter there dressed in funereal garb.

La triste consolación de Amán

"Ay! (le responden) si verdad recela
lo que en bosquejo el corazón imprime,
no en vano el alma en el temor se hiela,
aunque el vigor de tu poder le anime;
5   que es la fortuna, en sus regalos fiera,
al bien difícil, pero al mal ligera.

"Si de Judá te procedió la guerra,
justo el dolor y justo el recelo,
que cuando caye, caye humilde a tierra,
10   y cuando sube, sube altivo al cielo;
que polvo iguala, iguala a las estrellas,
postrado en él o levantado en ellas."

La oraciòn de la Reina Ester

Mientras la reina con la ansia interna
el rey y Amán a su convite inclina
y alegre espera de la fuente eterna
el santo arroyo de pidad divina;
5   con alma humilde, junto a las corrientes
de fuente inmensa, son sus ojos fuentes.

Aqual humor, que de abundante vena
del alta fuente a la interior mezclado,
regó la huerta de delicias llena,
10   que sus canales derrocó el pecado,
al mundo atrae, y brota nuevas flores
seca raíz y aliento sus olores.

El pensamiento, en éxtasis suave,
el vano objeto de otro bien destierra,
15   el celo abriendo con ardiente llave,
cuanto la culpa en sus engaños cierra;
y entre aquel ser de angélico contento
con dulce labio articuló su acento:

Haman's cold comfort

    "Woe!" they answer him, "If that which the heart
imprints in sketchy outline forebodes the truth,
it is not for naught the soul in fear freezes,
though the force of your position urge it on;
5   for fortune in its gifts is often cruel,
harsh towards the good, but to the wicked mild.

    "If it is from Judah that your conflict springs,
just is your grief and just the fear you feel,
for when Judah falls, he humbly falls to earth
10   and when he rises, rises proud to heaven;
for he is like the dust, he is like the stars,
prostrate in the dust, or raised up to the stars."

The prayer of Queen Esther

    Meanwhile the queen, wracked by internal anguish,
invites the king and Haman to her banquet
and in joyous hope awaits the sacred stream
of divine mercy from the holy fount-head;
5   her humble soul bowed low beside the torrents
from a boundless source, her eyes are flowing springs.

    That element which from the abundant vein
of a highmost spring, mingling with a lower,
irrigated the Garden full of delights
10   (for its flowing channels sin demolished)
reconciles the world and dried-up roots put out
new flowers and the air bursts with its new scents.

    From her thoughts, succumbed to gentle ecstasy,
she banishes the vain desire for other ends,
15   her passion releasing with a burning key
all that which sin in its deceits encloses;
and from within that angelic-natured soul
she gives voice with her sweet lips to these words:

"Eterno Ser que con piedosa mano
20   santos tesoros, pródigo, repartes,
y sin moverse en hemisferio humano
tu sol alumbra en más remotas partes,
mi vida no, la de tu pueblo mira,
viva por ti el que por ti suspira.

25   "Tu santo Nombre del lugar descienda,
que a nuestro amparo tu saber dispone,
y el fiero golpe su valor defienda
del que, atrevido, a la verdad se opone;
que no es objeto de tu sol la nube
30   y tu piedad sobre tus obras sube.

"Indigna yo de penetrar mi celo,
de baja tierra a la distancia mucha
de mis deseos encamina el vuelo
y el son humilde de mi llanto escucha;
35   que por tus llamas apurado el ruego,
será mi voz centella de tu fuego.

"Puede, Señor, al hombre su delito
negar la entrada, que a tu bien camina,
mas tu favor, que un mar es infinito,
40   lo más difícil con su fuerza inclina;
que al fin comete la maldad más fiera
quien a su culpa tu piedad no espera.

"Si en tu balanza la justicia igualas
con la maldad, ¿qué harán los que te ofenden?
45   Mira, Señor, que las mundanas alas
por sí no suben y sin ti descienden;
y cuando el hombre tu furor provoca,
la mayor pena recompensa es poca.

"Ve que el rigor de injusto atrevimiento
50   por su ministro no eligió tu celo
y que procura el más soberbio intento
tu santa Ley que sea olvido al suelo,
y aunque el pecado de Israel te incite,
si él no la guarda, el otro no la admite.

"Eternal Being who with merciful hand
20   generously bestows holy rewards on us
and without descending to the sphere of men,
illumine with your sun the remotest parts,
give heed, not to my life, but your people's life:
let them live for you who for your sake expire.

25   "Let your holy Name descend from the Place,
for our safekeeping is in your wisdom's care,
and may its valor ward off the cruel blow
from one who brazenly stands against the truth;
for to cloud is not the purpose of your sun
30   and your mercy rises over all your works.

"Unworthy am I to comprehend my zeal,
yet from lowly earth to distance far beyond
direct my desires upon their upward flight
and listen to the humble sound of my tears;
35   for when my plea by your flame has been consumed,
my voice shall be as a spark amidst your fire.

"The sins of man, Lord, may prevent his entry
when he makes his journey towards your goodness,
but your favor, which is an infinite sea,
40   bends with its strength what is most intractable;
for in the end he who ceases to have hope
in your mercy, commits the direst evil.

"If in your scales you set justice to balance
wickedness, what can they who offend you do?
45   Look, Lord, how these worldly wings of ours cannot
on their own rise up and without you descend;
and when man does provoke your wrath and fury,
the greatest punishment is but small reward.

"See how the cruelty of unjust insolence
50   has chosen not to use your zeal as agent
and how the most arrogant design intends
your holy Law be cast to earth, abandoned,
and though the sin of Israel incites your ire,
if she neglects it, he outright denies it.

55   "Si el menor instrumento el verdadero
        sujeto fue de sublimar tu gloria,
        el dulce efeto a mi deseo espero
        y tu grandeza, en mi humildad, notoria:
        ya nuevo aplauso escuchan mis oídos
60   y vencedores vueltos los vencidos.

        "Cuando Sisrá, con general espanto,
        armó soldados, tremoló banderas,
        piedoso oíste de tu pueblo el llanto,
        que en el castigo por su enmienda esperas,
65   y con la leche que bebió infelice,
        Iael le mata y Débora lo dice.

        "Si del egipcio el corazón más duro
        y sus siervos tu gloria exprimentaron,
        cuando, a la vara vuelta el agua en muro,
70   tus redimidos por la mar pasaron,
        sentimos hoy tanto el rigor más fuerte,
        cuanto es mayor que la aflición la muerte.

        "Aquél detuvo y éste se apresura,
        éste a la espada, aquél a servidumbre,
75   aquél fue rey, éste de un rey la hechura,
        él por engaño y éste por costumbre;
        y como al otro le cubrió el abismo,
        su intento a éste sea el lazo mismo.

        "Cuando injusto placer de objeto vano
80   despertó tu furor, viendo humillarse
        a lo que obró sin ti mortal la mano
        y de tu amor tus hijos olvidarse,
        si como padre su maldad sufriste,
        éste no alcance lo que tú no hiciste."

55 "If it could be that the smallest instrument
could be the right one to exalt your glory,
I have hope my wish will gain its sweet intent
and humbly wait on your greatness known to all:
already a new applause comes to my ears
60 and those once vanquished now are turned to victors.

 "When Sisera, inflicting general terror,
armed soldiers and raised up the banners of war,
you mercifully heard your people's lament,
for by punishing you hope to change their ways,
65 and with the milk that he fatefully imbibed,
Jael dispatched him, as Deborah relates.

 "If the hardest heart among the Egyptians
and his servants came to know your glory,
when by the rod the waters became a wall
70 and your people redeemed passed over the sea,
we know today that the harsher is the trial,
by so much worse is death than our affliction.

 "The first held back and the second hurries on,
this one to use the sword, that one to enslave,
75 the first was king, the second a king's minion,
he misguided and he through force of habit;
and just as the abyss engulfed the other,
may this one's intention be a snare to him.

 "When wrongful pleasuring in worthless objects
80 awoke your wrath, seeing them bow down before
what without you the hand of mortal fashioned
and your children lose the memory of your love,
if fatherlike you suffered their evil ways,
let him not achieve what you forbore to do."

Conclusión

Ah, del sumo Poder perfeto ejemplo,
piedad que ampara, amor que nunca olvida!
llegue al altar de tu divino Templo
quien mira en ondas de temor su vida,
5   que si piedoso su remedio ordenas,
su gloria nace de sus mismas penas.

Gusto el dolor, regalo es el castigo
que el justo prueba de tu santa mano,
siendo el tormento de aquel bien testigo,
10   nunca sujeto a movimiento humano;
porque es al alma escala el sufrimiento,
que toca el suelo y llega al firmamento.

Éste libró el rey de aquel conflito,
donde el blasfemo, en su poder seguro,
15   cercó Sión de ejército infinito,
negando aun ave penetrar su muro,
desengañado cuando en un instante
despojo fue de espada fulminante.

Éste al varón en sus miserias prueba
20   que humilde ve doblada recompensa;
por éste el justo en la encubierta cueva
en el ungido no vengó su ofensa;
al hombre escudo, a la ciudad es muro,
de golpe esento, de temor seguro.

25   Éste del mal las fuerzas diminuye
y con sus alas siempre al bien camina,
que en la esperanza su remedio arguye,
que firme funda en la piedad divina:
si tu poder, si tu valor es tanto,
30   al par del mundo te celebre el canto.

Conclusion

       Oh, perfect example of the highest Power,
       mercy which succors, love which never forgets,
       let him who sees his life sink in waves of dread,
       approach the altar of your divine Temple;
5   for if in mercy you ordain his ransom,
       out of his very pain is born his triumph.

       Sorrow is pleasure, reward the punishment
       that the just man endures at your holy hand,
       his torment bearing witness to that blessing,
10   which is to human feeling never subject:
       because suffering is a ladder for the soul,
       which stands on earth and rises to the heavens.

       He it was who released the king from that strait
       where blasphemy, secure in its own power,
15   encircled Zion with an infinite host,
       denying even birds entry to its walls,
       in an instant stripped of its illusions, when
       it became the victim of the flashing blade.

       He it is who shows the worthy in his depths
20   that, humble, he receives reward in double;
       for his sake the just one in the hidden cave
       did not take vengeance on the Lord's anointed;
       to men he is a shield, to the city a wall,
       from blows protected, from fear kept secure.

25   He it is who weakens the strength of evil
       and with his wings leads goodness ever on,
       for in hope he shows us his salvation,
       which on his divine mercy he firmly founds:
       if your power is such, if such your valor,
30   may you be throughout the world extolled in song.

Lamentaciones del profeta Jeremías

Lamentación 1:1

    ¿Cuál desventura, o ciudad,
ha vuelto en tan triste estado
tu grandeza y majestad
y aquel palacio sagrado
5   en estrago y soledad?

    ¿Quién a mirarte se inclina
y a tus muros derrocados
por la justicia divina,
que no vea en tus pecados
10   la causa de tu ruina?

    ¿Quién te podrá contemplar,
viendo tu gloria perdida,
que no desee que un mar
de llanto sea su vida,
15   para poderte llorar?

    ¿Cuál pecado pudo tanto,
que no te conozco agora?
Mas, no advirtiendo, me espanto,
que tú fuiste pecadora
20   y quien te ha juzgado santo.

    En ofenderle te empleas,
ya por antigua costumbre,
y en errores te recreas
y así no es mucho que veas
tus libres en servidumbre.

    Tus palacios y tus puertas
fueron materia a la llama
en esas calles desiertas,
por émulos de tu fama
30   en tus miserias abiertas.

The Lamentations of Jeremiah

Lamentation 1:1

What misfortune, O City,
has brought to such a sad estate
your greatness and your majesty
and that most holy palace
5   to ruin and to solitude?

Who is there that inclines to look
upon you and your fallen walls,
cast down by divine justice,
that does not see that in your sins
10   lies the reason for your downfall?

Who can bear to gaze upon you,
seeing your departed glory,
and not wish that his very life
would turn into a sea of tears,
15   so that he might lament for you?

What sin has power to do so much
that I no longer know you now?
But, since I do not know, I fear,
for you were indeed a sinner
20   and he who judged you holy.

You spend your time in his offense,
through a habit long established,
and take delight in evil ways,
and so it is of no surprise
25   to see your freemen all enslaved.

Your palaces and your portals
were fed as fuel to the flame
in those deserted thoroughfares—
in your wretchedness open wide
30   for those who envied your renown.

Por tus plazas y rincones
miro, por ver si pasea
alguno de tus varones,
porque crea a sus razones,
35   cuando a mis ojos no crea.

Mas vano es este deseo,
que animales sin razón,
sin dueño, balando veo,
que, no articulando el son,
40   certifican lo que creo.

Aunque se encienda mi pecho
llamando siempre, callaron
tus hijos en su despecho:
como sus dioses se han hecho
45   que por su engaño llamaron.

La causa porque caíste
y porque humilde bajaste
de la gloria en que te viste,
fue la verdad que dejaste,
50   la vanidad que seguiste.

Ya no eres la princesa
de todas otras naciones,
ya tu altivez es bajeza
tu diadema y tu grandeza
55   se ha vuelto en tristes prisiones.

Ya tu palacio real,
humilde, cubre la tierra
en exequía funeral;
la paz antigua es la guerra
60   y el bien antiguo es el mal.

Tú fuiste al Señor contraria,
de los pecados el fruto,
en tu cosecha ordinaria,
ha sido el mismo tributo
65   por quien te ves tributaria.

Through your homes and private places
I peer to see if one amongst
your worthies might still be passing,
so I might believe his telling
35 when I do not believe my eyes.

But this desire is vanity,
for I see animals, senseless,
masterless, wandering, bleating,
which, though they do not voice the words,
40 confirm what I know to be true.

Although my breast become inflamed
forever calling out, your sons
have in their despair gone silent,
as silent as the gods on whom
45 they in their self-delusion called.

The reason why you tumbled down
and why you descended, humbled,
from the glory wherein you were
lies in the truth that you forsook,
50 in the vanity you followed.

Now no longer are you princess
among all the other nations,
now your loftiness is baseness,
your diadem and your grandeur
55 have turned to dismal bondage.

Now your royal palace lies
ignoble, covering the earth
in funereal obsequy;
the age-old peace is turned to war
60 and the age-old good to evil.

If you rebelled against the Lord,
the fruits which you garnered
in your customary harvest
have been the selfsame tribute
65 which makes you tributary now.

No sólo viste perder
la honra que te adornó,
mas tus hijos perecer,
que el Señor los entregó
70   al más tirano poder.

Cómo se puede alentar
tu pueblo, entre su gemido,
llegando a considerar
lo que seguir ha querido,
75   lo que ha querido dejar?

Lamentación 1:12

O vosotros que pasáis
y el extremo a que he llegado
por dicha no imagináis,
vuestro paso apresurado
5   tened, porque me veáis.

De vuestra lástima fío,
que si con el océano
no puede medirse un río,
digáis que dolor humano
10   no puede igualarse al mío.

De aquello que se edifica
y más su firmeza alaba
su fin la fama publica,
que lo que el tiempo fabrica
15   el mismo tiempo lo acaba.

No fue mi ruina así,
que al punto que me olvidé
del cielo a quien ofendí,
sin tiempo el tiempo llamé,
20   para vengarse de mí.

Not only have you seen the loss
of the honor which adorned you,
but you have seen your children die,
for the Lord has delivered them
70   into the greatest tyrant's hand.

How can your people find comfort
for themselves, amid their wailing,
when they come to consider
what paths they have wished to follow,
75   what paths they have wished to forsake.

Lamentation 1:12

O you who pass by in the way
and do not take for good fortune
these dire straits to which I have come,
keep pressing on your pace, so you
5   may see me truly as I am.

I have faith in your compassion,
for if a river cannot be
compared with the mighty ocean,
acknowledge that no human grief
10   can equal the grief I suffer.

That which is built up and, more,
proclaims its own stability,
its end is published wide by fame,
for that which has been formed by Time
15   that selfsame Time brings to an end.

My downfall did not come that way,
for the moment that I forgot
heaven whom I offended,
I considered Time had no time
20   to exact its revenge on me.

Llamándome santidad,
los efetos de mis manos
eran justicia y verdad,
mas, como se han vuelto vanos,
25   siguieron la vanidad.

Llorando el daño Israel
del incauto atrevimiento
del ídolo de Betel,
yo, en lugar de escarmiento,
30   seguí los errores dél.

Yo fui la viña cercada
y del rocío celeste
era mi planta bañada,
mas, siendo mi fruto agreste,
35   fui de gentiles pisada.

La torre que en medio della
mi amado me fabricó
fue la Casa santa y bella,
y sin merecerla yo,
40   quedé perdida en perdella.

El bien fundado lagar,
tan firme en mi beneficio,
ha sido el sagrado altar
donde se vio derramar
45   la sangre por sacrificio.

Y viendo que mi pecado
el fruto era de mi gusto,
con justa razón airado
el Señor, como es tan justo,
50   con ira me ha vendimiado.

De Canaán he procedido,
siendo amorreo mi padre,
que este bien no ha conocido,
y como hetea mi madre,
55   entre inmundicia he vivido.

When in the name of sanctity
I clothed myself, justice and truth
were the product of my hands,
but since it turned to vanity,
25   vanity these have followed.

When Israel wept over the harm
done by the heedless, reckless act
which set an idol in Bethel,
I did not learn the lesson taught
30   but pursued its ways of folly.

I was the encompassed vineyard
and by the celestial dew
was my plant gently watered,
but when my fruit ran to wildness,
35   I was trampled by the Gentiles.

The tower which in the midst of it
my beloved built for me was
the beautiful and holy House,
and though I did not merit it,
40   in losing it I myself was lost.

The well-established winepress,
so steadfast for my benefit,
has been the sacred altar
whereon we have seen overflow
45   the blood shed for the sacrifice.

And seeing that my sinfulness
was the fruit of my own choosing,
with just and angry reason
the Lord in his great justice
50   with wrath has harvested me.

I am descended from Canaan,
an Amorite was my father,
who has not known this benefit,
and my mother being a Hittite,
55   I have lived in uncleanliness.

Volvió mi tiempo de amor
y el que desnuda me vio
me cubrió de su favor
y de precioso valor
60   joyas y prendas me dio.

La diadema, que segura
creía que estaba en mí,
la seda y la bordadura
hicieron volverme así,
65   confiada en mi hermosura.

De mis vestidos tomé
y de diversas colores
mis altares fabriqué,
y fui tras mis amadores
70   y el verdadero dejé.

Fui para mí tan cruel,
que sólo a quien me ofendía
he sido amante fiel
y el don que a mí me debía,
75   yo misma le he dado a él.

Por esto extendió su mano
el Señor, de mí ofendido,
y agora sé lo que gano
en despertar de mi olvido
80   con la espada del tirano.

Lamentación 1:13

El fuego de su venganza
mandó del cielo el Señor
contra mi necia esperanza,
cual rayo que en su furor
5   sólo en la muerte descansa.

•   •   •   •   •

My time of love returned to me
and he who saw I was unclothed
in his favor covered me
and bestowed upon me jewels
60   and gifts of high and precious worth.

The diadem, which I thought did
lie securely upon my head,
the silk and the embroidery
made me in this fashion change,
65   full-confident in my beauty.

I took of my finest vestments
and in many diverse colors
I set up and decked my altars,
and I pursued my paramours
70   and my true lover left behind.

I have been so cruel to myself
that only to him who harmed me
have I been a constant lover
and the gift which I owed myself
75   I myself have given to him.

Because of this, the Lord, whom I
offended, has stretched out his hand
and now I know what I have gained
on waking up from my neglect
80   at the blow of the tyrant's sword.

Lamentation 1:13

The Lord sent down from heaven
the fire of his vengeance
to countermand my foolish hope,
like a thunderbolt which in its fury
5   finds its repose in death alone.

•   •   •   •   •

Lo que en injusto cimiento
finge que el ser eterniza
refiere su atrevimiento
de su fuego el mudo acento,
10   la lengua de su ceniza.

Que, como se vuelve en hielo
el fuego que el alma alienta,
con justo furor el cielo
el material alimenta,
15   por dar venganza a su celo.

Y cuando el Señor llamaba
el que, temblando, le oía,
en la zarza se mostraba
y aunque toda en fuego ardía,
20   el fuego no la quemaba.

Si a los tres el horno ardiente
aun no tocó su vestido,
siendo un portento a la gente,
su fuego no les consiente
25   ser de otro fuego vencido.

Cuando el profeta pidió,
por su verdad, la señal,
al punto desengañó
al que adoraba a Baal
30   el fuego que descendió.

Viendo el Señor acabada
la obra del santo Templo
y el arca santa llevada,
del sabio rey, por ejemplo,
35   la humilde oración le agrada.

Mostrando cuanto estimaba
la ofrenda del justo ruego,
el fuego la arrebataba
y con temor de aquel fuego,
40   el sacerdote no entraba.

That which on unjust foundations
fancies it will last for ever
finds its brazenness unfolded
in the mute accents of its fire,
10   in the language of its ashes.

For, as the fire which inspires
the soul turns into ice,
heaven with rightful fury
finds fuel with which to stoke the flames
15   to avenge its jealousy.

And when the Lord called upon
him who in trembling heard him,
he showed his presence in the bush
and though this was engulfed in fire,
20   the fire did not consume it.

If it did not touch the raiment
of the three in the fiery furnace,
being a portent to the people,
his fire would not let them be
25   conquered by another fire.

When the prophet begged for a sign
to prove that he was the true God,
the fire which descended then
at once stripped of their illusions
30   those who followed the cult of Baal.

When the Lord beheld completed
the work of his holy Temple
and the holy Ark uplifted,
the humble prayer of a wise king
35   as an example pleased him.

Showing how much he did esteem
the offering of that just request,
the fire came and snatched it up,
and out of terror of that fire
40   the priest would not enter there.

Y así de una calidad
el efeto es diferente:
pues da vida a la verdad
y mata, como al presente,
45   el que vive en su maldad.

En mi camino engañoso
viendo tan libre pasar
mi paso presuntuoso,
su red estendió en lugar
50   en que fingí mi reposo.

Que si paloma volara
y con sus alas ligera
al cielo me levantara,
la red no me detuviera,
55   ni entre sus lazos quedara.

Y así pagué mi porfía,
llorando el bien que perdí,
sin pensar lo que perdía,
hasta que el cielo algún día
60   se quiera acordar de mí.

Lamentación 2:6

Cual huerto que de mil flores
con artificio la mano
plantó de varias colores
que no las secó verano,
5   ni el hielo con sus rigores.

Allí los frutos se miran
cuando las hojas defienden
al sol su luz, que retiran:
ellos la vista suspenden
10   y ellas flagrancia respiran.

And so of one same element
the effect can be divergent,
because it grants life to the truth
and kills, as in the present time,
45   him who thrives in his wickedness.

When he saw pass by so freely
my presumptuous footstep on
along the highway of falsehood,
he spread out his net in the place
50   where I thought to find my rest.

For if as the dove I could fly
and with his wings lightly, swiftly
lift myself up to heaven
the net would not detain me here,
55   nor in its bonds would I remain.

Thus I paid for my persistence,
weeping for the good I lost,
(not thinking what I was losing),
until such a day as heaven
60   may wish to remember me.

Lamentation 2:6

She is as a garden planted
with a thousand flowers of myriad
hues by the skillful hand of God
which the summer did not parch dry
5   nor the ice's harshness wither.

There many fruits are to be seen,
when their protecting leaves keep out
the light of sun which they repel:
the first enthrall the passer's eye,
10   the second exhale sweet fragrance.

El siempre verde amaranto
aviva allí su color;
vese inclinado el acanto
y la violeta que tanto
15 se adorna con su palor.

El lirio blanco y celeste,
riendo de que el rocío
llorando se manifieste,
al aire pide su brío
20 porque sus alas le preste.

Allí de aparencia hermosa
y de las flores princesa,
armada asiste la rosa
que enseña a guardar, curiosa,
25 con la virtud la belleza.

La granada abre el coral
que por mostrarse revienta
y en su corona real
la fe de un rey representa
30 en su vasallo leal.

La manzana en quien, al vivo,
la roja color se altera
y dentro el humor nocivo,
al hombre imita que, altivo,
35 le mata su primavera.

El racimo que, colgado,
la caña suave imita
cuyo licor moderado
alegra y sobrado quita
40 con la razón el cuidado.

El agua, que el nacimiento
de alto principio recibe,
deleita en su movimiento
y para el vuelo apercibe
45 sus alas al pensamiento.

The ever-verdant amaranth
enlivens there its color;
the bowed acanthus may be seen
and the violet, whose pallor
15   so fittingly adorns it.

The lily, celestial and white,
laughing that the morning dew
should manifest itself in tears,
begs the wind its liveliness
20   so that it might lend her wings.

There beautiful in appearance
and princess of all flowers,
sits the rose arrayed with arms,
teaching that we should keep beauty
25   pure and guarded round with virtue.

The pomegranate opens up
its coral, which bursts to show itself,
and in the royal crown it wears
it demonstrates the faith a king
30   may have in a loyal vassal.

The apple which, when on the bough,
to the red blush of anger turns
and noxious humor has within,
imitates the man who, overproud,
35   destroys its flowering season.

The bunch of grapes which, as it hangs,
imitates the mellow stalk
whose juice in moderation
brings joy and in excess deprives
40   man of his care and reason.

The water, which its origin
receives from a lofty source,
in its motion affords delight
and to our meditative thoughts
45   provides the wings with which to fly.

Éste, pues, donde asistía
el gusto casi inmortal
que por su trono escogía,
perdiendo su monarquía,
50   llora en silencio su mal.

Seca el sol, abrasa el hielo
cuanto, benino, criara
en sus influjos el cielo;
que el aire le desampara
55   y no le alimenta el suelo.

Su fuerza se debilita,
lo más tejido se rompe,
su vida el fruto limita
y el aire, que se corrompe,
60   las verdes hojas marchita.

Así el divino Poder,
que el huerto santo ordenó
con soberano saber,
las flores que en él plantó
65   eran de eterno placer.

Lamentación 2:7

El santo fuego que ardía
y el altar del sacrificio
que al cielo en llamas subía,
como abrasada edificio,
5   se vuelve en ceniza fría.

Como al que ofende el calor
y, no sufriendo el vestido,
aparta con él su ardor,
así su Templo escogido
10   de sí desecha el Señor.

This garden, then, in which there dwelt
pleasure near to everlasting,
where she chose to set her throne,
now her monarchy is ended
50   bemoans in silence her ill fate.

The sun parches, the frost withers
all that which in kindlier times
heaven would nurture with its powers;
for the cooling winds forsake it
55   and the earth nourishes no more.

Its vigor turns to weakness,
the most entangled growth breaks down,
the fruit cuts short its useful life
and the air, which putrefies,
60   causes the green leaves to wither.

And so has done the Power divine
who arranged the holy garden
with the sovereign understanding:
the flowers which he planted there
65   were for an eternal pleasure.

Lamentation 2:7

The holy fire which used to burn
and the altar of sacrifice
which sent up its flames to heaven,
like a building set ablaze,
5   are now turned to dead cold ashes.

As one whom the heat oppresses,
unable to bear his clothing,
casts off with them his burning heat,
so does the Lord cast from himself
10   the Temple which he had chosen.

Que el hombre que en santo celo
el corazón sacrifica,
siguiendo, altivo, su vuelo,
benino lo justifica
15   entre sus llamas el cielo.

Si en el errado camino
el apetito sin rienda
huye el auxilio divino,
es fingimiento su ofrenda
20   y su humildad desatino.

Quien huye la vanidad
y es de inocentes amparo,
siendo su amor la verdad,
con un sacrificio raro
25   obliga el alta piedad.

Que, cuando son los errores
de injusta vida el ejemplo,
de un año en otro mayores,
en vano llevan al Templo
30   ofrendas los pecadores.

Que, como es refugio al justo,
cuando son justos sus dones
y su voluntad su gusto,
es cueva para el injusto
35   donde se ocultan ladrones.

•   •   •   •   •

Viendo Jacob abrasado
de aquella estancia divina
el muro más levantado,
lamenta entre su ruina
40   la pena de su pecado.

Y dice: "O piedad paterna,
si del castigo tu mano,
con el amor, no se alterna,
será nuestro llanto en vano,
45   será nuestra pena eterna.

For the man who in holy zeal
makes a sacrifice of his heart,
pursuing his purpose proudly,
is in kindliness forgiven
15   by heaven when flames surround him.

If upon the way of error
appetite, knowing no restraint,
flees from divine assistance,
its offering is false pretense
20   and folly its humility.

He who flies from vanity
and is the help of innocents,
since his love is truth itself,
with a singular sacrifice
25   he commands God's highest mercy.

For, when misguided error is
the token of unrighteous lives,
growing the worse from year to year,
in vain do the sinners carry
30   their offerings to the Temple.

For, as to the righteous it is
a haven, when their gifts are just
and to do his will their pleasure,
so it is for the unrighteous
35   a cave where robbers lie in wait.

•   •   •   •   •

When Jacob sees burned to the ground
the loftiest of the ramparts
of that holy habitation,
he laments amid his ruin
40   the torment of his transgressions.

He says: "O Father of mercies,
if your hand that chastises
does not sometimes give way to love,
our weeping will have been in vain,
45   our sorrow will be eternal.

"Mira, Señor, destruídos
los límites más cubiertos,
al hombre no concedidos,
que, de tu gloria desiertos,
50   se quejan como ofendidos.

"En tu balanza divina
el peso de altos delitos
tanto al castigo se inclina,
que piden, como infinitos,
55   nuestra infinita ruina.

"Mira cuán débiles son
los frágiles fundamentos
de nuestra composición
y cómo en estos tormentos
60   lleva igual parte Sión.

"Nuestras maldades olvida
y acuérdate que Babel
pasó con mortal herida. . . ."
y antes que diga, a Israel
65   la voz se acaba y la vida.

La historia de Rut

Al tiempo que era Israel
por jueces gobernado,
siendo su daño el pecado,
su llanto el refugio en él.

5   Después que pasó el Jordán
con segunda maravilla,
de nueve heredó su silla
quien fue su nombre Abezán.

Faltando en el hombre el celo,
10   que alcanza el eterno fruto,
el campo negó el tributo,
sus influencias el cielo.

"Behold, Lord, utterly destroyed
the most closely guarded precincts,
where no entry was permitted man,
which, abandoned by your glory,
50   now lament as ones offended.

"In your divine scales of justice
the weight of misdemeanors
so tips down towards chastisement
that, being infinite, they cry out
55   for our infinite destruction.

"Behold how enfeebled are
the insubstantial foundations
of this construction that we are
and how Zion in the torments
60   we suffer, bears its equal share.

"Pass over our iniquities
and remember that Babylon
inflicted here a mortal wound. . . ."
and before he could continue,
65   Israel's voice with his life expired.

The story of Ruth

During the time when Israel
was governed by the judges,
when the cause of her hurt was sin
and tears her refuge in its midst.

5   After she passed over Jordan
by a second miracle,
he who was by name of Ibzan
inherited from nine his seat.

Since the zeal was lacking in man,
10   which secures the eternal fruit,
the field denied him its tribute,
heaven its kindly influence.

Al centro le contradice
la espiga en lo que señala,
15   cual hombre a quien no se iguala
la obra con lo que dice.

Es heno que inculto y vano
en el tejado creció,
que el hombre, en lo que juntó,
20   no pudo cargar su mano.

Falta el gusto y sobra el daño,
que quien el sustento olvida
del alma, en su misma vida
lo niega a la vida el año.

25   La tierra en su ingratitud
muestra el mal, el bien encierra,
que mal produce la tierra,
si muere en flor la virtud.

El verde honor, que en el prado
30   en oro el tiempo resuelve,
piedras son, si en piedra vuelve
al corazón su pecado.

El labrador ve perder
su esperanza entre el espanto,
35   y pues no sembró con llanto,
siembra su llanto al coger.

Varón de Judá, que entiende
del cielo la voluntad,
a los campos de Moab
40   volver sus años pretende.

De Betlén descansa allí
Elimelec, a quien son
sus hijos Maalón, Chilón,
y su consorte Naomi.

The ear of corn in what it shows
contradicts its inner being,
15 just like a man in whom the deeds
do not conform with what he says.

It is grass that wild and worthless
has grown upon the housetop,
for the man who reaped it could not
20 fill his hand with what he garnered.

Pleasure lacks and troubles abound,
for to him who neglects the food
of his soul, the year denies
his life the food of life itself.

25 The earth in its ingratitude
shows forth the bad, conceals the good,
for the earth yields a bad harvest,
if virtue perishes in flower.

Honor green, which in the field
30 should be by Time transformed to gold,
is turned to stones, if through his sin
the heart of man is turned to stone.

The farmer sees his expectations
brought to nothing in the horror,
35 and since he did not sow in tears,
he sows his tears at reaping time.

A man of Judah, who well grasps
what is the will of heaven,
seeks to direct his life away,
40 towards the fields of Moab.

In that place rests Elimelech
of the town of Bethlehem,
whose sons are Mahlon and Chilion
and whose wife is Naomi.

Canción, aplicando misericordias divinas y defetos proprios a la salida de Egipto hasta la Tierra Santa

En este fiero Egito
de mi pecado, donde el alma mía
padece la tirana servidumbre,
del tesoro infinito
5   de tu divina lumbre,
a mi noche, Señor, un rayo envía.
Sea tu santa inspiración mi guía;
que entre la luz del amoroso fuego,
me llame en el desierto, no cursado
10   de mundana memoria:
allí desnudo, por tu causa, el ciego
velo de error, el hábito pasado,
dichoso suba a contemplar tu gloria,
donde mi ser por milagroso efeto
15   en sí tranforme el soberano objeto.

•   •   •   •   •

La tierra prometida,
do mi temor, porque mi vida asombre,
gigantes finge en fuerzas desiguales,
a mi fe concedida,
20   traiga della señales,
que manifiesten tu poder al hombre:
colunas alce a tu glorioso Nombre,
donde tu Ley, para memoria eterna,
ultra del tiempo su verdad refiera,
25   que lo humano deshace;

veré tus montes, donde no se alterna
la edad del mundo, y dulce primavera,
alegre siempre, siempre satisface;
salve a mis ojos nueva maravilla,
30   salve mil veces, O sagrada silla.

**Song in which the poet relates the divine mercies granted him
and his own failings to the Exodus from Egypt to the Holy Land**

    In this cruel Egypt
of my sinfulness, in which this soul of mine
suffers the enslavement of a tyranny,
from the infinite treasure
5   of your radiance divine
send, Lord, a beam of light into my darkness,
Let your holy inspiration be my guide;
let it, amid the light of the loving fire,
call on me in the desert, unfrequented
10   by any worldly memory:
there, having for your sake stripped from me the blind
veil of error, the clothing of the past,
let me happy rise to behold your glory,
where the sovereign object will transform my being
15   by miraculous effect into itself.

     •   •   •   •   •

    May the land which is promised,
wherein my dread, to put my life in terror,
imagines giants of a strength unequaled,
the land my faith is granted,
20   bring forth from it the tokens
that will manifest your power to mankind:
let me raise up columns to your glorious Name,
on which your Law for your eternal memory
will tell of your truth beyond the span of time,
25   which undoes all human things;

    I shall see your hills, where the age of the world
knows no changeful revolution and sweet spring
is ever joyful and ever satisfies;
hail to the new miracle before my eyes,
30   hail to you, O sacred seat, a thousand times.

Canción, mientras no puedo
la voz formar que el tiempo no corrompa,
ni tocar con el dedo
que no se canse, ni las cuerdas rompa,
35 el arpa santa, el son, si diferente,
siempre al oído me será presente.

My song, while I have no power
to summon a voice which time will not corrupt,
nor, strumming with skilled fingers
which do not tire or cause the strings to break, play
35 the sacred harp, the sound of it, so different,
will be always present in my ear.

Notes

Tres poemas autobiográficos

The three "Autobiographical Poems" are taken from a manuscript in the collection of the *Etz Haim* Library, Amsterdam (MS 48 D 39) which was first published by I. S. Révah in "Autobiographie d'un Marrane, édition partielle d'un manuscrit de João (Moseh) Pinto Delgado," *Revue des études juives* 119 (1961).

In this work, the poet presents in poetry and prose form the events of his life and his spiritual journey from the Christian world of Portugal to Amsterdam. The fact that the poems that we present were written in Portugal, under the shadow of the Inquisition, lends them added interest, while their style is only marginally less developed than in the maturer Rouen works, which understandably show a greater depth of Jewish knowledge. The titles for all three poems derive from the poet's own prose text.

A la salida de Lisboa

The text is taken from MS fol. 3 v–6 r.

1 *la infame puerta*. The gates of Lisbon where the regime of the Inquisition holds sway; this immediately introduces the theme of the oppression of the crypto-Jew and the latter's need to maintain his faith in the most difficult of circumstances.

25 *nuestro pecado*. Pinto Delgado inclines to the Prophetic view that Israel's sufferings are due to her own failure to follow God's commandments.

36 *se incline*. The verb suggests both the restricted confinement imposed on the accused, keeping him bent double, and the torture used to "incline" his will.

37 *La doncella*. Israel is personified as a maiden, victim of an *auto de fe*.

The Inquisition tended to pursue in turn all those who were involved in a given case, whether implicated or merely witnesses; an example of this "chain of persecution" is given by J. Caro Baroja in "El proceso de Bartolomé Febos o Febo," *Homenaje a don Ramón Carande* (Madrid, 1963), 2: 59–91.

42 *su temor*. Lit., "her terror"; i.e., the object of her terror, the Inquisition.

46 *se olvida*. The victim is pushed beyond endurance to the point where he "forgets himself" and confesses.

52 The reference is to the confiscation of property by the Inquisition.

53 Here the poet develops in true biblical style the theme of God's vengeance on Israel's oppressors. In this stanza and the following there is an underlying reference to the Church's claim to be the heirs of Israel, one which the poet considers particularly unjustified in view of the conduct of the Inquisition (see 1. 57). They are as it were Esau trying to retrieve the inheritance they have forfeited (cf. Genesis 25).

55 *asirle la capa*. (1) cf. *quitar la capa*, "To take more than one's legal due." (2) "unmask" from *capa* in the figurative sense of "mask" or "protection," alluding to the seeking out of crypto-Jews by the Inquisition.

56 *la = capa* (l. 55), here "property," "fortune"; possibly also "mantle, (of office)"; cf. note l. 53.

65 *Los desterrados.* A variation of the idea of reversal of the state of affairs in the Messianic era.

75. For the designation of Christianity as idolatry, cf. Antonio Enríquez Gómez, *Romance al divín mártir,* passim.

77–80 Cf. Psalms 115:5–7 "They have mouths but they speak not: eyes have they, but they see not. . . . They have ears but they hear not . . . feet have they, but they walk not."

95 1 Samuel 18:7 "Saul hath slain his thousands and David his ten thousands."

97 The poet now addresses Israel, the Marranos "in captivity," taking up the theme outlined previously (see note 1. 25).

98 *Dio.* The usual Sephardi vernacular form for God, which avoids the plural-sounding ending of normal Spanish *Dios.*

108 *alcanzar tus efetos.* The idea of heavenly "recompense" contains a possible play on the material sense of *efetos,* "effects," i.e., the confiscated property they might hope to regain (cf. 1. 52 and note).

111 *pascuas.* The three Pilgrim Festivals of Passover, Pentecost, and Tabernacles.

116–17 Psalms 137:5 "If I forget thee, O Jerusalem, let my right hand forget her cunning." The sequence as a whole recalls that psalm ("By the waters of Babylon . . .").

116 *Dios.* Cf. note 1. 98; the normative form is used for the sake of rhyme.

121 The harrowing events themselves provide the instrument on which the lament of the poet is to be played, except that the pain is beyond expression. Note 1. 123, an allusion to Psalms 137:6 "let my tongue cleave to the roof of my mouth."

140 *la cuenta.* Double sense of (1) counting, (2) drawing up an account or balance sheet, hence metaphorically judgment after death.

143 *le ofrece. Se ofrece* may be intended, meaning "offering himself," i.e., in self-sacrifice.

152 *un Dios, un Pueblo, una Ley* recalls Hernando de Acuña's dictum *una Monarca, un Imperio y una Espada,* "one Monarch, one Empire and one Sword," which epitomizes the ideology of the Church Militant.

156 *el día.* The day of Messianic Redemption.

A la despedida de un amigo

The text is taken from MS fol. 7 v–9 v. In this poem, the poet, taking as his point of departure the situation of a friend who has reached the safety of Amsterdam, contrasts the benefits to be gained by such a step with his own vacillation in undertaking it. The sense of guilt explored here has been attributed to the poet's desire to pursue his literary ambitions, rather than any adherence to Catholicism. See A. D. H. Fishlock, "The Shorter Poems of João Pinto Delgado," *Bulletin of Hispanic Studies* 31 (1954).

3 *rebaños.* Plural suggests that the poet has in mind the other safe havens besides Amsterdam, e.g., in Italy and the Orient.

26 *el bien.* The blessing of God's protection, the goal attained by leaving.

32 *suave.* Counts as three syllables here.

48 *peregrino.* "Pilgrim" or "wanderer," Marrano word par excellence to describe the intense insecurity of the crypto-Jew in Iberia, used by the sixteenth-century writer Nuñez de Reinoso and Antonio Enríquez Gómez *inter*

alia. For the first, see C. H. Rose, *Alonso Núñez de Reinoso: The Lament of a Sixteenth Century Exile* (Rutherford, N.J.: Fairleigh Dickinson University Press, 1971).

61   *El día santificado*. I.e., *Yom Kippur*. The poet is clearly aware of its significance, though he is here prompted by his own particular sense of guilt to place it in prominence.

65   *La pascua*. Here Passover, the Festival of Freedom par excellence.

69–70   The poet may mean this literally; schooled principally on the Pentateuch, the Marranos were a prey to such misconceptions and imagine Jewish practice to be as described there. Even without this error there is the feeling in this passage that the poet's knowledge of Judaism, though considerable, is somehow incomplete, through being indirectly acquired.

81–82   The sense appears to be that the friend knows from his own experience that the only way to achieve one's true religious self and integration into Jewish life is by taking to the seas and escaping.

90   *forzoso*. If literary ambition was what prevented the poet's departure, then he is being dishonest in referring to *tan forzoso inconveniente* as its cause. In fact it is the poet's sense of his own self-deception which informs the passion of the poem's last stanzas.

104   *inmundancias*. I.e., under Christianity.

105   *aquellos*. People or things, that is, vain delights.

110   *volver atrás*. Literally "to go backward."

133–36   Better, the poet implies, to leave than call on God in one's hour of need.

En alabanza del Señor

MS source: fol. 42 r–45 r. This poem takes the second one a stage further to consider the religious and moral position of crypto-Jews living in the "idolatrous" state of Christianity, with the poet exploring the essentially Marrano theme of guilt regarding past failure to observe Judaism fully. The poet himself regarded this as the best of all his poems, a fact which attests to the intensely personal relevance of its theme. Note also that it is in *terza rima* form, which he does not appear to use anywhere else.

17   *la aparencia vana*. "Vain appearance": the familiar Golden Age theme of *engaño*, the deceptive nature of things of the world, is introduced here.

18   *dominan*. The subject is the same as that of *se pierden* and *inclinan* (1. 16), i.e., the poet's weak-spirited feelings *(sentidos, 1. 14)*.

25   *a pagar*. Also present is the idea of *apagar(se)*, "to be extinguished."

31   *de tu gracia aquel licor*, etc. Cf. the "water of life" image in Revelation 22:1; this sequence as a whole on the theme of grace and the purpose and direction of the soul echoes the writings of Pinto Delgado's Christian contemporaries. The tercet 31–33 relates to the previous one: there can be no possible redemption *(descargo, 1. 30)* without God's grace.

33   *la nieve*. MS omits *la*, necessary for meter and balance (cf. Révah ed., p. 124).

34   *protento*. The "portent" in question is *gracia* (1. 31), a goal which even the keenest lose sight of (1. 36). Another image of "failure" occurs in line 39.

40 ff.   The poet appears to have in mind, not the physical escape of the previous two poems, but a moral "flight" of the soul in the direction of God; it is in this dimension that the problem truly lies and without confronting it, the

physical escape to freedom is meaningless (cf. the conclusion to the second poem).

47 *desenfunado*. From the Portuguese *desenfunar-se*, "to cease being vain or haughty"; the word is not attested in Spanish, see Martín Alonso, *Enciclopedia del idioma* (Madrid, 1958).

52 ff. The poem focuses on the figure of the *mísero*, the wretched Marrano who gives himself to the outward observance of Christianity and is spiritually deformed by it. The poet identifies himself with him.

53 *mármol duro*. Christian images which are the object of veneration. The repetition of *a duro* (1. 54) suggests the corrupting effect of this practice.

55 *el inocente*. Whether he gives cause for suspicion or not, the "innocent" man is still prey to the Inquisition, because of the activities of the *malsín* or "tale bearer" who is likely to betray him. The character of the *malsín* (a word apparently of Hebrew origin) is a familiar one in the period and recurs in the poems of the Marranos.

80 *lazo*. This is the link which the *mísero* maintains with Judaism and which leads to his condemnation by the Inquisition, thereby bringing him the spiritual benefits of martyrdom.

82–83 *lleve . . . / finjase*. The subject is *mundo* (1. 79 above). For clarity, "they" is used in translation (also ll. 84, 85, 86, etc.).

89 *su manto*. "Cloak," suggests priest's habit; also "veil" or "cover."

94–95 *el tiempo . . ./el tiempo y la mitad*. See Daniel 7:25 and 12:7, "time, times and half a time," a phrase made much of in calculating the date of the Messianic Coming (cf. Enríquez Gómez, *Romance*, 1. 441 and note).

96 The Ingathering of the Exiles, in all probability to Iberia rather than the Land of Israel.

100 *el de llaves áspero monarca*. The Pope, the symbol of whose office is the keys of Saint Peter.

109 ff. The language and tone here are very reminiscent of Pinto Delgado's version of Lamentations (see below, pp. 98 ff.), particularly the elegy on the destruction of Jerusalem.

110 *vuelve a abrazar*. MS omits *a*.

127–28 Psalms 90:4 "For a thousand years in thy sight are but as yesterday when it is past."

132 Cf. Jeremiah 12:10 "Many pastors have destroyed my vineyard."

133–35 The poet expresses here the nub of the Marrano dilemma.

138 *miseria*. Cf. *mísero* line 52 et seq.

139–41 God uses men in order to punish Israel for her sins, but they remain his instruments, not his equals; they are thus subject to experience his wrath in their own punishment (see ll. 142–45 below).

148–50 The poet evokes Isaiah's vision of God, Isaiah 6:3–6.

151 *el ignorante*. The same as the *mísero* already mentioned: the poet elaborates on the process of his spiritual decline (cf. 1. 54) until he is ensnared in corruption and sin (1. 157).

153 *en muertos confiado*. The "dead" in question are Jesus and the saints of the Church.

156 *él será dios*, etc. The poet's point is that "idolatry" leads the worshiper to an over-exalted view of his own powers, since he has made the "god" he worships.

157 Cf. Psalms 57:6 "They have prepared a net for my steps."

157–60   The crypto-Jew, whatever his own sins, becomes caught up in the sinfulness and corrupting ambition of the leaders of the society in which he lives.

158   *quien*. In view of *el sucesor* (1. 160) a specific leader of the Church or Inquisition may be intended—Tomás de Torquemada and one of his successors as Chief Inquisitor? In any case it is clear that the poet views their activities as an affront to heaven (1. 159).

161–62   The judaizer is being offered, through confession and reconciliation with the Church, a heavenly reward which is distasteful to him.

164–65 *deseara . . ./tormento*. The aim of the whole inquisitorial process was the saving of the victim's soul: his death—e.g., in an *auto de fe* or under torture—would not impede, rather further that aim, hence ensuring the victim did not suffer ''torture'' in afterlife. The irony is that this process in fact renews the Marrano's Jewish faith and gains his salvation within that faith (see 1. 168).

172   *metal*. Gold, the most precious of metals.

Poema de la Reina Ester

This and the remaining examples of João Pinto Delgado's poetry given in this volume are taken from the same collection *Poema de la Reyna Ester. Lamentaciones del Propheta Ieremias. Historia de Rut, y varias Poesías* (Rouen, 1627). All the works are on biblical themes, the poet refashioning his source with the declared aim of reconciling the Holy Text with contemporary literary style. This he succeeds in accomplishing by omitting none of the content of the original, while adding much in the way of poetic embellishment and comment, often derived from Talmudic sources, in a way which, bearing in mind the taste of the Golden Age, is never irrelevant or inappropriate. For a study of the Rouen poems, see A. D. H. Fishlock's thesis, ''The Poems of João Pinto Delgado,'' University of London, Ph.D., 1952.

El sueño y las lástimas de Mardochay

The first passage from *Poema de la Reina Ester* (Rouen edition, pp. 40–46) is the dream of Mordecai and his lament on hearing of the decree against the Jews (Esther 4:1). The dream is present in the Apocrypha addition to Esther 10, but Pinto Delgado derives his version from the Yalkut of Simeon Qara Hadarshan, which he knew via the Latin translation of Louis-Henri d'Aquin *(Scholia Rabi Salamonis Iarchi in Librum Esther* [Paris, 1622]; also contains excerpts from Talmud *Tractate Megillah* and Rashi on Esther). There are numerous textual comparisons between the two works, in addition to which the poet has been influenced in the placing of the dream here rather than before the eunuchs' plot in Esther 10 by the Yalkut's commentary to Esther 3:15, the verse immediately prior to Esther 4:1 (see *ed. cit.*, pp. 29–30). For detailed analysis see A. D. H. Fishlock, ''The Rabbinic material in the *Ester* of Pinto Delgado,'' *Journal of Jewish Studies* 2 (1950–51). Note that the meter is the *sexteto*, rather than the more grandiose *octava real*.

7–12   The idea that the threat to the Jews is punishment for idolatry during the time of Nebuchadnezzar derives from Rashi *apud* Esther 4:1, with reference to a second dream which Pinto merges with the first (d'Aquin ed., pp. 8–9).

13–16   As an example of how closely the poet follows d'Aquin's Yalkut, cf. "vidit in somnis Mardocheus ingentem tempestatem, immanem terrae motum, & vocem terribilem per totam terram diffusam, & magnam formidem omnibus hominibus iniectam" (ibid., p. 30).

17 ff.   The contending dragons symbolize Haman and Mordecai, while the fountain is Esther (see Apocryphal Esther vv. 6–7).

43   The lament which follows is in the biblical tradition of the intercession of Abraham on behalf of Sodom (Genesis 18:23–33) and Moses for Israel (Numbers 14:11–21).

45   There may also be a play on *envueltos* as meaning "involved," i.e., in bringing about the Jews' downfall; *mal* in the sense of "harm," "misfortune."

48   *fin . . . fin.* A typical example of Pinto's use of chiasmus.

52   *el instrumento de soberbia.* I.e., the instrument by which pride is punished.

57–58   The reference is to Abraham and the "sacrifice" of Isaac (Genesis 22).

61 ff.   In this description of the sufferings of Israel and the vindictiveness of her enemies there are echoes of Jeremiah, Psalms, and Job.

73–78   An allusion to Jeremiah and his Lamentation (see *llanto,* 1. 78).

79–82   The reference is to the pronouncement of the Holy Name of God by the High Priest in the "holy of holies," the inner sanctum of the Temple, on the Day of Atonement in order to petition on behalf of the people for their sins.

91   *Cuál . . . agravio?* A subtle piece of irony: what looks like an expression of universal sympathy is confirmed by the next line as one of universal rejoicing at the suffering of the Jews.

112   *su repuesta.* Literally "his reply," i.e., the reply he expects to receive.

115–20   Esther 4:2.

La triste consolación de Amán (Rouen ed., p. 76)

This short passage corresponds to Esther 6:13 where Haman seeks the advice of his wife and friends, who by their words unwittingly (in this version) heap praise on his enemies. It splendidly illustrates how Pinto, in making use of Rabbinic sources, exploits his own talent for manipulating antitheses and poetic images in succession. See Fishlock, "Rabbinic Material in *Ester*," and E. M. Wilson, "The Poetry of João Pinto Delgado," *Journal of Jewish Studies* 1 (1948–49).

9   *caye, caye.* The repetition appears in d'Aquin's translation of the *Tractate Megillah:* "Iudaei namque cum *cadunt,* ad terram usque *cadunt.*" The source continues: "At vero cum *ascendunt,* ad coelum usque *ascendunt*" (p. 33). This supplies the parallel repetition of *sube, sube* (1. 10) while both parts of the quotation together give the contrast *tierra / cielo* (9, 10).

11   *al polvo . . . estrellas.* This contrast of dust and stars, while present in the Talmud itself has not come through in d'Aquin's version (see above), the poet's probable sole source for the Talmud; he has had recourse in fact to the Commentary of Rashi on Esther 6:13 (*ed. cit.,* p. 12).

La oración de la Reina Ester (Rouen ed., pp. 77–81)

The prayer of Esther is an interpolation of the poet's own (though possibly inspired by the prayer in the Apocryphal Esther 14), between the end of chapter 6 and the beginning of chapter 7 of the Book of Esther, where the Queen awaits the arrival of the King and Haman at the second banquet to which she has invited them. It is a fine expression of the poet's faith in the certainty of God's mercy on the righteous of Israel.

6   *fuente*. Both literal and metaphorical senses are exploited here: "spring" and "source," as the culmination of a series of images of water.

9   *la huerta*. The image of the garden (here the Garden of Eden) is a favorite one of Pinto Delgado's, cf. *Lamentaciones* 2:6 (below).

11–12   The idea here is that tears which spring from virtuous thoughts (especially repentance) are a force for the renewal of life.

21   This is intended as a denial of the Christian concept of God working through human agents, rather than directly to the individual as in Judaism, a detail which reinforces the Jewish nature of Pinto's poem. One notes the absence of any correlation between the person of Esther and the Virgin, which is drawn to greater or lesser extent in the works of Christian writers on the theme, e.g., Lope de Vega's *La hermosa Ester*. See A. D. H. Fishlock, "Lope de Vega's *La hermosa Ester* and Pinto Delgado's *Poema de la Reyna Ester*: A Comparative Study," *Bulletin of Hispanic Studies* 32 (1955).

25   *lugar*. "Place": this relates to the use of *makom* in the Hebrew (Esther 4:14), which is traditionally taken as a designation of God, in a book of the Bible which is notable for its lack of direct reference to the Deity.

50   The enemies of the Jews have as it were taken it upon themselves to punish them, without relying on God to do so or, conversely, acting as his agents.

57   *espero*. Both senses of "hope" and "wait" are intended.

61–66   Judges 4–5: Sisera and the Song of Deborah.

73–78   A comparison is drawn between Haman and Pharaoh, with the argument that if God saved Israel from the latter who only sought to enslave her, he will *a fortiori* save her from one who hastens to destroy her utterly. This leads to the final point (79–84) that God would not surely allow to happen a punishment which he in his mercy would stop short of inflicting.

79–84   The incident of the Golden Calf (Exodus 32).

Conclusion (Rouen ed., pp. 109–11)

The poem ends with five forceful stanzas on the theme of the virtue and reward of suffering, an affirmation of God's power and mercy.

12   *escala*. Cf. Genesis 28:12: Jacob's dream is here treated *a lo divino*.

13–18   The reference is to Hezekiah and the siege of Jerusalem by the Assyrians under Sennacherib, whose army was miraculously struck down by a plague when on the point of victory (2 Kings 19).

19   *varón*. David; for his sparing of Saul's life (21–22), see 1 Samuel 24.

Lamentaciones del profeta Jeremías

João Pinto Delgado's *Lamentaciones* may justly be considered his masterpiece: we see the poet's consistent themes of the tribulations of Israel as punishment and the poet's faith in God's redemption, expressed with consummate mastery of his art, in which subtlety combines with simplicity of expression, complex rhetorical device with sincerity of emotion, and the tone ranges from pathos to astringent moralizing in the manner of the Old Testament prophets. The poem consists of glosses of some seven to twenty-five *quintillas* on each of the verses of the first two chapters of the Lamentations of Jeremiah. Each section or *lamentación* is preceded by a prose translation of the verse in question, usually in the version found in the Ferrara Bible, with some occasional borrowing from Cassiodoro de Reyna's Protestant ''Bear'' Bible and the Vulgate. The use of the Ferrara Bible looks like a gesture of affirmation of the poet's Jewishness, while by contrast he shows a preference in the poem itself for the interpretations of the Vulgate—indicating perhaps the hold of his upbringing on his aesthetic taste and outlook. Since the prose translation is only of marginal interest to the general reader, it has been omitted, while for purposes of reference an English translation is given in these notes in the Authorized Version. For a study of the *Lamentaciones,* see A. D. H. Fishlock, ''The *Lamentaciones* of João Pinto Delgado,'' *Atlante* 3 (1955); also, for comparison, the Christian version of Quevedo, *Las lágrimas de Hieremías castellanas,* ed. J. M. Blecua and E. M. Wilson (Madrid, 1953).

Lamentación 1:1 (Rouen ed., pp. 114–17)

''How doth the city sit solitary, that was full of people! how is she become as a widow! she that was great among the nations, and princess among the provinces, how is she become tributary!'' (Lamentations 1:1)

1–5   The poet turns the exclamations of the original into a question, which together with three more in the following stanzas form an intricate rhetorical pattern. The immediate concentration on the moral theme contrasts with Quevedo's version, *Las lágrimas de Hieremías castellanas,* which concentrates at this point on the lack of people in the city (i.e., the visible evidence of abandonment).

6.   *se inclina.* (1) ''to bend, bow the head''; (2) ''to be inclined to do something.''

13.   *un mar/ de llanto.* Pinto's favorite image of the ''sea of tears,'' here enriched in its pathetic effect by the enjambement.

23–24   *recreas/. . . veas.* Note how the effect is varied by an occasional change in the rhyming pattern: A B AA B instead of A B A B A as elsewhere.

32–33   For the idea of the poet/prophet seeking out someone to tell him what had happened, cf. Jeremiah 5:1.

44   *se.* Rouen ed. *le,* which would give the translation ''As [silent as] their gods they [Israel's enemies] have made them.''

46   *caíste.* The image of falling recurs in *Lamentaciones* with reference to sin and its consequences; cf. l. 53 below.

51   *princesa.* Here Pinto follows the Vulgate's use of the word *princeps,* rather than *señora* as in Ferrara and the poet's own prose version of this verse.

64.   *tributo.* Conceit: the tribute paid is in produce, the evil produce of sin which has led to Israel's enslavement.

67   *honra.* There is perhaps here an echo of the honor conventions of the Golden Age: the loss of honor by the 'princess' is disaster in itself.

Lamentación 1:12 (Rouen ed., pp. 172–74)

''Is it nothing to you, all ye that pass by? behold, and see if there be any sorrow like unto my sorrow, which is done unto me, wherewith the Lord hath afflicted me desolate and faint all day.'' (Lamentations 1:12)

1 ff. The speaker here is Jerusalem; Pinto takes the difficult first words of Lamentations 1:12 *lo alechem* ("not unto you") as a statement, in accordance with Talmudic interpretation, not as a question as in the Authorized Version. This accords with the poem's religious moral, i.e., such misfortune will not happen to others, since they, unlike Jerusalem, have not sinned.

3   *dicha*. The passers-by are wrong to see her fate as "bad luck" and not the punishment of God which it is; doubly so as it is actually Israel's good fortune to be thus treated by God.

5   *porque me veáis*. By moving on, the witness will gain a clearer perspective, as from a distance, of the situation he beholds.

24   *se han vuelto vanos*. The subject must be *efetos* since *vanos* is masculine; hence, since the produce of the hands has ceased to be justice and truth and become vanity, the hands themselves have gone in pursuit of vain or worthless deeds.

28   *el ídolo de Betel*. See 1 Kings 12–13 (the incident which leads to the withering of Jeroboam's hand).

31   *viña*. The image of the vine or vineyard has been suggested by the Vulgate version of Lamentations 1:12 "quoniam vindemiat me": "since he has harvested me as the vintage"; cf. also Isaiah 5:1–2 and Ezekiel 15:6.

36   *La torre*. Both the identification of the tower (of David) with the Temple and of the wine press with the Altar of Sacrifice in the following stanza are derived from Cornelius a Lapide, *Commentaria in quatuor prophetas maiores* (Paris, 1622), col. 84 on Isaiah 1–2 (quoting Origen).

38   *Casa*. The usual term in Sephardi Spanish for the Temple.

47   *el fruto*. Play on the idea of the fruit which is the object of desire (overtones of Genesis) and that which is the result of that desire.

67   *colores*. Masculine in Mod. Span. and usually only feminine in the Golden Age with reference to complexion; its use here perhaps underlines the personification of Jerusalem as a splendidly bedecked woman.

68   *fabriqué*. The primary sense is of "building," with here the secondary idea of "arraying" or "decking out."

74   *que a mí me debía*. The subject of the verb is "I"; in giving her love to her enemy she has given him the love or self-respect she owed herself.

Lamentación 1:13 (Rouen ed., pp. 174–78)

"From above hath he sent fire into my bones, and it prevaileth against them: he hath spread a net for my feet, he hath turned me back: he hath made me desolate and faint all the day." (Lam. 1:13)

6–10   The poet links Nimrod's Tower of Babel (Genesis 10) with the towers of Jerusalem; the interpretation of "bones" (Lamentations 1:13) as "towers" derives from the Targum via Cornelius a Lapide, *Commentaria*, col. 519.

10   *lengua*. Both sense of "tongue" are intended: the tongues of fire speak volumes through the ruin they leave behind.

15   *celo*. The word is well chosen; besides "jealousy" it means "zeal," thus reinforcing the idea that the fire of vengeance or judgment matches the fire of religious devotion which has now cooled. A further development is seen in the biblical references of the following stanzas which are examples of fire not harming those who keep faith with God—the fire of Divine Presence.

16–20   Moses and the Burning Bush, Exodus 3:1–4.

21–25   The three young men and the furnace of Daniel 3:12–30.

26–30   Elijah and the prophets of Baal, 1 Kings 18:17–40.

31–40   Solomon's prayer and God's acceptance of his sacrifice in the Temple, 2 Chronicles 6 and 7:1–3.

41 ff.   The poet returns to his text for the image of the net.

52   *ligera*. "Lightly," "unimpeded," hence "swiftly."

Lamentación 2:6 (Rouen ed., pp. 240–43)

"And he hath violently taken away his tabernacle, as if it were of a garden; he hath destroyed his places of assembly. . . ." (Lamentations 2:6) In contrast with the previous "lamentation," this one provides an example of the secular treatment of a theme in the Golden Age manner.

2   *la mano*. God's hand: the image of God as gardener is used by the poet in his version of Lamentations 2:1.

6–8   The fruit is visible because the leaves keep the sun out of the onlooker's eyes, but also because they protect the fruit and allow it to thrive.

11 ff.   The plants are clearly chosen for their symbolic value: for example, the amaranth suggests immortality, the acanthus humility, and the violet modesty.

16–17   *El lirio . . . /el rocío*. Cf. Hosea 14:5 "I will be as the dew unto Israel: he shall grow as the lily."

26   *el coral*. A common *culto* word for "mouth."

27   *revienta*. The two senses of the English "bursting" are present in the Spanish.

28   *corona*. The base of the pomegranate is in the form of a crown, making it the symbol of royalty and loyalty to kings.

31   *al vivo*. "In the flesh," i.e., when not picked.

32   *se altera*. (1) "alters"; (2) "becomes angry."

33   *el humor nocivo*. A reference to the bitterness of the pips within the otherwise pleasant fruit; the allusion to Adam is clear.

36   *el racimo*. Grapes stand for the good things of life.

37   *la caña*. "Stem" or "stalk" but also (1) "sugar cane" (from which alcoholic drinks like rum are made); (2) a measure of wine; (3) possibly also a tall cylindrical wineglass (as for drinking *manzanilla*): the ripening grapes imitate or anticipate the wine which is made from it later.

41   *El agua*. The symbol of divine grace; cf. Christian imagery as in Revelation 22:1.

42   *principio*. Both (1) "beginning," "origin," and (2) "principle."

Lamentación 2:7 (Rouen ed., pp. 245–49)

"The Lord hath cast off his altar, he hath abhorred his sanctuary, he hath given up into the hand of the enemy the walls of her palaces. . . ." (Lamentations 2:7)

1 ff.   For the image of fire cf. Lamentación 1:13 above; here it develops as a fine example of Pinto's elegiac style (l. 36 ff.).

12   *el corazón sacrifica*. Cf. Psalms 51:17 "The sacrifices of God are a broken spirit: a broken and a contrite heart, O God, thou wilt not despise": the interpretation of this as meaning martyrdom is shared by Enríquez Gómez (see *Romance*, l. 336).

21–22   Cf. Jeremiah 7:5–7 concerning charity towards the stranger, the orphaned, the widowed, and the innocent.

26 ff.   This and the following stanza derive from the strictures of Jeremiah
7:10–11.

40   *pena*. (1) "pain"; (2) "punishment."

La historia de Rut (Rouen ed., pp. 317–19)

This extract is from the opening stanzas of Pinto Delgado's poem which re-
counts the story of Ruth. It illustrates his use of Talmudic material to enhance
the poetic expression of his theme rather than as example or adornment: he
draws on the idea in the *Midrash Rabbah* that Elimelech left Israel to avoid
giving charity to others when famine produced shortage, not as a direct conse-
quence of the famine itself. This idea informs the whole moral cast of the poem,
while the expression is in the spiritualized mold which we have seen elsewhere
as typical of the poet's style. For detailed study of the Rabbinic influence in this
poem, see E. M. Wilson, "The Poetry of the João Pinto Delgado," *Journal of
Jewish Studies* 1 (1948–49).

2   *jueces*. As Ruth 1:1 "when the judges judged": a period when in particu-
lar Israel went in pursuit of false gods, according to the Rabbis.

5–6   The entry into Canaan of the Israelites, Joshua 4, seen as a second
miracle (cf. Exodus from Egypt and crossing of the Red Sea).

8   *Abezán*. One Jewish tradition places the events of Ruth in the time of
Ibzan's judgeship (Judges 12:8); see *Midrash* III.6.

14   *la espiga*. This is the "blasted corn" of Isaiah 37:27; much of the force
of the following parenthesis derives from the ambiguity in the references to the
hypocrite, who is only revealed as Elimelech by the juxtaposition of *Varón de
Judá* (l. 37) with the description of the worthless *labrador*/hypocrite of the
preceding stanza (also the repetitions of *hombre* and *vida*).

17–18   *Es heno que . . ./en el tejado creció*. See Isaiah 37:27 (also Psalms
129:6–7). The subject of the verb *(es)* is ambiguous, either the *espiga* of line 14
or the *hombre* of line 19: the very ambiguity leads to a concentration of imagis-
tic expression through the linking of the metaphors of the two successive stan-
zas.

41   *descansa*. The mitigation of Elimelech's sin is seen by the Rabbis as
lying in the fact that he did not intend his sojourn in Moab to be permanent.

42–43   The ostensibly banal listing of names conceals within it an antithesis
between Elimelech who went out of Judah to sin and Naomi who returned in
virtue.

Canción . . . a la salida de Egipto hasta la Tierra Santa (Rouen ed., pp. 349–55)

The opening and concluding stanzas of this poem are given in order to illus-
trate the poet's skill in transposing personal experience (cf. "Autobiographical
Poems") to the plane of fully developed allegory in the form of a *camino del
alma*, or "journey of the soul," after the manner of Luis de Granada. There are
also echoes of the writings of Philo of Alexandria here; see A. D. H. Fishlock,
"The Shorter Poems of João Pinto Delgado," *Bulletin of Hispanic Studies* 31
(1954).

8–9   A reference to the Burning Bush, Exodus 3:2.

18   Cf. the spies' report of giants in the Promised Land, Numbers 13:32–33.

T W O

Antonio Enríquez Gómez

Antonio Enríquez Gómez was born in Cuenca, New Castile, in about 1600 of "mixed" parentage, New Christian father and Old Christian mother. The judaizing element in his family, however, is undeniable: his grandfather, Diego de Mora, was arrested for judaizing in 1588 and died in an Inquisition jail (he was the leader of a thriving crypto-Jewish community in Quintanar de la Orden); and his father, Diego Enríquez de Mora, was arrested and condemned by the Inquisition shortly before 1624 and went into exile in France where, his first wife having died, he took a wife from the Jewish community of Amsterdam. On the other hand, Antonio married a woman of Old Christian stock, Isabel Basurto, in 1618. By 1624 he was established in commerce in Madrid. During this period he made several business trips to France, to his father in Nantes and his uncle in Bordeaux. At the same time he was gaining a reputation for himself as a poet and playwright in Madrid and frequenting the circle of Lope de Vega: when the great poet died, he contributed a sonnet in his honor to Juan Pérez de Montalbán's anthology *Fama póstuma* (1636).

Called to give evidence at the trial of one Bartolomé Febos (for judaizing) in 1634, he must have thought it prudent to leave for France, which he did towards the end of 1635 or early 1636. He followed what one might call the "Marrano trail" by way of Peyrehorade (southwest France), Bordeaux, and Rouen (1644). In France, he occupied himself with both politics and literature: on the one hand, he allied himself with the Portuguese delegation in France to fight for the recognition of Portugal's recent independence from Spain, and on the other, he had all his nondramatic works printed there, the majority by Laurent Maurry, Pierre Corneille's printer in Rouen. The Rouen works include *El siglo pitagórico* (1644), a satire employing the Pythagorean idea of transmigration of souls and including a picaresque novel; *La*

Incumbit capiti Cælo dimissa Corona
Non alia uates Cingit Apollo Suos·

Portrait of Antonio Enríquez Gómez from *Academias morales de las Musas*
(Bordeaux: Pedro de la Court, 1642)

culpa del primer peregrino (1644) on the theme of Adam and the Fall; and *Política angélica* (1647), a veiled attack on the Inquisition under the guise of orthodox Catholic argument. His principal collection of poetry and plays, *Academias morales de las Musas*, appeared in Bordeaux in 1642, and his panegyric *Luis dado de Dios*, directed to Louis XIV, was published in Paris in 1645: on its title page is displayed the poet's title of Knight of the Order of Saint Michael, a signal honor for a foreigner, though precisely for what it was conferred is not known. Enríquez Gómez's two major poems of commitment to Judaism also date from this period, the unpublished *Romance al divín mátir, Judá Creyente* on the martyrdom of Lope de Vera y Alarcón in 1644, and *Sansón Nazareno*, an epic poem on the Samson story. Both are concerned with the themes of martyrdom and Messianic redemption.

Towards the end of 1649, Enríquez Gómez returned to Spain, for reasons either of homesickness or unfinished commercial business, but not because he rejected Judaism—he had plans to leave again for Naples. In Spain he took on the alias of Fernando de Zárate (identified by some with the fervent Catholic playwright of that name). He was burned in effigy in Seville by the Inquisition in 1660 and eventually arrested in person in 1661. On 18 March 1663, he died while awaiting sentence and two years later was reconciled in effigy with the Church.

Antonio Enríquez Gómez's talents lay in two directions, the satirical and the purely poetical, as one may see from the outline of works mentioned above. In the first, he set out to rival the wit of the archenemy of judaizers, Francisco de Quevedo, though it cannot be said, some fine barbs aside, that it was a contest which he won. On the other hand, he stands up much better in comparison when he breaks away from the Quevedo mold into his own somewhat original use of biblical sources, Job and Ecclesiastes, as seen in *Academias morales* and *La culpa del primer peregrino*. The *Romance al divín mártir* also shows the poet putting his talent for wit and incisive argument to good use in addition to expressing his main religious themes. We see the other side of the poet at its best in *Sansón Nazareno*, both in the Gongorine description of Samson's first love and in the final moments of the hero in the last canto. Lastly, we may say that, while perhaps not the most profound of poets, Antonio Enríquez Gómez has the capacity to express his feelings, particularly his religious feelings and his identification with Judaism, with a sincerity and skill whose effect is often moving.

Cuando contemplo mi pasada gloria

Cuando contemplo mi pasada gloria
y me veo sin mí, duda mi estado
si ha de morir conmigo mi memoria.
    En vano se lastima mi cuidado,
5   conociendo que amar un imposible
contradice del cuerdo lo acertado.
    ¿Qué importa que mi pena sea terrible,
si consiste mi bien en mi destierro,
decreto justo para ser posible?
10   Despeñado caí de un alto cerro,
pero puedo decir seguramente
que no nació de mi tan grande yerro,
    Lloro mi patria y della estoy ausente,
desgracia del nacer lo habrá causado,
15   pensión original del que no siente.
    Si pudiera mi amor de lo pasado
hacer de olvido un pacto a la memoria,
quedara el corazón más aliviado.
    Mas es esta enemiga tan notoria,
20   que porque sabe que me da disgusto,
muerte me da con mi pasada gloria.
    ¡O quién supiera (aun por camino injusto)
dónde la hierba de olvidar se cría,
para morir tal vez con algún gusto!
25   A la Tesalia fuera y sufriría
(por borrar las especies desta fiera)
que me abrasara el que ilumina el día.
    Sin memoria quedara, de manera
que pudiera juzgar con la visiva
30   de más amor y ciencia verdadera.

    •   •   •   •   •

No tengo, no, segura confianza
de ver lo que perdí: ¡qué necio he sido!
el bien que yo perdí tarde se alcanza.
    Perdí mi libertad, perdí mi nido,
35   perdió mi alma el centro más dichoso,
y a mí mismo también, pues me ha perdido.

When I consider that glorious past of mine

When I consider that glorious past of mine
where I am found no more, the remembrance
of my state, I fear, is bound to die with me.
In vain my anxiety gives vent to grief,
5   knowing that to love something impossible
is to deny what a sane man knows is true.
What does it matter that my pain is fearsome,
if my banishment is for my own good
(the decree seems just enough that it be so)?
10   Cast headlong down, from a lofty peak I fell,
but I can with all certainty declare
that such a grievous fault was not born of me.
I mourn my homeland, from her I am absent,
an accident of birth must have been its cause—
15   the cross of origin the unsuspecting bear.
If only my love of that which is past could
make with memory a pact of forgetting,
my heart would know a state of greater comfort.
But so implacable is this enemy
20   that because he knows he sorely vexes me,
to death he taunts me with my glorious past.
O would I knew (even by some unlawful means)
where the herb that brings oblivion is grown
so I might die perhaps and find contentment.
25   To Thessaly I would go and suffer there
(so as to erase the visions of that beast)
the one who lights the day to consume me.
Without memory I would remain, so that
I might form a judgment through the seeing power
30   of greater love and knowledge of a true kind.

•   •   •   •   •

I do not have, no, that certain confidence
that I shall see what I have lost: foolish me,
the good I lost, too late will be regained.
I lost my liberty, lost my only home,
35   my soul lost the happy place where it belonged,
and me too, for it has been the loss of me.

¿Cómo puedo aguardar ningún reposo,
si el reloj de mi vida se ha quebrado,
parándose el volante perezoso?
40   Dejé mi albergue tierno y regalado
y dejé con el alma mi albedrío,
pues todo en tierra ajena me ha faltado.
    Fuéseme sin pensar mi aliento y brío,
y si de alguna gala me adornaba,
45   hoy del espejo con razón no fío.
    Mi sencilla verdad, con quien hablaba,
si la quiero buscar, la hallo vendida:
dejóme y fuese donde el alma estaba.
    La imagen en el pecho tengo asida
50   de aquel Siglo Dorado, donde estuve
gozando el mayo de mi edad florida.
    Una contraria y deslucida nube
turbar pretende el sol de aquella infancia,
adonde racional origen tuve.
55   ¡Ay de mí! que perdí (sin arrogancia)
la ciencia más segura y verdadera,
aunque algunos la den por ignorancia.
    Perdí mi estimación, parte primera,
del cortesano estile noble llave,
60   adonde el juicio halló su primavera.
    Hablaba el idioma siempre grave,
adornado de nobles oradores,
siendo su acento para mí suave.
    Eran mis penas por mi bien menores,
65   que la patria, divina compañía,
siempre vuelve los males en favores.
    Gané la noche, si perdí mi día,
no es mucho que en tinieblas sepultado
esté quien vive en la Noruega fría.
70   Perdí lo más precioso de mi estado,
perdí mi libertad: con esto digo
cuanto puede decir un desdichado.
    ¡O tú, cualquiera bárbaro enemigo,
fundamento cruel de mi fortuna!
75   si gloria quieres, sirve de testigo.
    Sin esperanza me dejaste alguna
de volver a cobrar lo que por suerte
el cielo me otorgó desde la cuna.

How can I expect to ever gain respite,
if the timepiece of my life has been shattered,
the idle balance wheel stopping in its tracks?
40   I left behind my sweet and tender dwelling
and left behind my free will with my soul,
for on foreign soil I stand bereft of all.

Without a thought, my breath, my strength went from me,
and if some finery I once used to wear,
45   today, with reason, I mistrust the mirror.

My simple truth, with whom I was wont to speak,
if I seek to find her, I now find betrayed:
She forsook me and went to where my soul was.

Clasped tight to my bosom I hold the image
50   of that Golden Age, in which I found myself
enjoying the Maytide of my blooming years.

One contrary and obscuring cloud attempts
to perturb the sunlight of that infancy
where I did have my rational origin.

55   Woe is me, for I lost (without arrogance)
the most certain of knowledge and the truest,
though some there are who account it ignorance.

I lost my standing, the most important part,
the illustrious key to the style of courtier,
60   out of which true judgment draws its origin.

It spoke to me in a language ever grave,
embellished by tongues of noble orators,
its accents for me being gentle on the ear.

Through my good fortune, my sorrows were the less,
65   for one's homeland, that divine companion,
always turns misfortunes into favors.

If my day's light I lost, the night I gained,
for it is of slight account that he who lives
in cold Norway in darkness should be shrouded.

70   I lost the most precious part of my estate:
I lost my liberty; by this I mean
all that a wretched creature can express.

O you, whatever harsh enemy you be,
the cruel foundation of what Fate has dealt me,
75   if fame you seek, serve now as my witness.

Without any hope whatever you left me
that I might recover that which by chance
heaven from the cradle endowed me with.

Conténtate de verme desta suerte
80   que ya no me ha quedado, si me miras,
más firme bien que el aguardar mi muerte.
Si por ella, bárbaro, suspiras,
ruega que viva, pues viviendo ganas
las saetas, cobarde, que me tiras.
85   Salieron, sí, mis esperanzas vanas,
pues pensando volver a mi esfera,
con la esperanza me llené de canas.
Allá dejé mi alma verdadera,
no vivo, no, con la que allí tenía
90   (o se ha trocado en otra la primera).
Hallo extranjera la que llamo mía,
pues veo rebelados los sentidos,
huyendo de tan justa compañía.
Fábula vengo a ser de los nacidos,
95   no es mucho que lo sea, pues llegaron
a aborrecer verdades los oídos.
No suelen, no, los campos que adornaron
el mayo y el abril helarse al noto,
como todos mis miembros se me helaron.
100   Ni el brazo suele (aunque al honor le importe)
segar con mano fuerte los vitales,
como mi herida dio sangre en el Corte.
No gime entre las selvas y cristales
la tórtola su amada compañera,
105   como yo mis fortunas y mis males.
Ave mi patria fue, mas ¿quién dijera
que el nido de mi alma le faltara
y que las alas de mi amor perdiera?
Si pérdida tan grande se alcanzara
110   con suspiros, con lágrimas y penas,
con mi sangre otra vez la conquistara.
Mas ¡ay dolor! que sin piedad condenas
los lazos que te ha dado la crianza,
adonde nunca tu pasión refrenas.
115   Entendió mi perdida confianza
volver a poseer lo que era suyo
y cerróse la puerta a la esperanza.
Con justa causa y con razón arguyo
de cobarde al deseo inobediente,
120   pues vive cuando de sus brazos huyo.

Take your delight in seeing me this way,
80   for now I am left, if you can look and see,
with no sure joy save that of awaiting death.
    If after that you crave, cruel barbarian,
pray that I live, for by my living you gain
the arrows which you cowardly loose at me.
85   All of my hopes turned out, yes, to be vain ones,
for in thinking I might see my sphere again,
with nurtured hope I turned all my hair to gray.
    Yonder I did leave behind my true soul,
I do not live with the one that I had there
90   (or the first one has changed into another).
    A stranger I find that one I call mine,
since I find my feelings have turned rebellious,
fleeing away from such true company.
    I have become a fable among born men;
95   it is of little account that I should be so,
for my ears have come to abhor all things true.
    Those fields that May and April do adorn
are not wont to freeze under the southern wind,
as the limbs of my body all have frozen.
100   Nor is the arm wont (though honor be concerned)
to scythe through a man's vitals with such swift strength,
as my wound drew blood from me there in the Court.
    Nor laments amid the woods and crystal streams
the turtledove his beloved companion,
105   as I bemoan my fortune and my troubles.
    Such a bird my homeland was, but who would say
that it should be without the nest of my soul
and that it should lose the wings of my love.
    If such a grievous loss could be regained
110   through sighs, through tears, through heartfelt affliction,
with my own blood I would once more achieve it.
    But oh the pain! For you pitiless condemn
the bonds which your upbringing has given you,
for which you never can hold back your feelings.
115   This lost confidence of mine bethought itself
to take possession once more of what was his
and saw the gateway to hope closed firmly shut.
    With just cause and reason do I accuse
of cowardice my disobedient desire,
120   for it lives on when from its arms I flee.

A penas largas me lloré presente
no a leves males lastimaba cuanto
alumbra ese topacio transparente.
    Si mi sepulcro labro con el llanto,
125 ofrézcase en las aras de su pira
tan continuo pesar y dolor tanto.
    A los aires enciende si suspira
mi corazón, pues de centellas lleno,
líquidos Etnas por los ojos gira.
130   Si estuviera el sentido tan ajeno,
como lo está de recobrar su fama,
pudiérase beber este veneno;
    Mas ¡ay de mí! en la extranjera llama
aun no estoy mariposa que muriendo
135 goza la luz de lo que adora y ama.
    En diferente clima entré riendo,
imaginando como tierno infante
que era mi patria la que estaba viendo.
    Halléme rodeado en un instante
140 de más Babeles que en Senar compuso
el soberbio rigor de aquel gigante.
    Hallé mi cuerpo convertido en uso,
que el que muda de patria decir puede
que a mudar de costumbre se dispuso.
145   Si en los frases y términos excede
el propio al extranjero su idioma
por guerra babilónica me quede.
    Bien la patria perdida el brío doma,
pues cuando se acredita el movimiento
150 de lo que fue, ni aun los amagos toma.
    Hablo y no me entienden y esto siento
tan sumamente, que me torno mudo,
barriendo si fe mi entendimiento.
    Y si a vengarme del agravio acudo,
155 el más vil de la tierra le deshace
a la paciencia su divino escudo.
    Ninguno de razón me satisface,
todo es a fuerza de pasión tirana
cuanto conmigo la malicia hace.
160   ¿Quién de mi patria santa y cortesana
me trujo a conocer diversas gentes,
ajenas de la mía soberana?

For copious tears I wept here, long and deep,
not for trifling woes did I stir to pity
all that which gives light to the limpid topaz.
If I am digging my own grave with weeping,
125   let there be offered up on the altar of
its pyre such ceaseless sorrow and such great pain.
    The four winds are set ablaze when my heart
heaves a sigh, for being full of living sparks,
it pours out liquid Etnas through my eyes.
130   If I were as far removed from emotion
as I am from regaining my lost honor,
I could bear to drink down this poisonous draft.
    But, woe is me, for in this alien flame
I am not even a moth, which in dying
135   enjoys the light of what it adores and loves.
    Laughing, I went off to a different clime,
fondly imagining, like a tender child,
that what I was seeing was my own homeland.
    In an instant I found myself surrounded
140   by more Babels than on the plain of Shinar
that giant of unyielding pride constructed.
    I found my body put to other usage,
for he who changes country can truly say
that he has exposed himself to change his ways.
145   Given in its turns and phrases one's own tongue
the foreigner's surpasses, may his language
be to me still like Babylonian chaos.
    Well does to lose one's country tame the spirit,
for when we have acknowledged the passing of
150   what has been, it does not even rise to threats.
    I speak and they do not understand me: this
I feel so keenly that I am struck dumb,
sweeping aside, unsure, my understanding.
    And if I resort to vengeance for the wrong,
155   the basest in the land sets it all to rights
by dint of patience which is his holy shield.
    None with reason can give me satisfaction,
all that evil malice perpetrates on me
is done by force of tyrannizing passion.
160   Who from my sacred and gentle motherland
brought me to the knowledge of divers peoples,
all alien to that sovereign one of mine?

No hay más seguros deudos y parientes
que las piedras del noble nacimiento,
165   que son siempre seguros y obedientes.
    Cuando me paro a contemplar de asiento
lo que al presente soy y lo que he sido,
la ansia se me dobla y el tormento.
    Cuando me veo solo y perseguido,
170   reparo si yo soy el que merezco
la imagen de mi ser en tanto olvido.
    Y si me llaman, sin sentido ofrezco
la vista al nombre, hallándome engañado
de ver que aun a mí mismo me parezco.
175   Si me recuerdan de mi perdido estado,
como si algún letargo me dejara,
respondo con semblante alborotado.
    Y si en mi rostro el sabio reparara,
leyera en letras de color de cera
180   la pasión del espíritu en mi cara.
    Perder la libertad, ¿quién lo sufriera,
sino la ley de honor, que siempre ha sido
en el honrado superior esfera?
    Bien pudiera volver favorecido,
185   mas eso fuera bueno si llevara
lo mismo que saqué del patrio nido.
    Si con volver mi fama restaurara
a la Libia cruel vuelta le diera,
que morir en mi patria me bastara.
190   Pero volver a dar venganza fiera
a mis émulos todos fuera cosa
para que muerte yo propio me diera.
    Ampáreme la mano poderosa,
que con ella seguramente vivo,
195   libre desta canalla maliciosa.
    Bien sabe el cielo que con sangre escribo
del corazón estos renglones puros,
que al fin el cuerpo es animal nocivo.
    El no puede sentir estos seguros
200   dolores del espíritu, que el alma
los llora dentro de sus propios muros.

There are no more constant relatives and kin
than those stones that built one's noble birthplace,
165 for they are ever faithful and obedient.
    When I stop to consider with sound judgment
what I at present am and what I have been,
the anguish, the torment weigh on me the more.
    When I see myself alone and persecuted
170 I consider whether I deserve to be
so much the image of abandonment.
    And if they call me, with senses numbed, I raise
my eyes to hear my name, suffering under
the delusion that I still look like myself.
175   If they remind me of my lost estate,
as if a kind of lethargy had left me,
I reply with agitated countenance.
    And if a wise man were to observe my face,
he would read in letters of a waxen hue
180 my spirit's passion written upon my face.
    Who would suffer the loss of one's liberty,
save for the law of honor, which ever was
the loftier part of the man of honor?
    Well could I return enjoying favor,
185 but that would be good only if it removed
that same thing that I took from my native home.
    If with my return I could restore my name,
I would consign it to the Libyan desert,
for to die in my own land would be enough.
190   But to return to exact fierce vengeance
against all my rivals would be a thing
which I would give my own life to achieve.
    May the powerful hand of God come to my aid,
for through it shall I securely live,
195 free from this rabble who are full of malice.
    Heaven knows full well that with my blood I write
these pure lines drawn from my heart, for in the end
the body is nothing but a noxious brute.
    It is incapable of feeling these true
200 afflictions of the spirit, for the soul
within its own walls sheds for them its tears.

Y pues se queda mi destierro en calma,
tomen ejemplo en mí cuantos pretenden
en tierra ajeno vitoriosa palma.
205   Que no hay segura vida
cuando la libertad está perdida.

La culpa del primer peregrino

1 Diálogo de Adán y Eva

Habla Adán:

Hermoso dueño mío,
en cuya nieve el alba
va formando la rosa
sobre campos de nácar;
5   Lilio cándido y bello,
que entre coral se guarda
de los cristales puros
que arrojan las montañas;
Tus ojos de paloma
10   me son, esposa amada,
dos verdaderos nortes,
por do se rige el alma.
Tus dorados cabellos
parecen a las cabras
15   del monte a quien los siglos
darán docta albanza;
Tus pechos dos mellizos,
que retozando en gama
se apacientan en lirios
20   por valles de esperanzas.
Guerto cerrado y bello
es tu vergüenza casta,
florido albergue hermoso
del abril de tu gracia.
25   El ampo de la aurora
es tu hermosa garganta
y de diez azucenas
tus bellas manos blancas.

And since my exile floats on a sea now calmed,
let them find in me example all those who
seek in foreign lands the palm of victory.
205   For there is no life of certainty
when one has lost one's liberty.

The sin of the first pilgrim

1 Dialogue of Adam and Eve

Adam speaks:

Beautiful mistress of mine,
on whose snowy whiteness the dawn
moves, fashioning the rose's bloom
upon fields of mother-of-pearl;
5   Lily, pristine white and fair,
who amid coral keeps her store
of the pure crystal waters
that the mountains hurtle down;
    Your eyes, like those of the dove,
10   are to me, my beloved bride,
two veritable northern stars
by which my soul its bearing finds,
    The golden tresses of your hair
appear as a flock of goats
15   on the mountain which the ages
shall surely laud with learned praise.
    Your breasts are like two twins
that, frisking as if they were does,
feed among the lilies along
20   valleys full of expectations,
    A garden enclosed and handsome
is your modest chastity,
a beautiful flowering shelter
of the springtide of your grace.
25   The whiteness of Aurora
is your handsome towerlike neck,
and of ten lilies are composed
your beautiful hands of white.

La mano poderosa
30   en sola aquesta planta
límite puso al día
que sale de tu cara.
    Este vedado fruto,
que constante se guarda,
35   a muerte nos condena,
si el alma le profana.
    Es árbol prodigioso,
pues tiene entre sus ramas
reservados misterios
40   que para Dios se guardan.
    El árbol de la vida
es este, cuya gracia
manjar intelectivo
comunica a las almas.
45   Los labios apliquemos
a su moral sustancia,
pero no al de la muerte,
coronado de nácar.
    Aunque le ves hermoso,
50   su pálida manzana
tiene un gusano dentro
que tu sepulcro labra.
    Si no tocamos nunca
su tez arrebolada,
55   viviremos eternos
en esta selva sacra.
    Seremos desta gloria
las formas soberanas,
inteligencias puras
60   del superior alcázar.
    Con glorioso dominio
tú reina y yo monarca,
ilustre honor seremos
de criaturas humanas.

        •   •   •   •   •

65   Todo consiste, esposa,
en no tocar la planta
que en disfrazada muerte
su púrpura retrata.

The powerful governing hand
30 in that blossoming plant alone
set a boundary on the daystar
that rises from your countenance.
This which is the forbidden fruit
is kept watch over constantly
35 and it condemns us both to death
if our souls come to profane it.
This is a tree of wonders,
for it holds amongst its branches
mysteries of a secret kind
40 which are reserved for God alone.
This tree is the Tree of Life
and its quality of grace
imparts to the human soul a dish
of intellectual delight.
45 Let us put forth our lips to take
full in its moral sustenance
but not to touch that which means death,
that is crowned with mother-of-pearl.
Although it appears fair to you,
50 this apple of a pallid hue,
it contains a worm within it
which toils to make a grave for you.
If we do not ever touch
its skin which shines aglow with rouge
55 we shall live on eternally
in this forest hallowed of God.
We shall be the sovereign beings
of this glorious creation,
intelligences unsullied,
60 from the loftiest fortress realm.
With glorious dominion
you, the queen, and I, the monarch,
shall be the illustrious pride
of all human creation.

•   •   •   •   •

65 All this depends, my bride, upon
our touching in no way the plant
which portrays its royal purple
in tones which are but death disguised.

    Fuera deste precepto,
70   todos mis reinos manda,
    que no niega laureles
    quien no ha negado el alma.
      Abre el clavel partido
    que dulces perlas guarda
75   y en músicos conceptos
    mi corazón regala.
      Al sol de tu hermosura
    vive con esperanzas
    el mayo que me asiste,
80   el abril que me ampara.
      Rendido mi albedrío
    se dedica y consagra
    por víctima amorosa
    al cielo de tu gracia.
85   Oiga yo tus amores,
    que dos que se idolatran
    se beben los suspiros
    y con hablar descansan.

Responde Eva:

    Amado dueño mío,
90   tan justamente amado,
    que alabarte sería
    si no lisonja, agravio;
      Dulce y querido esposo
    del alma que consagro
95   a tu espíritu noble
    y corazón gallardo;
      Compañero divino
    que con imperio sacro
    a honrar vienes el orbe
100   por decreto sagrado;
      Origen de mi ser,
    pues tuve por descanso
    dormir en tu cordura,
    despertar en tu lado;

With exception of this precept,
70   govern over all my kingdoms,
for laurels need not be denied
one who has not denied her soul.
  Open your parted carnation
which guards the sweetest pearls within
75   and with harmonious concepts
delightfully regale my heart.
  Under the sun of your beauty
they come to life replete with hope,
May which comes to my attendance
80   and April which comes to my aid.
  My free will, already captive,
devotes and consecrates itself
to be love's victim, sacrificed
to the heaven of your fair grace.
85   Let me hear your love's expression,
for two who idolize each other
each other's living breath imbibe
and with the spoken word find rest.

Eve's reply:

  Beloved master of mine,
90   so rightly my beloved that
to praise you would be an affront,
if it were not flattery;
  Dearly loved and gentle husband
of my soul, which I consecrate
95   wholly to your noble spirit
and to your generous heart;
  My heaven-born companion
who with sacred dominion
have come to honor this planet
100   by a decree of holy source;
  You, the fount-head of my being,
for through your resting I achieved
in your wisdom a sleeping pause
in your side an awakening;

105   Tu voz y requiebros
       castamente he escuchado,
       en sus dulces acentos
       halló mi amor descanso.
           Como de selva en selva
110   viene saltando el gamo,
       así tu voz ha ido
       al corazón llegando.
           De amor estoy enferma
       y del alto collado
115   de la gracia divina
       por ti voy preguntando.
           "Deidades luminosas,
       ¿habéis visto mi amado?"
       "¿Quién es tu amado?" dicen
120   los planetas sagrados.
           "Es mi amado" respondo,
       "en diez mil señalado,
       rubio como el sol mismo
       y como el alba blanco.
125   "Su cabeza es el oro
       que ofir dispara a rayos
       y sus cabellos crespos
       que tiran a topacio.
           "Sus dos hermosos ojos
130   son de paloma, y tanto
       que nadan sobre leche
       donde se están bañando.
           "Es rey de todo el orbe
       y el Paraíso sacro
135   huerto de Eden divino
       le sirve de palacio."
           Pero ya que los cielos
       a quien Dios ha mandado
       que deste jardín puro
140   se alimenten sus astros,
           quisieron que te viese
       (rarísimo milagro,
       pues de padre y esposo
       gozas el nombre claro),

105   Your voice and your endearing words
      I have in chasteness listened to:
      in their sweet-resounding accents
      my love has its ease encountered.
      Just as the roebuck comes leaping
110   from wooded peak to wooded peak,
      likewise your voice has traveled
      to where it has reached my heart.
      I am sick of love for you
      and from the lofty eminence
115   of the grace of God divine
      I have come asking after you.
      "Brightly shining deities,
      have you seen my soul's beloved?"
      "Who is your soul's beloved?"
120   declare the sacred planets.
      "My beloved," I reply to them,
      "is chiefest among ten thousand,
      fair, ruddy as the sun itself
      and white as is the dawn of day.
125   "His head is as the finest gold
      that shoots out rays of ophir
      and his locks are bushy curls
      that are of a shade of topaz.
      "His two beautiful eyes are as
130   the eyes of doves and so much so
      that they appear to swim on milk
      while in it they are bathing.
      "He is the king of all the orb
      and sacred Paradise itself,
135   the Garden of Eden divine,
      serves him for a royal palace."
      But since it is that the heavens,
      whom God himself has commanded
      that from this garden undefiled
140   their stars should find their sustenance,
      have willed that I should find you
      (a miracle exceeding rare,
      since in the good name of father
      and of husband you rejoice)

145   con pacto intelectivo
el mandamiento santo
sobre mi alma pongo
por último descanso.
    Si este vedado fruto
150 por preceto sagrado
se adorna de la ciencia,
de nuestra alma presagio,
    no es justo, esposo mío,
que apliquemos los labios
155 a su alimento horrible,
cuando sin él estamos?
    Si deste mandamiento
me fías lo sagrado,
custodia sera el pecho,
160 templo del desengaño.
    En el amado mío
ha de quedar guardado
por siglo de siglos:
testigos son los astros,
165   las flores y las fuentes
y deste jardín sacro
los espíritus puros,
custodios soberanos
que guardan su hermosura
170 con movimiento alado.

2   La injusticia en el mundo
(El Primer Peregrino disputa con la Sabiduría Divina)

    No menos me ha causado pesadumbre
ver la desigualdad que tiene el mundo,
entre la niebla de la vasta lumbre.
    En Salomón este derecho fundo
5 y pues el orbe no admitió remedio,
menos el hombre en término segundo.
    Dame si puedes un divino medio
que ajuste esta balanza bulliciosa,
con que se ponga la razón en medio.

145   in intellectual accord
I enjoin upon my soul
to keep the holy commandment
as my ultimate refuge.
    If this fruit, which is forbidden
150 by a holy-ordered precept,
is richly endowed with knowledge
which is the emblem of our souls,
    is it not right, husband of mine,
that we should put forth our lips
155 to taste its dread-inspiring food
when we are not possessed of it?
    If of this commandment you do
assure me of its holiness,
its custodian shall be my breast,
160 that temple of disillusion.
    In that beloved one of mine
it is sure to be watched over
through age of ages for ever:
of this the stars are witnesses;
165   So too the flowers and the springs
and the pure, unsullied spirits
who live in this sacred garden
and are the supreme guardians
that protect her beauteous state
170 with gentle fluttering of wings.

2   *The world's injustice*
(The First Pilgrim argues with Divine Wisdom)

    No less has it caused me great sorrow to see
the inequality which reigns in the world,
amid the mists that surround the sun's great light.
    The wisdom of this I found on Solomon
5 and since that orb has not seen fit to change it,
still less has man who here stands in second rank.
    Grant to me, if you can, some means divine
that will set these turbulent scales to rights,
so reason might be established in their midst.

10 Veo la iniquidad artificiosa
sobre la cumbre de la humana vida
abatir la justicia poderosa.
 Veo que reina la soberbia, asida
al trono de Babel, lisonjeando
15 la tiránica acción del homicida.
 Veo el pobre los bienes mendigando
y al rico siendo, escándalo del cielo,
sin virtud los tesoros aumentando.
 Cáusame gran dolor, más desconsuelo,
20 que un necio mande sin razón un sabio,
fundando necedades en el duelo.
 ¿Quién, di, podrá sufrir un desagravio
hijo del mismo duelo aborrecido,
honra llamando su atrevido agravio?
25 ¡Ay de mí! que nací desposeído
del derecho sagrado, pues se ofrece
el rico a sepultarme con olvido.
 Cuatro cosas mi anima aborrece:
pobre soberbio, trono sin justicia,
30 sexo sin honra y viejo que apetece.
 Cinco abomino: falsedad, delicia,
adúltero, homicida y poco menos
un malsín sobornado de codicia.
 Adónde asiste el premio de los buenos,
35 si el siglo de los malos prevalece
y están los pueblos de maldades llenos?
 La justicia ni luce ni parece
y en los tronos adustos de Etiopía
la verdad por dinero se obscurece.
40 O ¡quién supiera autorizar la copia
del estado del mundo con la vida,
lectura del espíritu más propia!
 Aquella Providencia sin medida,
alma del mundo, como Causa eterna
45 remedie esta política perdida.
 Su esencia inconmutable y abterna
cure la llaga deste monstruo horrible,
pues solo puede como Causa interna.
 Si el Sabio dijo, con dolor terrible,
50 que vio salir por yerro del imperio
un daño general, ya fue visible.

10 I see iniquity with all its clever arts,
sitting upon the summit of human life,
strike down powerful justice to the ground.
 I see that haughty pride reigns, sitting firmly
on the throne of Babel, and encouraging
15 the tyrannous action of the murderer.
 I see the poor man begging for worldly goods
and the rich man, as an affront to heaven,
through no virtue increase his store of treasure.
 Great sorrow, nay affliction, has it caused me
20 that through no reason a fool should rule the wise,
founding his foolish wisdom on the duel.
 Who, tell me, can allow an act of vengeance
that springs straight from that selfsame hated duel,
calling his brazen affront by honor's name?
25 Woe is me, who was born utterly bereft
of that sacred right to justice, for the rich
are sworn to bury me in oblivion.
 There are these four things that my soul abhors:
a poor man who is proud, a throne without justice,
30 women without honor and lusting old men.
 Five things I abominate: falsehood, desire,
adultery, murder and little less than these,
a talebearer suborned by covetous greed.
 Wherein lies the reward of the righteous,
35 if the world gives greater heed to the wicked
and the nations are full of iniquity?
 Justice neither shines nor does it show its face
and among the dismal thrones of Ethiope
truth is clouded over with money's pall.
40 Oh, would that I could reconcile this copy
which is the state the world is in with the life
which is more fitting reading for the spirit!
 May that Providence which is without measure,
the soul of the world, as the eternal Cause,
45 remedy this policy of perdition.
 May his immutable and everlasting
essence heal the wound from this horrid monster,
for being the internal Cause, alone it can.
 If the wise king said with tremendous sorrow
50 that he saw, through error, spring from a throne
a general hurt, it was yet clear to see.

Este sin duda ha sido aquel delirio
que Salomón lloraba en el sujeto
más cómodo a la pena y al martirio:
55   Que el malo prive, sin tener respeto
a la causa primera, y que domine
sobre el sabio, el prudente y el discreto;
        Que todo se gobierne y encamine
por gusto de un soberbio poderoso
60   y que sin Dios los pueblos arruine;
        Que el pobre desvalido y temeroso,
armado de virtud, pierda la vida
a manos de un tirano codicioso;
        Que la verdad esté tan desvalida,
65   que muera el que la dice sin remedio—
la política santa está perdida;
        Que el interés se ponga de por medio,
alentando la bárbara codicia
y que se llame soberano medio;
70   Que a manos de la hidrópica delicia
toda virtud acabe y que el dinero
se llame inteligencia de justicia.
        ¿Esta desigualdad tuvo primero
el siglo antecedente? no es posible,
75   y si la tuvo, otro gobierno espero.
        Que esté la vanidad tan insufrible
que se oponga a las leyes soberanas,
parece a la razón cosa increíble.
        Que no respeten a las obras canas
80   jóvenes vicios, locos atrevidos—
¿cuándo se han de acabar estas manzanas?
        ¿Hasta cuándo los necios presumidos
el fruto comerán de su pecado,
al árbol, no del bien, del mal asidos?
85   Hasta cuándo, hasta cuándo el hombre honrado
el virtuoso, el solo, el peregrino,
ha de ser oprimido y agraviado?
        Hasta cuándo este Job casi divino
dirá que le han quitado su derecho,
90   torciendo la soberbia su camino?
        Deja que sea en lágrimas deshecho
mi triste corazón; deja que llore
por agua fuego, que me abrase el pecho.

It is this no doubt that was the folly
that Solomon lamented in this being
most wont to suffer pain and martyrdom:
55   That the wicked should enjoy favor, having
no respect for the first Cause, and dominate
over the wise, the prudent and the discreet;
That all should be governed and directed
for the pleasure of a powerful sovereign
60   and that he, Godless, bring the nations ruin;
That the unprotected and timorous poor,
armed though they be in virtue, lose their lives
at the hands of a rapacious tyrant;
That truth should find itself so without defense
65   that he who speaks it goes to his certain death—
God's holy government has been abandoned;
That self-interest should interpose itself,
fanning the flames of barbarous avarice
and that this be called the sovereign way of God.
70   That at the hands of over-bloated lust
all virtue should meet its end and that money
should be known as the very soul of justice.
Did the preceding age before us know
this inequality? it is not possible;
75   yet if so, may it be ordered otherwise.
That vanity should be so overweaning
that it should stand against the sovereign laws
seems a thing that reason can scarcely credit.
That hoary-headed deeds should not be honored
80   by youthful vices, rebellious madmen all—
when shall these apples of discord cease to be?
How long shall the foolish men of arrogance
eat of the fruit their sinfulness gives birth to,
tethered to the tree of evil, not of good?
85   How long, how long must the man of honor,
the virtuous, the lonely, the wanderer,
be sore oppressed and the victim of great wrongs?
How long shall this Job, a man almost divine,
say that they have taken away his birthright
90   when pride has turned him aside from his true path.
Allow this sad soul of mine to break down
utterly in tears; allow it to weep
fire not water, so that it consume my breast.

    Deja que la Fortuna se enamore
95 de mi propia desdicha interiormente
    y que sus penas líquidas adore.
    Déjame destilar como una fuente
    dolores puros, cuyos hondos mares
    publiquen mi furor exteriormente.
100 Déjame blasonar de mis pesares,
    déjame que al martirio ofrezca luego
    el corazón en cándidos altares.
    Que el malo viva y muera con sosiego,
    que el bueno muera y viva con tormento,
105 no lo puedo sufrir, mi error es ciego.
    Si tengo racional entendimiento,
    con justa causa en cólera anegado,
    peligra mi atrevido sentimiento.

Sansón Nazareno

Sansón encuentra a la tamatea

    Este, pues, prodigioso nazareno
    bajaba a Tamatá, del filisteo
    ciudad, y fatigando un valle ameno,
    parece organizado lilibeo;
5 de la estrella de Venus tan ajeno,
    venía el fuerte, el valeroso hebreo,
    que a una fuente los pasos conducía,
    pisando los crepúsculos al día.

    Sobre una alfombra de menuda grama,
10 tapete de la alegre primavera,
    dormida vio la que, nevando cama,
    era ninfa de toda la ribera;
    líquida por las flores se derrama
    de un arroyo la plata lisonjera,
15 siendo la fuente, por su verde calle,
    laúd del prado, cítara del valle.

  Allow that Fortune fall enamored of
95 my own misfortune within its inmost parts
  and that it may adore its liquid torments.
  Allow me to distill out like a fountain
  pure suffering, whose bottomless ocean will
  declare my frenzy to all external parts.
100 Allow me to display to all my sorrows,
  allow me to offer then in martyrdom
  my heart upon altars of a purest white.
  That the wicked should live and die in peace,
  that the righteous should die and live in torment—
105 that I cannot bear, my error makes me blind.
  If I have any rational understanding,
  with just cause these my rebellious feelings
  run the risk of being drowned in anger.

Sansón Nazareno

Samson meets the Timnaite

  So it was that this prodigious Nazirite
  was going down to Timnah, city of the
  Philistines, and sweeping down a pleasant vale,
  he seemed like a flying column all arrayed;
5 the strong, the valorous Hebrew, as he came,
  was so far removed from the star of Venus
  that his footsteps he directed to a spring,
  treading down the twilight shadows of the day.

  Upon a carpet of unworthy couch grass,
10 a rug laid out by merry-hearted Spring,
  he espied asleep one who, as she turned white
  as snow her bed, was a nymph of all the shore;
  the eye-deceiving silver of a streamlet
  in liquid state gushes forth amid the flowers,
15 the spring as it runs down its verdant path being
  the meadow's lute, the cither of the valley.

    Era la diosa oráculo sagrado
de cuanto Adonis veneró su estrella,
dulce beldad del niño dios alado,
20   y del cielo gentil la luz más bella;
cuanto la aurora cándida ha llorado
su sol resuelve en líquida centella,
pero, al querer su rosicler beberla,
en su concha el Amor concibe perla.

25   Orfeos ruiseñores laureada
música dan al nuevo sol dormido,
solfa de contrapuntos ajustada
en el coro sagrado de Cupido;
sobre cinco azucenas recostada,
30   bebe de Delo el resplandor mentido,
temiendo el sol que, abriendo los dos soles,
del cielo abrase antorchas y faroles.

    De un delgado cendal, velo de nieve,
la Venus de cristal se halló vestida,
35   cuyo armiño del Líbano se atreve
a ser aurora de su dulce vida;
el coral de su boca perlas bebe,
viva rosa de nácar encendida,
cuyo clavel viviente en sus abriles
40   trasciende con dos hojas los pensiles.

    Dalestina es su nombre, en quien los cielos
la imagen de Diana retrataron,
y al galán de torcidos paralelos,
en forma humana, de la luz bajaron;
45   dos transparentes cristalinos velos
cubren lo que los dioses envidiaron,
siendo el favonio a cada movimiento
errante sumiller, vagando el viento.

    Bajaba el joven de la excelsa cumbre
50   de una muda atalaya coronada
de los primeros rayos de la lumbre,
que a la délfica luz fue consagrada;

This goddess was the oracle divine
of whatever Adonis her star revered,
a sweet beauty of the wingèd boy-god's train,
20   and of the Gentile heaven the fairest light;
all that which the glowing white of dawn has wept
her sun resolves into a flashing liquid spark,
but as her rosy blush desires to drink it,
in her conch shell Love conceives a shining pearl.

25   Nightingales, each one an Orpheus, laureled
music bestow upon the new sun sleeping,
a sol-fa of counterpoint in harmony
warbled by the sacred choir of Cupid;
reclining as she lay upon five lilies,
30   she drinks in the gainsaid splendor of Delos,
the sun fearing that, opening her two suns,
she might consume each torch and lamp of heaven.

In a slender cloth of silk, a veil of snow,
the shining crystal Venus appears bedecked,
35   whose ermine borrowed from Mount Lebanon dares
to be the white aurora of her sweet life;
the coral of her mouth drinks a string of pearls,
a vivid rose aflame with mother-of-pearl
whose living pink when it springs open exhales
40   sweet odor across two petals' hanging gardens.

Dalestina is her name, in whom heaven
portrayed the very image of Diana
and brought down from the light in human form
the gallant of the distorted parallels;
45   transparent crystalline veils, two in number,
cover that of which the gods were envious,
while Favonius at every movement acts
as errant chamberlain, as the wind roams free.

The youth descended from the lofty summit
50   of a mutely silent watchtower adorned
by the first appearing rays of the light
which was consecrated to the Delphic lamp;

bajó de la opulenta pesadumbre,
y viendo entre las flores recostada
55   la nueva Aurora, en dulce parasismo,
inmóvil se quedó sobre sí mismo.

Neutra la vista, duda retirarse,
retratada en el propio sentimiento,
y temiendo la imagen engañarse,
60   queda engañado el simple entendimiento;
mueve los pasos, teme el empeñarse,
crece el incendio, arde el pensamiento,
y entre la dulce llama que le enciende,
Venus le ciega, Marte le defiende.

65   Al blanco escollo, al animado bulto,
guía sus pasos la tercer estrella,
por ver si puede, entre la llama oculto,
templar de amor la líquida centella;
el mudo arroyo, cristalino culto
70   de la dormida Flora, intacta y bella,
le ofrece, entre el aljófar que desata,
si puente de cristal, arco de plata.

La línea de Neptuno pasó, cuando
donde un sitial de blancos alelíes,
75   el vendado rapaz le fue mostrando
viviente el sur en concha de rubíes;
ciégale al paso que le va guíando,
quedando, entre las rosas carmesíes,
la flor vital de nuestro Adonis fuerte
80   laurel de Amor, corona de la muerte.

Vióla de trino, que mirarse puede
el sol, en brazos de su luz dormido,
y el vendado cometa le concede
paces al sueño, treguas al sentido;
85   la ninfa, que los términos excede
al vigilante espíritu encendido,
sacudiendo el temor con bizarría,
las pestañas abrió y alumbró el día.

he descended from the rich and weighty mass
and seeing reclining amongst the flowers
55   the new Aurora, in a sweet paroxysm
he stood immobile, deep in intensive thought.

He wonders whether to withdraw, his vision
neutral, retreating into his own feelings,
and fearing the image to be illusion,
60   he tarries, his simple intellect beguiled;
he takes a pace, he fears to engage himself,
the fire increases, his thoughts are set ablaze
and amid the sweet fire that makes him kindle,
Venus blinds him, while Mars springs to his rescue.

65   Towards the reef of white, towards the living
shadowy shoal, the third star directs his steps
to see if, amid the hidden flame, it could
temper with love the liquid flashing spark;
the speechless stream, the crystal adoration
70   of the sleeping Flora, pure and beautiful,
offers him, amid the misshaped pearls it casts,
if a bridge of crystal, yet a silver arch.

The line of Neptune had he passed over, when,
from a bench composed of white gillyflowers,
75   the youth whose eyes are bound revealed to him
the living south set in a shell of rubies;
he blinds him more with each step he leads him on,
the vital flower of our strong Adonis
remaining amid the crimson roses as
80   the laurels of love, the crown of his self's death.

He saw her at an angle, for thus the sun
may view itself, in its own light's arms asleep
and the comet whose eyes are bound grants to him
respite for his dreams, truces for his senses;
85   the nymph, who passes beyond the boundaries
to reach the burning spirit of awakening,
shaking off sleep's fear with splendid valor,
opened her eyelids and gave light to the day.

Divisa al joven, y la siempre bella
90   deidad, que veneró nevada espuma,
si exhalación no fue, pareció estrella,
volando al coro de la esfera suma;
rémora fue el arroyo, que a prendella
con vara de cristal, si no de pluma,
95   cortés salió, y a echalle se le atreve
cadenas de cristal, lazos de nieve.

El verdadero Apolo, conociendo
de Dafne el vuelo, sobre el margen para,
el alma por los ojos ofreciendo,
100   siendo el amor de sus finezas ara;
ella, viendo su amante, que vertiendo
afectos iba de su alegre cara,
sobre la fuente o líquido arroyuelo
inmóvil se quedó, ninfa de hielo.

105   En el mudo silencio, en el suave
éxtasis que las almas encendía,
abrir pretenden con divina llave
puerta a la voz, de la pasión espía;
el aire rompe con acento grave
110   un dulce ruiseñor, cuya harmonía,
trinando quejas y celando espumas,
a Venus llama entre nadantes plumas.

La oración y muerte de Sansón

"Dios de mis padres—dice—, Autor eterno,
de los tres mundos soberanos Atlante,
incircunscrito, santo y abeterno,
Dios de Abrahán, tu verdadero amante,
5   Dios de Isaac, cuyo altísimo gobierno
en la divina Ley vive triunfante,
Dios de Jacob, de bendiciones lleno,
oye a Sansón, escucha al Nazareno.

<pre>
        She spies the youth and the ever-beautiful
90   deity, whom snowy foam paid reverence,
        if she was not a shooting star, a star did seem,
        flying to join the choir of the highest sphere;
        an obstacle was the stream, which to take her
        with a wand of crystal, if not of feathers,
95   courteously came forward and attempted
        to throw on her chains of crystal, bonds of snow.

        This veritable Apollo, perceiving
        the flight of Daphne, halts upon the margin,
        offering through his eyes his soul as sacrifice,
100   for love is the altar where his feelings burn;
        she, observing her admirer pouring forth
        his affections through his bright and pleasing face,
        by the edge of the spring or liquid streamlet
        remains immobile, a nymph of frozen ice.

105   In the unspeaking silence, in the gentle
        ecstasy which was their souls inflaming,
        they seek the way to open with divine key
        a door for the voice, which is passion's spy hole;
        a sweet nightingale with her solemn accents
110   rends the air, whose song's harmonious accord,
        trilling love's complaints and concealing foams,
        calls to Venus amid its swimming plumage.
</pre>

The final prayer and death of Samson

<pre>
        "God of my fathers, eternal author,
        Atlas who sustains the three sovereign worlds
        uncircumscribed, holy, from everlasting,
        God of Abraham, who was your true lover,
5   God of Isaac, whose most exalted conduct
        lives triumphally on in the divine Law,
        God of Jacob, who was rich in blessings,
        listen to Samson, hear the Nazirite.
</pre>

"Unico Criador incomprehensible,
10   Señor de los ejércitos sagrado,
Brazo de las batallas invencible,
por siglo de los siglos venerado,
Causa, sí, de las causas invisible,
perfeto Autor de todo lo criado,
15   pequé, Señor, pequé, yo me condeno,
misericordia pide el Nazareno.

"Restituye, Señor, la prodigiosa
fuerza de mis cabellos a su fuego;
alienta con tu mano poderosa
20   el valor que perdí, quedando ciego;
tócame con tu llama luminosa,
pues a la muerte con valor me entrego;
dame aliento, Señor, para vengarme
y tu auxilio eficaz para salvarme.

25   "Yo muero por la Ley que tú escribiste,
por los preceptos santos que mandaste,
por el pueblo sagrado que escogiste
y por los mandamientos que ordenaste;
yo muero por la patria que me diste
30   y por la gloria con que el pueblo honraste;
muero por Israel, y lo primero
por tu inefable Nombre verdadero.

"Yo me ofrezco a la muerte porque sea
redimido mi pueblo en este día
35   de la dura potencia filistea,
arbitrio de la misma tiranía;
sacuda el yugo la nación hebrea,
goce este triunfo con la sangre mía,
salva a Israel, Señor, sea mi vida
40   víctima santa y lámpara lucida.

"Ea, Señor eterno! agora, agora
es tiempo que tu espíritu divino
favorezca esta mano vencedora,
para que acabe el duro filistino!

"One and only Creator, whose greatness
10   cannot be encompassed, holy Lord of hosts,
mighty arm unconquerable in battle,
through ages throughout ages venerated,
Cause, indeed, of all causes, invisible,
perfect Author of all that is created,
15   I have sinned, Lord, I have sinned, I myself
condemn: have mercy on the Nazirite.

"Restore to me, O Lord, the prodigious
strength of my hair to its full fiery force;
breathe new life through your powerful hand into
20   the valor which I lost, when I was blinded;
touch me with your radiant-shining flame,
for with valor do I give myself to death;
give me the courage, Lord, to avenge myself
and to save myself, your all-achieving help.

25   "I die for the sake of the Law which you wrote,
for the holy precepts which you commanded,
for the sacred people whom you have chosen,
and for the commandments which you ordained;
I die for the homeland which you gave to me
30   and the glory with which you graced your people;
I die for Israel's sake and before all else
for the sake of your true, ineffable Name.

"I offer myself to death in order that
my people may be redeemed upon this day
35   from the harsh dominion of the Philistine,
a judgment wrought on tyranny itself;
let the Hebrew nation shake off the yoke,
let it enjoy this triumph through my own blood;
grant Israel salvation, Lord, let my life be
40   a holy offering, a brilliant, shining lamp.

"Waken to my plea, eternal Lord, now, now,
is the moment when your divine spririt
should lay its favor on this conquering hand,
so that it may blot out the harsh Philistine!

45 ¡Muera esta gente idolatra que adora
en medio fauno de metal marino,
no quede dellos en el templo un hombre,
mueran los enemigos de tu Nombre!

"¿De qué sirve, Señor omnipotente,
50 esta nación de sangre filistina?
¿Qué gloria sacarás desta vil gente
en maldades y vicios peregrina?
¡Ea, Señor! acabe incontinente
esta fábrica fiera dragontina!
55 ¡Muera Sansón con cuantos filisteos
sustentan estos nichos cananeos!"

Dijo, y eslabonando pavoroso
los brazos a los ejes de diamante,
a pesar del cimiento poderoso
60 y del soberbio alcázar arrogante,
a pesar del salón artificioso
y la argamasa de betún ligante,
sudando sangre, el joven sin segundo
levantó las colunas del profundo.

65 Dio dos golpes con ellas, arrancando
los ángulos sin luz de la techumbre,
y la bóveda opaca rechinando
se deslizó de su eminente cumbre;
a plomo en un instante fue rodando
70 la inmensa de los orbes pesadumbre
y cayendo el profundo firmamento,
dio dos pasos el mundo de su asiento.

Delirando la fábrica rompida
al ruido, al estallido que rechaza,
75 la nave entre la furia desasida
se rompe, descoyunta y desengaza;
la multitud de gente sumergida,
a quien el edificio despedaza,
sepultada en el óvalo del mundo,
80 urna la sorbe el caos en el profundo.

45   Let this idolatrous people who adore
a semi-fawn of metal from the sea die,
let not one of them remain in the temple,
may they perish, these enemies of your Name.

    "What purpose do they serve, omnipotent Lord,
50   this nation of the race of Philistines?
What glory do you reap from this vile people,
for their vices and their wicked deeds renowned?
Listen, Lord, bring to an end without delay
this hideous dragontine construction!
55   Let Samson die and with him die as many
Philistines as holds each Canaanite recess!"

    Thus he spoke and linking with an awesome strength
his arms around the diamantine axes,
in spite of the foundations firm and mighty
60   and that fortress rising proud and arrogant,
in spite of that hall with artifice contrived,
and the mortar of fast-binding bitumen,
sweating blood, the youth who knew no rival
raised from their place the columns of deepest hell.

65   Twice he dashed them both together, tearing out
the dark-shrouded angles of the lofty roof
and with horrendous creaking the gloomy vault
slid down from the summit of its eminence;
in an instant there came tumbling headlong down
70   the vast and weighty mass of heavenly orbs
and with the falling of this deep firmament
the earth moved two paces sidewards from its place.

    While the broken fabric in mad frenzy raves,
with roar and thunderous report resounding,
75   the nave in midst of all that unleashed fury
is sundered, dislocated, and dismembered;
Submerged, that great multitude of people,
whom the falling edifice cuts asunder,
buried within the oval bowels of the earth,
80   for an urn the chaos sucks them down to hell.

De un golpe solo treinta mil gentiles
mató Sansón, logrando victorioso
en vida y en muerte sus cuarenta abriles,
todos ceñidos del laurel famoso;
85   redimieron sus años juveniles
la casa de Israel y el poderoso
dominio de la sangre filistea
quedó sujeto a la potencia hebrea.

Romance al divín mártir, Judá Creyente, martirizado en Valladolid por la Inquisición

Entre los fieros dragones
de aquel Tribunal soberbio,
cuya oliva fue la espada
sin arca de testamento,
5   el mártir más peregrino
el confesor más entero,
el farol más encendido,
el más divino intelecto
que vio el sol, que tuvo el mundo,
10   soldado del tercio viejo
de Sinai, padeció tantos
y desiguales tormentos,
que resucitó el valor
de los fuertes Macabeos.
15   Circuncidóse en la carcel,
cual otro Abraham, él mesmo
escribiendo con su sangre
el carácter más supremo.
Salió al suplicio domando
20   sofisticos argumentos,
hidras sin alma que viven
de la vanidad del viento.
Como oveja fue llevado,
según el sagrado texto,
25   al teatro riguroso
de los abismos del fuego.

With one single blow, thirty thousand gentiles
Samson slew, in life and in death achieving
the triumph of his span of forty summers,
all of which were with the famous laurel crowned;
85   his youthful years accomplished the salvation
of the House of Israel, and the powerful
dominion of the race of Philistines
remained henceforth subject to the Hebrews' sway.

Ballad in honor of the divine martyr, Judah the Believer, martyred at Valladolid at the hands of the Inquisition

Amid the fearsome dragons
of that arrogant Tribunal,
whose branch of olive was the sword
and not the Ark of Covenant,
5   the most wonderful of martyrs,
the most perfect of believers,
the most brilliant of beacons,
the most divine of intellects
the sun has seen, the world has known,
10   soldier of the ancient army
of Sinai, suffered so many
intolerable tortures
that he recalled the bravery
of the steadfast Maccabees.
15   He circumcised himself in jail,
as Abraham had before him,
writing himself in his own blood
the letters of the highest bond.
He went to his death, triumphing
20   over their subtle arguments,
like hydras without souls that feed
on the vanity of the wind.
Like a lamb he was brought down,
as written in the holy text,
25   to that scene of cruelty
where raged the fires of the abyss.

No se halló engano en su boca.
pues iba a voces diciendo:
"¡Viva el Nombre de Adonay,
30   sacro Auto del universo!"
El fiero vulgo atrevido,
como torpe, horrible y fiero,
porque no se reducía
a los precetos de Venus,
30   balas de ira le arrojaba,
articulando este pueblo,
si no la vida, el agravio,
si no la muerte, el incendio.
Llegó al tálamo de Bel,
40   en cuyo atrevido lecho
se desposaron los justos
con la Ley y los precetos.
Allí la lógica ciencia
de un teólogo moderno,
45   la mestafisica simple,
quiso darle por veneno:
—¡O, tú,—dice el varón justo—
que con inorante celo
reducir quieres al sol
50   en un círculo pequeño!
¡O, tú, sabio de Babel,
que, sin tener fundamento
tu babilónico estudio,
guerra publicas al cielo!
55   si me confiesas que Dios
a su peregrino pueblo
dio Ley, ¿para qué me dices
que la deje torpe y necio?
Si la dio para salvarme,
60   ¿qué salvación tener puedo
en la que me da tu gracia
fabricada por ti mesmo?
Si Dios dio Ley a Israel
con un carácter eterno,
65   ¿cómo ha de poder quitarlo
el sacrilegio idumeo?

No false words were upon his lips,
for he went calling out aloud
"Long live the Name of Adonai,
30   holy Author of all that is."
The insolent and cruel mob,
hideous, dull and bestial,
because he refused to bow down
before their laws of Venus,
35   threw upon him bales of anger
and these people, as they did so,
offered him not life but insults,
not death but the inferno.
He reached the bridal bed of Baal,
40   upon whose couch of arrogance
the men of righteousness were wed
with the Law and her commandments.
There, as with a poison, he sought
to feed to them the reasoned science
45   of a modern theologian,
the simplest metaphysics.
"Oh, you," spoke the virtuous saint,
"who blind through your misguided faith,
seek to confine the sun above
50   within but a tiny circle!
Oh, you, the wise man of Babel,
who, though your Babylonian
studies lack all firm foundation,
dare to declare war on heaven,
55   if you concede to me that God
gave a Law to his wandering
people, why then do you tell me
to foolishly abandon it?
If he granted it to save me,
60   then what salvation could I find
in that which your mercy gives me,
since you yourselves have fashioned it.
If God gave a Law to Israel
with an eternal character,
65   how could this be taken away
by the sacrilege of Edom?

Si no tiene salvación
esta Ley, ¿de qué provecho
fue a Israel, pues nada vale
70   la que está sin fundamento?
Si él dice: "Ley sempiterna
os di," ¿qué delirio nuevo
termino puso a su mano,
comentándole lo eterno?
75   Si es perfecta, como dice
el músico más supremo,
¿qué mayores perfecciones
hallar en otra podemos?
Si en el monte de Sinai
80   se oyeron voces del cielo,
¿quién sera tan atrevidio,
que le rehuse los ecos?
Deidad incommunicable,
como nos declara el verso,
85   no tiene fin ni principio,
siendo su Nombre abeterno.
Lo infinito de la causa
no comunica al efecto
aquella unidad sagrada
90   del primer entendimiento.
Si la Ley es la palabra,
esa venera su pueblo,
y, siendo infinito Dios,
a su palabra me atengo.
95   Si esta unidad increada
no tiene ningún defecto,
la Ley, palabra de Dios,
no lo tendrá en ningún tiempo.
Si esta luz intelectiva
100   alumbra sol de si mesmo,
¿qué luminaria se opone
a turbarle los reflejos?
Si Dios y el hombre firmaron
este sacro testamento
105   y se nos da por escrito,
¿cómo ha de haber otro nuevo?
No guardarlo puede el hombre
en lo que toca al concierto;

What could this Law profit Israel,
if it cannot bring salvation,
since such a Law is worth nothing,
70   if it lacks a firm foundation.
If he says: 'An eternal Law
I gave you,' what novel madness
is this that seeks to stay his hand,
telling *him* what is eternal?
75   If, as the supreme musician
tells us, the Law is perfect,
what greater qualities than these
could we find in another law?
If upon the Mount of Sinai
80   voices from heaven were heard,
who would be so foolish as
to deny the echoes from them?
The invisible Godhead,
as the verse of scripture tells us,
85   has no beginning, has no end,
since his Name is 'ab eterno.'
That sacred unity of God
who is the prime intelligence
does not impart to the effect
90   the infinity of the Cause.
If the Law is the word of God,
that then will his people honor,
and, given God is infinite,
I will myself cleave to his word.
95   If this increate unity
possesses no defect at all,
the Law, which is the word of God,
will at no time have any.
If this light of understanding
100   lights up a sun all on its own,
what luminary would interpose
to disturb its bright reflections?
If God and man together signed
this holy, binding covenant
105   and it is set down in writing,
how can there be any other?
Man can choose not to keep his part
of the agreement he has made,

pero, de parte de Dios,
110   siempre vive el firmamento.
        Los que siguen otro rumbo,
como alteran los preceptos,
como sienten mal de Dios,
luchan con los elementos.
115   Si dices: "La Ley fue santa,"
tu te engañas poco cuerdo;
pues, lo que una vez fue santa
no puede dejar de serlo.
        La ley del mundo mayor,
120   el orden del universo,
con la palabra de Dios
guarda la Ley que le dieron.
        Pues, si el orden natural
observaron tierra y cielo
125   sin variar la palabra
del mandamiento primero,
        ¿por qúe este mundo menor,
a la imagen de Dios hecho,
no ha de guardar la Ley santa
130   que escribió Dios con su dedo?
        Su Nombre, dice Isaias
es uno; pues, si el decreto
de la unidad es palabra,
una es la Ley por derecho.
135   Si hay otra, ya la palabra
faltó con el cumplimiento;
y Ley que deroga el culto
hace mudable a su Dueño.
        Dalla con limitación
140   fuera macular to regio,
ignorando siendo Dios
la revelación del tiempo.
        Decir Dios Ley para siempre
oístes desde los cielos;
145   y no guardar su palabra
era engañar a su pueblo.
        Pues, si en Dios no puede haber
este insolente argumento,
¿por qúe, bárbaro, lo sigues
150   con errores manifiestos?

       but as far as God is concerned
110   the signature holds ever good.
         Those that follow other pathways,
       such that they change the commandments
       or seek rebellion against God,
       are fighting elementary truths.
115   If you say: 'The Law was holy . . .'
       you are foolishly mistaken,
       for what was at one time holy
       cannot cease to be so now.
         The law of the macrocosm,
120   which regulates the universe,
       obedient to the word of God,
       keeps the Law which it was given.
         So then, if the natural order
       is observed by heaven and earth,
125   without their altering one word
       of the first of the Commandments,
         why should we, the microcosm,
       who were made in God's own image,
       not adhere to the holy Law
130   which God wrote down with his own hand?
         His Name is one, according to
       Isaiah; then, if the decree
       that God is one is holy writ,
       then by rights there is but one Law.
135   If there is any other Law,
       God has failed to keep his word
       and a Law which worship alters
       renders changeable its Master.
         To have given it with limits
140   would be to stain his majesty
       ignoring the fact that God is
       the revelation for all time.
         You heard the voice of God declare
       from heaven a Law for ever,
145   thus for him not to keep his word
       would be to deceive his people.
         If this unseemly argument,
       then, is inappropriate to God,
       why, barbarian, do you persist
150   in the paths of proven error?

La unidad siendo distinta
no es unidad en hebreo,
y Ley dividida en dos
no tiene seguro asiento.
155   Quererme tú reducir
a tres distintos sujetos,
multiplicando deidades
con sus festivos desvelos,
    es decirme que la Causa
160 se iguala con los efectos,
y lo propio es para mí
dividirla en tres que en ciento.
    Ridículamente osado,
retóricamente necio,
165 te opones a quien te dice:
"Yo, el primero, yo, el postrero."
    Si son tres dioses en uno
los profetas se perdieron,
pues adoraron el uno
170 y los dos no conocieron.
    Si distintos eran antes
y uno se adoró en el Templo,
errado anduvo aquel culto
en el primer mandamiento.
175 Si cuando adoras al uno
son todos tres aquel mesmo,
los dos que miras distintos
no son de ningún provecho.
    Dios es uno, y su palabra,
180 su espíritu y Nombre eterno
en una esencia infinita
sin distinción la creemos.
    Para conocer la fe,
un solo Dios verdadero
185 no tiene necesidad
de materiales sujetos.
    No ver a Dios y creerlo
es una fe con misterio,
sin rozarse con lo humano
190 nuestro divino intelecto.

A unity which is diverse
is no unity in Hebrew,
thus, a Law which is in two parts
lacks any firm foundation.
155   To try to force me to believe
in three separate individuals,
multiplying deities, each
with their festive observances,
160   is like trying to tell me that the
Cause is equal to its effects;
thus I might as well divide it
into a hundred as in three!
How ridiculously brazen,
how rhetorically foolish
165   to oppose the One who told you:
'I am the first, I am the last.'
If he is three godheads in one,
the Prophets sadly went astray,
since they worshiped only one God
170   and did not know the other two.
If there were more than one before
and in the Temple one was worshiped,
that religion walked in error
as regards the First Commandment.
175   If when you worship the One God,
all those three are combined in him,
then those two that you see separate
really serve no useful purpose.
God is but one and in his word,
180   his spirit and eternal Name,
which is one infinite essence,
we believe without distinction.
In order that his faith be known,
a God who is the one true God
185   does in no way require the help
of any material agents.
Not to see God and yet believe
is to have a faith with mystery
without our divine perception
190   being touched by what is human.

De las tres adoraciones,
dulía y perdulía, podemos,
no olvidando la latría,
sacar nuestros argumentos.
195   Si la fe consta de impulso,
¿qué padrino es el madero
para conciliar una alma
con su Criador en el cielo?
Fe con mezcla material
200   es imán que halaga el hierro,
y fe con alma de piedra
cadáver fue de su dueño.
La fe santa, la fe pura
es la que observa el hebreo,
205   pues conoce un solo Dios
por luz del entendimiento.
Las demás son vanidades
de los sabios destos tiempos,
y es locura a lo divino,
210   intervalos del ingenio.
Fe que aplica los oídos
a perdonar con defectos
por la autoridad de un hombre,
fe puede ser de los necios.
215   Sólo Dios, dice Mosseh,
os perdonó en el desierto,
castigando alguna parte
del pecado del becerro.
Sólo Dios, dice Isaías,
220   tiene el meromixto imperio
en el hombre, y sólo Dios
puede perdonar defectos.
El sólo, dice David,
pudo redimir su pueblo;
225   luego redención con sangre
más es muerte que remedio.
Si Dios no tiene poder
sin atropellar un bueno,
para redimir al mundo,
230   la vida estuvo en el muerto.

We can found our argument on
the three kinds of adoration—
worship of the saints and Virgin,
not forgetting what is God's due.
195 If faith is spiritual at base,
how can wood act as our guardian
and help us reconcile our souls
with their Creator in heaven?
Faith that has material taint
200 is a magnet that lures to sin,
and faith that has a heart of stone
makes a corpse of him who owns it.
The holy faith, the pure faith
is the one the Hebrew observes,
205 for he knows of only one God
as the light of understanding.
All the rest is the vanity
of learned thinkers of these times
and madness in religious vein.
210 lapses in the thinking mind
A faith that turns its attentions
to mitigating errors through
the authority of one man
could only be the faith of fools.
215 It was only God, says Moses,
who pardoned you in the desert,
punishing you in some degree
for the sin of the Golden Calf.
Only God, Isaiah says,
220 holds that unchallengeable sway
over mankind, and only God
can grant pardon for our failings.
Only God, says David, could give
salvation to his people;
225 thus, a redemption bought with blood
is no solution, simply death.
If God does not have the power
to grant redemption to the world,
without trampling a good man down,
230 only the dead would possess life.

No está de parte de Dios,
según vuestro sentimiento,
aquel poder soberano
que tiene desde abeterno.
235   Pues, si un Dios con condiciones
gobierna vuestro intelecto,
claramente se conoce
que no es Dios ni puede serlo.
¿Qué necesidad tenía
240   el Legislador excelso
de ver sangre derramada
para perdonar los pueblos?
Si es inocente la sangre,
derremarla no es bien hecho;
245   si es culpada, su delito
puede pagar, no el ajeno.
Comió Adán una manzana,
y, para salvar su yerro,
¿queréis vosotros formar
250   quien le beba este veneno?
Y cuando esto fuera ansi,
¿que redención le daremos
al mundo, pues hoy los hombres
se condenan poco cuerdos?
255   ¿Qué ha redimido esta sangre,
si los malos y los buenos
están en peor estado
que antes de morir tuvieron?
Si la Ley siendo guardada
260   tiene salvación de precio,
¿que precio tiene la sangre
comparada a los preceptos?
Ultimamente la Ley,
que tengo dentro en mi pecho,
265   es de Dios, y su palabra
no es material alimento.
Del Tribunal de Antioco
salgo a morir en el fuego
por el Nombre del Señor,
270   a quien mi alma encomiendo.

According to your opinion,
God does not have within his grasp
that sovereign capability
that he has held eternally.
235   If a God hedged by conditions
rules over your intellect, then
it clearly will be recognized
that he is not God, nor could be.
What necessity has he, who
240   is the supreme Giver of laws,
of seeing blood set flowing
so the nations may be pardoned?
If the blood is innocent,
it is not good that it be shed;
245   if guilty, he may pay the crime,
for himself but not for others.
Adam ate the apple, and now,
in order to expunge his sin,
do you wish to find another
250   to drink this poison for his sake?
And just supposing this were so,
what redemption shall we offer
the world, since today we see men
madly heading for damnation?
255   What redemption has this blood bought,
if both the wicked and the good
are in a worse condition now
than when they were condemned to die?
If the Law, through being kept,
260   offers salvation as its prize,
what is the value of that blood
compared with the commandments?
In the last recourse, the Law
which I cherish within my breast
265   comes from God and his word provides
nourishment that is not material.
From the Tribunal of Antioch
I go to die amid the flames,
for the sake of the Lord's Name,
270   to whom I now commend my soul.

Peregrino en Israel
seré yo por nacimiento,
despreciando por la Ley
la sangre de mis aguelos.
275   Cual otro Sansón, asido
de las colunas del templo,
he de morir por vivir,
aunque pese al filisteo,
En el horno de Babel,
280   uno de los tres mancebos
seré, alabando la Causa
por quien vivo y por quien muero.
Esa llama abrasadora
que ha de devorar mi cuerpo
285   será mi carro triunfal,
pues es de Elías mi celo.
La vida negando a Dios
ni la busco ni la quiero;
los bienes sin la Ley santa
290   ni los admito ni precio.
Lo que está en el corazón
con la boca lo sustento,
y, porque le conste al mundo,
¡naciones, yo soy hebreo!
295   ¡Judío soy, castellanos!
La Ley de Mosseh confieso
dada en el monte Sinai
por el Autor de los cielos.
¡Ea, antiocos profanos,
300   ejecutad el decreto
de la vil Inquisición,
tribunal de los infiernos!
No quiero misericordia;
que si con ella le niego
305   a Dios la Ley que me ha dado,
su gracia divina pierdo.
¡Muera yo sin profanar
su santo Nombre supremo!
¡Sea confesora el alma
310   si ha de ser mártir el cuerpo!

As one who is by birth, so shall
I be a pilgrim in Israel
and thus reject for the Law's sake
the blood of my forefathers.
275   Just like another Samson, bound
to the columns of the temple,
I shall die so that I may live,
though the Philistines regret it.
In the Babylonian furnace,
280   I shall be one of those three youths
glorifying the Cause of all,
for whom I live, for whom I die.
That all-consuming flame
which must devour up my body
285   will be my chariot of triumph,
for my faith springs from Elijah.
I do not seek nor do I want
a life pursued denying God;
nor do I accept or value
290   wealth that is without the Law.
That which lies deep within my heart
I do uphold with my own mouth;
and so the world may clearly see,
you nations, I am a Hebrew!
295   I am a Jew, Castilians!
I profess the Law of Moses,
which was given on Mount Sinai
by the Author of the heavens.
Ho! profane Antiochians,
300   come and execute the decree
of the vile Inquisition,
the Tribunal of Hell below.
I do not want your clemency,
for, if through it I did deny
305   the Law which God has given me,
I would lose his divine favor.
Let me die without profaning
his supreme and holy Name!
Let my soul affirm its belief,
310   if my body must be martyred!''

Esto dijo, y los verdugos,
atándole en el madero,
para arder el sacrificio
le echaron un Mongibelo.
315 Empezó a crujir la carne,
y, rechinando los huesos,
viva la voz en el alma,
ansí dijo el Macabeo:
—Divino Señor, que asistes
320 en el Trono en el excelso
Tribunal que vio Isaías
de los serafines bellos;
Dios de Abrahám, Dios de Isaac,
Dios de Jacob, Rey eterno,
325 cuyo Nombre incircunscrito
sólo consta de sí mesmo;
Causa de todas las causas,
Criador de tierra y cielo,
sin principio y sin fin,
330 y un solo Dios verdadero;
esta vida que me distes
por sacrificio te ofrezco,
y un corazón abrasado
en las aras deste incendio:
335 como nos dice David,
es sacrificio perfecto.
Que muero por tu Ley, dicen,
mas no entienden el conceto,
que, si muero por quien vivo,
340 ya vivo de lo que muero.
Amante soy de tu Ley
y de tal suerte la celo,
que muero por adorarla:
¡mira, Señor, si la quiero!
345 Estos martirios que paso,
estas penas que padezco,
como amante las admito,
como esposo las venero.
Vida me ofrecen sin ella,
350 ¡como si un amante hebreo
tuviera sin ella vida,
pues todo sin ella es muerte!

This he said, and tying him to
the stake, the executioners
piled on him a mountain of wood
to set the sacrifice ablaze.
315 His flesh began to crackle
and whilst his bones were creaking,
the living voice rose from his soul
and thus the Maccabean spoke:—
 "Divine Lord, who sits on your throne
320 amid the supreme Tribunal
of the beauteous seraphim,
which the prophet Isaiah saw;
 God of Abraham, God of Isaac,
God of Jacob, eternal King,
325 whose unfathomable, boundless Name
consists of nothing but itself;
 the ultimate of all causes,
Creator of heaven and earth,
having no beginning nor end,
330 a God who is alone the true;
 this life which you have given me
I offer you in sacrifice,
together with a heart consumed
on the altar of this fire:
335 as the words of David tell us.
this is the perfect sacrifice.
 They say I die for your Law's sake,
but they do not grasp the concept,
for if I die for whom I live
340 that death already gives me life.
 I am a lover of your Law,
and so much do I adore her
that I die for love of her—
look, O Lord, how much I love her!
345 This martyrdom I undergo,
these tortures I am suffering.
as a lover I accept them,
as a husband I adore them.
 They offer me life without her—
350 as if any Hebrew lover
could ever live without her,
for without her all is death!

Por vieja la repudieron,
¡y el oro de sus cabellos
355   más que los rayos del sol
alumbran el universo!
Sus ojos son de paloma,
azules pero no negros,
y de dos blancos mellizos
360   tiene sus hermosos pechos.
Sus palabras son divinas
y sentencias sus conceptos,
y con su sabiduría
tuvo ser el ministerio.
365   Por adorarla me matan,
pero, yo seré en el fuego
el ave simple que sabe
morir y vivir a un tiempo.
Como ésta es de Dios esposa,
370   poco importa que esté muerto
el cuerpo, siendo imortal
el alma que a Dios ofrezco.
Desta materia caduca
en el muno el venidero
375   veré al Señor, pues el polvo
serafín es con aliento.
Vivo entre el fuego voraz,
el espiritu que tengo
en el crisol de la carne
380   purificará su celo.
Divinamente inspirado,
te digo, pueblo soberbio,
a quien amenaza a rayos
el airado Dios del cielo,
385   que ya del libro sagrado,
intelectivo cuaderno,
la divina profecía
viene apresurando el tiempo.
¡Ay de ti! pueblo sin Dios,
390   aquel que idolatras ciego
en los páramos del mundo,
que te amenaza Dios mesmo!

They cast her off for being old—
yet the shine of her golden hair
355   lights up all the universe
more brightly than the sun's own rays!
    Her eyes are like those of the dove,
although they are not black but blue,
and she has beautiful breasts
360   that are as two white twins.
    The words that she speaks are divine,
her opinions, worthy maxims
and through her divine wisdom
was priestly rule established.
365   They kill me for adoring her,
but I shall be amid the fire
that simple bird who at one time
knows how to live and how to die.
    Since she is the bride of God
370   it matters little that this my
body will be dead, for the soul
I offer God is immortal.
    Departing from this weary flesh,
in the world of the hereafter
375   I shall see the Lord, since my dust
will be a seraph, breathed with life.
    Alive amid the raging fire
the spirit that is within me
will purify its fervor out
380   in the crucible of the flesh.
    Inspired by a divine force,
I tell you, arrogant people,
whom the wrathful God in heaven
menaces with bolts of thunder
385   that the divine prophecy
of that sacred book, the notebook
of revelations, already
comes hastening towards its end.
    Woe betide you, godless people,
390   you that blindly worship idols
in the wastelands of the world,
for it is God who threatens you.

La América por el norte
en fin al año noveno
395 alzará pendón, talando
con ciento y cuarenta leños
los mares del medio dia.
descubriendo un varón cuerdo
tres islas en trece dias.
400 castigos de muchos reinos.
Antes de cuarenta y nueve
habrá guerra en un consejo
y no pocos alborotos
en el estado plebeyo.
405 Los que viven en el agua
con los sitas y agarenos,
si no se confederaren,
tendrán simulado feudo.
Tres lustros y cuatro dias
410 tendrán guerra dos imperios,
trepando los orientales
al olímpico elemento.
¡Ay del mundo! cuando lleguen
sesenta y seis anos ciertos,
415 adonde será el hambre
el castigo mas pequeño!
Veránse en setenta y cinco
salidas a un mismo tiempo
por las bocas de dos hombres
420 dos leyes con ritos nuevos.
Morirán por defenderlos
un millón y curatro cientos
bárbaros en desiguales
batallas de sangre y fuego.
425 Cerca de setenta y seis
temblarán catorce templos
y caerán los edificios
con los ídolos al centro.
Alborotarán el mundo
430 dos hipócritas mancebos
y con fingidos milagros
harán creer a los necios

From the north, America
at the end of the ninth year
395   will raise its banner and lay waste
the seas of the meridian
    with one hundred and forty ships,
while a wise captain discovers
three islands in thirteen days,
400   the scourge of many kingdoms.
    Before the year of forty-nine,
in a council there will be strife
and not a few disturbances
among the lower orders.
405   Those that live upon the water
if they do not confederate
with the Scythians and the Turks,
will share in their feigning fiefdom
    For three 'lustra' and four days
410   two empires will be locked in war,
in which the Orientals climb
to the Olympian element.
    Woe to the world when the certain
year of sixty-six arrives.
415   when hunger will be seen to be
the least of all the punishments!
    In seventy-five there will be heard,
issuing forth at the same time
from the mouths of two different men
420   two religions, each with new rites.
    One million and four hundred
barbarians will die in order
to defend them in ferocious
battles of flowing blood and fire.
425   About the year of seventy-six,
fourteen temples will tremble
and these buildings will tumble down,
with their idols in their midst.
    Two hypocritical young men
430   will put the world in tumult
and with their spurious miracles
will make the ignorant believe

que son de Dios inviados
para convertir los pueblos;
435 pero, sus mismos amigos,
antes que pase año y medio,
  en la plaza de Babel
manifestarán sus yerros
y morirán publicando
440 sus fingidos fundamentos.
  Siete tiempos y tres años
tendrá Nembrot el imperio,
y la vasta idolatría,
dividida en treinta reinos,
445 diluvios de sangre humana
sembrarán por los desiertos.
La cuarta bestia terrible
bramará desde su asiento,
  y al otavo mes del año,
450 cuando un cometa ligero
saliere del aquilón,
temblarán todos los peublos
  Dividida en cuatro partes,
la horrible fiera en el viento
455 sembrará sus esperanzas
y morirá sin remedio.
  El verso de Daniel
resplandecerá ligero
y una gente perseguida
460 gozará de sus reflejos.
  Tubal, dividido en dos
principes de nacimiento
si no turbado, atrevido,
si no villano, plebeyo,
465   llamará los peregrinos,
y por fin del año sexto,
revueltas las religiones
de los malos y los buenos,
  se conocerán los hombres
470 que tuvieron parentesco
con los tribus escogidos,
fuera de los nueve y medio.

         that they have been sent by God
         so they may convert the nations;
435   but, before a year and a half
         have passed, their very own comrades
             will in the square of Babylon
         demonstrate their iniquities
         and they will die proclaiming loud
440   their groundless articles of faith.
             For seven times and three years
         Nimrod's dominion will endure
         and divided into thirty
         kingdoms widespread idolatry
445   will scatter floods of human blood
         about the wildernesses.
         The terrifying fourth Beast will
         bellow fiercely from his station
             and in the eighth month of the year,
450   when a brightly shining comet
         will appear in the northern sky,
         the nations all will quake with fear.
             In four parts riven asunder,
         the horrifying Beast will cast
455   his expectations to the wind,
         then meet inevitable death.
             The words of the prophet Daniel
         will shine in full resplendence
         and a persecuted people
460   will bask in its reflected light.
             Tubal, divided among two
         princes who are by origin,
         if not subversive, audacious,
         if not of the people, lowly,
465   will call the wandering people in,
         and at the end of the sixth year,
         when the religions of the good
         and evil have been overturned,
             all people will acknowledge those
470   who by descent were kindred of
         the chosen tribes of Israel,
         besides the nine and a half tribes.

     Dividiránse el Oriente
naturales y extranjeros,
475 y por fin de siete y tres
quedarán sin fundamento
     la casa de Babilonia
y el Tribunal del Secreto.
El águila con la luna,
480 el león con el cordero,
     con el elefante, el gallo
y otros ocultos misterios,
a los tres años cabales
de los dos primeros tiempos,
485   volverán a revolverse
alborotando soberbios
todo el ámbito del mundo.
Mas los principes pequeños
     que administraren justicia
490 se librarán del incendio.
Un rey tendrá su corona,
tres provincias serán reino,
     y en el año de noventa
saldrá a luz un nuevo imperio,
495 con los términos indianos,
no visto ni descubierto.
     Y, contando la palabra
'semana' por jubileo,
que el profeta Daniel
500 profetizó con secreto,
     si no cumplidas, escritas
en el 'descanso seteno',
las setenta llegarán,
cuando se viere en el cielo
505   siete cometas errantes
que, cual relámpago o trueno,
se desharán en tres horas,
echando llamas de fuego.
     Veráse un monstruo en el Asia
510 en figura de hombre fiero,
siendo por tres años solos
el oráculo indigesto

Natives of the land and strangers
will divide up the Orient
475   and at the end of seven and three
the dynasty of Babylon
   and the Tribunal of Secrets
will crumble at their foundations.
The eagle mounting to the moon.
480   the lion lying with the lamb
   and with the elephant the cock and
other hidden mysteries,
when three years exactly are passed,
following the first two ages,
485   will come and come to pass again,
stirring up in their sublime way
the whole circumference of the world.
But, all those minor princes
   who have administered justly
490   will be saved from the inferno
A king will have his royal crown,
three provinces his dominions,
   and in the year of ninety
a new Empire will see the light,
495   with its boundaries in the Indies,
not witnessed nor revealed before.
   And if we understand the word
a 'week' to mean a Jubilee,
as the prophet Daniel foretold,
500   though he kept his meaning hidden,
   (if not fulfilled, yet written down
in the expression 'seventh-day rest'),
the seventy weeks will come to pass
when in the sky there will be seen
505   seven swiftly moving comets,
which, just like lightning or thunder,
will in three hours consume themselves,
while issuing flames of fire forth.
   In Asia a marvel will be
510   seen in the guise of a wild man,
who will be for three years only
the bewildering oracle

de los bárbaros gentiles;
y sus ritos y preceptos,
515   ley nueva de aquellos siglos.
obedecerán diez pueblos.
El Nilo sudará sangre,
y en medio del Mar Bermejo
se verán dos querubines
520   en forma de dos mancebos,
de la gente repelida
soberanos mensajeros.
Veránse lustres armados
por los páramos del viento
525   y en todas las curatro partes
del territorio pequeño.
No habrá paz en todo el mundo,
y entre la guerra el hebreo
llamará, siendo la augustia
530   en los mortales del suelo
la mayor, la más horrible
que los humanos padecieron
dende que el Autor divino
crió todo el universo.
535   Por la parte del oriente,
amanecerá un Lucero,
nueva Estrella de Jacob,
Principe de Paz eterno.
Con la vara de su boca
540   domará los idumeos.
y en la gran Jerusalaim
tendrá su divino asiento.
Saldrá de allí la palabra
y de Sión el concepto;
545   y la Ley y el Nombre santo
temerán todos los pueblos.
En Jaacob serán benditas.
las gentes, y en este tiempo
morirá la idolatría.—
550   Esto dijo y murió luego.

of the barbarian gentiles;
and ten nations will obey
515   his rituals and his precepts,
the new religion of that age.
   The Nile will flow with blood again
and in the midst of the Red Sea,
two cherubim will be espied
520   in the form of two young men
   who will be the sovereign messengers
of the rejected people.
Resplendent armies will be seen
in the cold regions of the wind
525   and in each of the four corners
of the little territory.
There will be no peace in the world
and amidst the war the Hebrew
   will cry out loud, since the anguish
530   felt by the mortals of the earth
will be the worst, most hideous
that human beings have suffered
since the time the divine Author
created all the universe.
535   In the direction of the east,
there will dawn a splendorous Light,
a new Star come out of Jacob
the eternal Prince of Peace.
   With the rod of his mouth he will
540   subjugate the Idumeans
and he will have his divine seat
in Jerusalem's great city.
   From there shall go forth the word
and out of Sion the Idea;
545   and all the peoples shall revere
his Law and his holy Name.
   In Jacob shall the nations
all be blessed and in this time
idolatry will cease to be."
550   Thus he spoke and then expired.

Notes

Cuando contemplo mi pasada gloria

This poem comes from *Academias morales de las Musas* ([Bordeaux, 1642], pp. 59–67), a collection of poems and plays presented in the manner of a literary contest in a pastoral setting: the poem is put in the mouth of the shepherd Albano, who throughout represents the poet himself. Both the name of the character and the initial line recall Garcilaso de la Vega; respectively, the lamenting shepherd of the Second Eclogue and the first line of Sonnet I, "Cuando me paro a contemplar me estado." The practice of reworking the poetry of others was common in the period (versions of the same poem exist by Lope de Vega and the Duke of Sesas); the interest for us lies in the cryptic expression of the exile's love for his country of birth, which can be glimpsed behind the *exercise de style*.

2   *duda mi estado*. Literally, "my state fears": the poet views his past as one might contemplate the ancient ruins of a state whose memory lives on only in one who is stricken to death with grief.

7   An allusion to the poet's self-imposed exile for reason of safety; note the image of Adam's departure from Eden underlying this passage, an image to which the poet frequently has recourse (see *La culpa* below).

12   *no nació de mí*. Enríquez often uses the idea of Original Sin as a metaphor of the *converso* condition, brought about by his parentage and "blood" rather than necessarily by his own doing; cf. also ll. 13–15 below. On the use of the metaphor of Original Sin, see J. G. García Valdecasas, *Las "Academias morales" de Antonio Enríquez Gómez* (Seville, 1970).

34   *Perdí mi libertad*. Enríquez Gómez equates the loss of homeland with loss of liberty itself—cf. sonnet on the theme *A la perdida libertad de la patria* ("On the lost liberty of the homeland"); the idea is bound up with that of losing one's "center" (see l. 35), one's alloted place in the cosmological scheme of things.

46   *Mi sencilla verdad*. The simple virtues associated with the "Golden Age" of the past, here personified (cf. l. 50).

52 ff.   The golden image of the past is marred by the loss of honor occasioned by the circumstances of his flight. In a society as preoccupied with the dictates of the code of honor as was seventeenth-century Spain, the loss of honor brought about by Inquisitorial investigation represented a severe blow to the individual.

56   *ciencia*. Cf. *el árbol de la ciencia,* the "tree of knowledge" of Genesis.

59   *estilo*. "Title" or "way of life"; cf. note to l. 52 on honor, the *sine qua non* of social success. There is a reflection here of the idea of the courtier (the epitome of *juicio*, "judgment," l. 60) derived from the Italian Renaissance (see Castiliglione's treatise on the subject, *Il libro del Cortegiano)*.

69   *Noruega*. Norway seen as the archetypal land of "cold exile."

73–74   The poet appears to address his oppressor in the person of the *malsín* ("talebearer") responsible for his troubles; see also note to Pinto Delgado, *En alabanza del Señor,* l. 55.

77–78   *lo que . . . el cielo me otorgó*. The poet may be thinking of his cultural heritage or in a more specific sense the property which his mother left him but which was confiscated by the Inquisition on account of his father's prosecution (see biography).

86   *esfera*. "Sphere" where one belongs, hence "home"; cf. note to ll. 34–35.

102   *el Corte*. The seat of the Court, hence the capital, Madrid; *sangre* in the same line suggests loss of honor, rather than literally "blood."

106–8   The image of the nest inverts that of the plundered nest of Garcilaso's First Eclogue, lines 324–37.

112 ff.   The poet addresses himself here (or possibly *dolor*, his pain): by seeking his own death, he appears to "condemn" the very ties with his homeland which give rise to his suffering.

115   *mi perdida confianza*. Cf. l. 31 ff.

130–31   *Si estuviera el sentido . . ./como lo está*. The subject literally is *el sentido*, "my feeling," seen as being distant from the poet. The inversion (as compared with the translation) is intended to heighten the conceit.

133 ff.   The poet now turns to the theme of exile and the sense of alienation it brings.

140   Genesis 11:1–9.

142   *convertido en uso*. Turned into something that others use or abuse; *uso* also means "custom," giving rise to the play of ideas in the next two lines.

145–47   Not understanding the language of those around him, the exile takes refuge in his sense of the superiority of his own tongue.

150   *ni aun los amagos toma*. As an illustration of the extent of his alienation, the poet shows the exile as not understanding threats or insults made to him and therefore unable to act in accordance with the code of honor which is second nature to him. What is more, he sardonically notes, ll. 155–56, the foreigner prefers to resolve difference by reasoning, instead of by the sword.

158–59   The poet concludes that all his troubles abroad spring from his "passion" for his homeland, leading back his first theme for the final part of the poem.

160–61   *Quién . . ./me trujo?* The form of the question seems to suggest that the poet has the *malsín* in mind again—which individual was it who betrayed him?

163   *la mía soberana*. The "sovereign people" he has in mind is probably the Spanish, though possibly the Jews might be intended.

166   The poet returns to his original motif.

181 ff.   The idea of the loss of honor as a metaphor of the New Christian's situation is taken up again and developed.

186   *lo mismo que saqué*. That is to say his dishonor, which he wants removed.

191   *émulos*. "Rivals"; Enríquez Gómez usually denotes his literary enemies by this term, as in Prologue to *Sansón Nazareno*. What is cliché there appears to be in earnest here.

202 ff.   The poet's conclusion is that exile is not the ideal solution; cf. his return to Spain (see biography, p. 139).

205   *libertad*. See note to l. 34.

La culpa del primer peregrino

1 Diálogo de Adán y Eva

This sequence is taken from *La culpa del primer peregrino* ([Rouen, 1644], pp. 13–16), a poem which, with the Fall of Adam as its point of departure, elaborates a debate between the *Peregrino* (Man, cf. Pinto, *Despedida*, note 1. 48) and Divine Wisdom on the eternal questions of good and evil, punishment and reward, and allied themes; in it Wisdom replies to Man's doubts with the palliatives of conventional religion, while there is a certain dramatic tension between the interlocutors which lifts it beyond the banal. More interesting is the poet's use of biblical sources—Job, Ecclesiastes, and Song of Songs—in a manner which by its literalness appears to pay homage to the very language of the source and which breathes new life into the poetic conventions of the Golden Age (cf. the elaborate style of *Sansòn Nazareno* [see below, p. 165 ff.]). While the use of the Bible as poetic source is not as unusual in the period as may be thought (see Blecua and Wilson, *Las lágrimas de Hieremías castellanas),* its use in a nonmystical, indeed nonreligious, manner is. Enríquez's robustly secular approach amounts to a de-Christianization of his cultural experience. It is of interest also to compare the following *Diálogo* with the first extract from *Sansón Nazareno* as examples of the pastoral genre, biblical and secular.

1 ff. Adam is cast in the role of Solomon addressing the Shulamite as in Song 4; cf. ll. 57, 62 below.

3–5 *la rosa sobre campos . . ./Lilio.* Cf. Song 2:1 "Yo soy el lirio del campo, y la rosa de los valles" (Reyna version); A.V. "I am the rose of Sharon, and the lily of the valleys."

9 Cf. Song 4:1 "tus ojos, de paloma"; A.V. "thou hast doves' eyes."

13–16 Cf. Song 4:1 "tu cabello, como manada de cabras que se muestran desde el monte de Galaad"; A.V. "thy hair is as a flock of goats, that appear from Mount Gilead." In Enríquez's euphemistic reference to Gilead, there may be an allusion to Jeremiah 8:22; alternatively, one tradition identifies Gilead with Gilboa, thus an allusion to David's lament of 2 Samuel 1 ("how are the mighty fallen") may be intended.

17–19 Song 4:5 "Tus dos tetas, como dos cabritos mellizos de gama, que son apacentados entre los lirios"; A.V. "Thy two breasts are like two young roes that are twins, which feed among lilies."

21–24 Song 4:12 "Huerto cerrado eres . . . fuente cerrada, fuente sellada"; A.V. "A garden inclosed . . . a spring shut up, a fountain sealed." The evident eroticism of this stanza (as of the sequence as a whole) contrasts with Fray Luis de León's interpretation of this verse as a reference to the Virgin, in his translation of Song of Songs.

25–26 Song 7:4 "Tu cuello, como torre de marfil"; A.V. "Thy neck is as a tower of ivory"; cf. Song 4:4 "torre de David." Possibly the image of the fingers as ten lilies (27–28) reflects "thousand bucklers" hanging on the tower of David (4:4).

30 *aquesta planta.* I.e., "the tree of knowledge" (Genesis 2:7).

42 *gracia.* (1) the external attractiveness of the Tree; (2) the grace or benefit bestowed by adhering to the commandment regarding it

50 *pálida.* "Pallid," the color of death; also "yellowish," suggesting the color of the fruit itself.

54   *arrebolada*. "Rouged" (*arrebol* = rouge), suggesting a woman's face, made up to be superficially attractive. Also, by way of *arrebol*, the red glow of the sky from the setting sun, one comes back to the conventional woman/sun analogy.

68   *púrpura*. (1) "royal purple," cf. l. 62; (2) a conventional euphemism for blood.

retrata. Play on *retractar*, "to retract" may also be intended: death, as it were, withdraws life's glory/blood.

72   (1) Eve has not held back her love for Adam nor has she yet (2) "sold her soul," succumbing to the corruption Enríquez sees as endemic in court circles: there is of course irony in this worldly-wise observation of Adam.

75   *conceptos* "Concepts" or "conceits."

109-12   Song 2:8-9 "La voz de mi Amado. He aquí que éste viene saltando sobre los montes, saltando sobre los collados. (9) Mi Amado es semejante al gamo, o al cabrito de los ciervos"; A.V. "The voice of my beloved! behold, he cometh leaping upon the mountains, skipping upon the hills. (9) My beloved is like a roe or a young hart." Note that the poet's version has the voice "leaping"; cf. "beloved" in A.V. and Reyna.

113 ff.   The following sequence recalls the Shulamite's night search for her beloved through the streets of Jerusalem, Song 3:1-5.

113   Song 5:8 "de amor estoy enferma"; A.V. "I am sick of love."

117   Eve addresses the stars; cf. watchmen and daughters of Jerusalem, Song 3:3, 5.

121-24   Song 5:10 "Mi Amado es blanco, rubio, más señalado que diez mil"; A.V. "My beloved is white and ruddy, the chiefest among ten thousand."

125-27   Song 5:11 "Su cabeza, oro fino, sus cabellos crespos, nergros como el cuervo"; A.V. "His head is as the most fine gold, his locks are bushy, and black as a raven," Enríquez omits the "vulgar" reference to the raven and portrays the lover as fair headed.

129-32   Song 5:12 "Sus ojos como de las palomas, que están junto a los arroyos de las aguas: que se lavan con leche, que están junto a la abundancia"; A.V. "His eyes are as the eyes of doves by the rivers of waters, washed with milk, and fitly set."

149 ff.   The poet suggests slyly Eve's attitude of "yes, but—" to Adam's expressed instructions: Enríquez Gómez takes many opportunities in his works to portray the subversive power of woman, as in *Sansón* and in the satirical *Siglo pitagórico*.

160   *desengaño*. (1) the disillusion or disapointments of love; (2) the enlightenment or awakening which follows a state of moral misapprehension (see Introduction, p. 30); what is a banality for Eve (sense 1) is a moral profundity for Adam ultimately (2).

164   Cf. l. 117; with the sequence *astros, flores, fuentes, espíritus* (here, the birds) the whole of nature is encompassed in a summation typical of the period (highly developed in the plays of Calderón).

2   *La injusticia en el mundo*

This extract is part of the Third Dialogue of *La culpa* (*op. cit.*, pp. 89–93). The Old Testament sources—Ecclesiastes (with Proverbs) and Job—are used to convey respectively the theme of the folly of the world Man has made for himself and the impotence of Man in the face of the obstacles he finds to his happiness and to justice. In this portrait of the anguish of Man's existence the poet also draws on his own skill as a social satirist. The verse form used is *terza rima*.

3   *la vasta lumbre*. The sun, cf. Ecclesiastes 1:3 *et passim*, "under the sun." Note: since it is the tone of the biblical sources, rather than the actual words, which the poet is following here, only A.V. will be quoted, without the Spanish translation.

6   *en término segundo*. "A little lower than the angels" (Psalms 8:5).

10–12   Ecclesiastes 8:14 "There is a vanity which is done upon the earth; that there be just men, unto whom it happeneth according to the work of the wicked; again, there be wicked men, to whom it happeneth according to the work of the righteous."

14   *Babel*. Used by Enríquez as the symbol of tyranny (particularly in the form of the Inquisition).

19–24   These two strophes, in the manner of an aside, may seem to lead the poem into bathos, but we have already noted the importance of the code of honor in Spanish life of the period: it is thus natural that the poet should epitomize Man's folly in terms of this scourge, which derives from it.

25–26   Job 27:2 "[God] hath taken away my judgment"; A.V.'s "judgment" means the right to be judged fairly and this is the sense of Enríquez's *derecho*. Note that the poet's use of the word derives directly from the Reyna translation: since it does not appear in any of the other available Bibles, it provides an indication, among others, that Enríquez used Reyna as his biblical source.

27, 31   An imitation of Proverbs 6:16 ff. "These six things doth the Lord hate: yea, seven are an abomination unto him. . . ."

33   *un malsín*. See note to *Cuando contemplo*, l. 73–74.

41   *la vida*. The spiritual life, conditioned by thoughts of judgment after death. This world is but a copy (*copia*, l. 40) of that "life" from which it should be drawn, as it were, like a painting.

32 ff.   One notes here the influence of the Christian view of the inherent sinfulness of the world as a result of Original Sin; on the other hand, nowhere in the poet's work is there any suggestion that it is redeemable through Jesus.

46   *abterna*. I.e., *ab eterna* "from everlasting."

49   *el Sabio*. Solomon, the reputed author of Ecclesiastes (see Ecclesiastes 1:1).

50–51   Ecclesiastes 10:5–6 "There is an evil which I have seen under the sun, as an error which proceedeth from the ruler: (6) Folly is set in great dignity. . . ." "Folly" occurs in l. 52.

53   *el sujeto*. Man, whose lot is suffering. However, it is possible that by *martirio* (l. 54) the poet has religious martyrdom in mind, in view of the importance he accords it in the *Romance* and *Sansón Nazareno* (see below).

66   *la política santa*. Cf. title of Enríquez Gómez's treatise *La política angélica*, in which he attacked the Inquisition's persecution of New Christians as being contrary to the Church's declared principles. Perhaps this whole argument may be taken as a covert attack on the Inquisition, artfully disguised behind orthodox theology (as in the above-mentioned treatise).

67   *el interés*. "Self-interest," a typical butt of Enríquez's satire, but also a charge often leveled at the Inquisition.

74 *el siglo antecedente*. I.e., in Eden, before the Fall.

86 *peregrino*. The use of this word may support the "Marrano" interpretation suggested above, 1. 66.

88 Job 27:2, as 1. 26 above; the sense is given by line 90—how long will Man complain that his punishment is undeserved? Even Job was guilty of pride in this respect. An alternative interpretation (cf. above) is that, as in the poems of Pinto Delgado, the suffering of the Marrano is being ascribed to his inadequate observance of Judaism—due to his "pride."

94–96 Fortune is depicted as a lover who is moved to tears by the tears of the loved one; *sus penas*, etc.—i.e., those of the speaker's misfortune *(desdicha*, 1. 95).

100–101 An echo of Psalms 51:17 "The sacrifices of God are a broken spirit: a broken and a contrite heart, O God, thou wilt not despise" (also quoted in *Romance*, 1. 336).

Sansón Nazareno

Sansón encuentra a la tamatea

The poet's description of the meeting of Samson and the Timnaite comes from Canto I (Stanzas 36–49) of *Sansón Nazareno*, an epic poem (published in 1656 but written in all probability in 1649) which recounts the familiar story of Judges 13–16 somewhat in the vein of Tasso's *Gerusalemme Liberata*, while serving at the same time as the vehicle for the expression of the poet's religious commitment, his faith in the Messianic redemption, and his belief in the virtues of martyrdom—themes which will be seen again in the *Romance*. Through the character of Samson, the erring Nazirite, the poet explores his own failure to adhere adequately to Judaism, for which only the perfect sacrifice of martyrdom (as he sees Samson's death) can make amends. That aspect of the poem will be seen in the second extract which follows, while the first shows how Enríquez Gómez takes the opportunities provided by his source to launch into poetic display in the manner of Góngora. The metrical form is *octava real*, as appropriate to the epic genre.

1 *(et passim) nazareno*. Literally "Nazarene"; cf. Jesus of Nazareth: the confusion of this word with "Nazirite" derives from the Christian tradition which sees Samson as a prefiguration of Jesus, a view which, this linguistic error apart, Enríquez Gómez manifestly does not share (see Canto VII and discussion in my thesis "Two poems of Antonio Enríquez Gómez," University of London, 1976, pp. 133–37).

4 *lilibeo*. A word of obscure meaning but which is frequently used by the poet in the sense of a small squadron of venturing soldiers seeking to accomplish feats of battle.

11 *nevando*. *Nevar*, "to snow" is used here as shorthand for the analogy of clothes with the whiteness of snow; this device is typical "Gongorism," which has to be paraphrased rather than translated.

13–16 The description of the stream recalls the Petrarchan *topos* popularized by Garcilaso (see Introduction, p. 28), while the execution here recalls Góngora's *Soledades*, 1:538–68 (e.g., image of *calle*, "street," 1. 15, cf. *Sol.* 1:542; *cítara del valle*, 1. 16, cf. *Sol.* 1:563).

18   *su estrella*. Venus is the star in question; hence the goddess Venus (or Aphrodite) who loved Adonis (same line).

19   *el niño dios alado*. Cupid, cf. 1. 28 below.

24   Cf. birth of Venus in a conch shell.

29   *cinco azucenas*. For the same metaphor for the hand cf. *Diálogo de Adán y Eva*, 1. 27.

30   *Delo*. Delos, an important center of the cult of Apollo, hence a reference to the sun (Apollo being the Greek sun-god). The sun's splendor is said to be *mentido*, "false," since it is less bright than the sun which is the Timnaite, who thus appears to be the real sun. This typically *culto* conceit is further developed by the play in the following lines (31–32) on the idea of her eyes as also being like suns.

34   *cristal*. "Crystal," hence white, by way of the accepted analogy of foam/water with snow (see Introduction, p. 29).

36   *aurora*. "Dawn," "dawning"; the white light of the very early dawn is intended (cf. other images of white here).

39   *clavel*. The flower "pink," which can be crimson, as intended here.

abriles. A mild pun on *abril* "April" and *abrir* "open".

40   *pensiles*. (1) "hanging"; (2) "beautiful gardens."

41   *Dalestina*. The name appears to be the poet's own invention, possibly derived from *Palestina*, the country.

42–44   The woman is Diana, the moon-goddess (cf. images of white above), while being at the same time the sun Apollo *(el galán*, 1. 44), described here as having descended from earth in human form. The phrase *de torcidos paralelos* 'of twisted parallels' (1. 43) refers to the distance of the sun in the highest sphere of the planets, or to the fact that one cannot look straight at the sun.

47   *favonio*. The westerly wind, the zephyr.

48   *errante*. Both "wandering" and "erring."

50   *atalaya*. "Watchtower" or "guard" in such a tower (as Samson appears to be at that moment).

52   *délfica*. "Delphic" referring to Apollo, at whose sanctuary on Mount Parnassus the famous oracle resided.

53   *pesadumbre*. "Weightiness" in the sense of "anxiety," etc.: the abstract noun referring to Samson's apprehension is used in its literal original sense, derived from *pesar*, "weigh," for the hillock where he stands.

58   *retratada*. For *retractada* "retreating"; however the sense of *retratada*, "drawn," "portrayed" may be there, the image of love seen as being mirrored in the feelings of the beholder.

66   *la tercer estrella*. Venus, the third planet in the solar system.

69   *cristalino*. Cf. *cristal*, 1. 34 above, and note.

72   Another good example of *culto* conceit: the water looks like a silver arch even if it is only a "bridge" of foam; at the same time it provides the hero with a real crossing place. Note the counterpoint of the two hemistiches, using *si*—a favorite *culto* device.

81   *de trino*. An astrological reference, *trino* ("trine") being the aspect of two planets 120 degrees apart, giving *de trino*, "at an angle"; the "planets" in question here are Samson and Dalestina, both of whom are the sun (hence the idea of it looking at itself), since he is Apollo, the sun-god (1. 97 below), and she like the sun as previously described.

90   *que veneró nevada espuma.* Subject and object are ambiguous: (1) foam (*espuma*) reveres her since she is white; (2) she reveres foam, i.e., Venus born of the foam, hence love.

109   *un dulce ruiseñor.* The nightingale is another expected element in the conventional *topos;* cf. note 11. 13–16.

111   *espumas.* See note 1. 90, above.

La muerte de Sansón

The final stanzas of *Sansón Nazareno* (Canto XIV, 58–68), the hero's prayer of repentance and his heroic death (Canto XIV), successfully marry the expression of sincere religious feeling with the epic style: the great critic Menéndez y Pelayo, who was not greatly taken with Enríquez Gómez's baroque style, considered it worthy of note *(Historia de los heterodoxos españoles,* 2d ed. [Madrid, 1965], 4:319). The first five stanzas given here were also included in A. Durán's *Romancero y cancionero sagrados,* Biblioteca de autores españoles, vol. 35.

1 ff.   The invocation of the names of the Patriarchs may be biblically inspired or derived from Jewish Liturgy *(Amidah)* as is the case in the *Romance,* 11. 323–34; indeed, there is reason to believe that this passage is a reworking in heroic style of the other work, which precedes it slightly in date.

2   *los tres mundos.* The three spheres, material, intellectual, and celestial, of which the universe is composed according to Aristotelian philosophy.

25–28   Samson is seen by the poet as the defender of the Law in his role as Nazirite; at the same time he is the representative of all those of Jewish faith who fight against religious tyranny and ultimately, in his failings and repentance, the expression of the poet's personal religious feeling. It seems that the poet, whatever the practical motivation for his return to Spain, saw the risks involved as leading to a potential martyr's death, for which he was fully prepared. There is no doubt that just prior to his return he underwent a period of intense religious feeling, as *Sansón Nazareno* and the *Romance,* in particular, bear witness.

46   The reference is to Dagon, the Philistine's god, whose name is associated with Hebrew *dag* ("fish"); the term *medio fauno* ("semi-fawn") suggests a vaguely classical, hence pagan, association.

54   *dragontina.* The word is Enríquez's own invention, suggesting both Dagon (see previous note) and "dragon."

56   *nichos.* In his description of the temple, at the beginning of the canto, the poet depicts the galleries and "chapels" from floor to ceiling packed with Canaanite tribes of all different kinds.

58   *los ejes de diamante.* The columns of the temple are likened to the "axes" on which the world turns; this anticipates the description below of the fall of the temple in terms of a universal destruction (69–72).

76   *desengaza = desengarza,* literally "unravel."

81–84   As frequently in this poem, the poet returns after each excursus or elaboration in his own style to his source in the Bible, here paraphrased but recognizable: Judges 16:30 "so the dead which he slew at his death were more than they which he slew in his life."

Romance al divín mártir, Judá Creyente, martirizado en Valladolid por la Inquisición

Enríquez Gómez's *Romance* is uniquely outspoken in its Jewish stance, as compared with the poet's other writings, which are orthodox in appearance and express only covertly his true beliefs, a fact which, as with Pinto Delgado's "Autobiographical Poems," is accounted for by its being solely in manuscript. It takes as its subject the death of Lope de Vera y Alarcón at the hands of the Inquisition of Valladolid in 1644; his martyrdom caused widespread interest among Marranos and Jews abroad because he came to Judaism, having no New Christian connections, under pressure of the circumstances of his trial, during the course of which he circumcised himself with a bone and adopted the name of *Judá Creyente*, "Judah the Believer." The poem is in two parts, an anti-Christian polemic and a prayer which develops into a prophecy of the Messianic Coming. In the latter, one may see the influence of Gonçalo Annes Bandarra's *Trovas*, which were interpreted as foretelling the restoration of the Portuguese throne in 1640 (a movement in which the poet was involved) as well as that of the Talmud, by way of the *Chronologia Hebraeorum* of Genebrardus. In personal terms the poem is a working through of the poet's religious identity, always pro-*converso* but not until this point positively crypto-Jewish, as a result of the crisis in his life in the period 1647–49 when his friends in the Portuguese entourage in Paris (including the judaizer Manuel Fernandes Vilareal) returned to Portugal, leaving him to decide about his own future. He had also tried to publish in 1647 his attack on the Inquisition, *Política angélica*, which offended in Portuguese and French quarters, as well as becoming involved with the Prince de Condé then in rebellion against the French Crown. All this appears to have made him *persona non grata* in France: one may readily imagine the desire for religious certainties which such a situation produced. The resulting poem was as popular as its subject: two complete copies of the manuscript are extant (Oxford and Amsterdam), while a partial copy and a fourth complete one are known to have existed at one time (see respectively C. Roth, "Le Chant du cygne de Don Lope de Vera," *Revue des études juives* 97[1934]: 97–113, and I. S. Révah, *Ecole pratique des Hautes Etudes, IVe Section Sciences historiques et philologiques*, Annuaire, 1966). Miguel de Barrios makes at least two references to the poem in his writings, no doubt attracted, as a Sabbatian, by its Messianic content. The present edition is based on the manuscript in the Bodleian Museum, Oxford (MS Opp. Add.4º, 150 with ocasional reference to the other extant manuscripts. For a full description of the text, see my thesis "Two poems of Antonio Enríquez Gómez," University of London, 1976; see also "Antonio Enríquez Gómez's 'Romance al divín mártir, Judá Creyente,'" *Journal of Jewish Studies* 26 (1975).

15–18   This detail of Lope de Vera's story and others are recorded in one of the principal sources of information regarding the martyr, namely a letter sent by the Inquisitor Moscoso to the Marquesa de Monterey, which somehow came into the hands of the Jews of Amsterdam (cf. Isaac Cardoso, *Excelencias de los hebreos* [Amsterdam, 1679], pp. 363–34). One copy is in the British Library (MS Or. 8098). The other main source, also in the British Library (MS Egerton 2058) consists of a highly biased account of events, probably issued by the Inquisition to justify its actions and proclaim the infamy of its victim.

24 *el sagrado texto*. Isaiah 53:7 "he is brought as a lamb to the slaughter, and as a sheep before her shearers."

35 *de Venus*. I.e., "venal," "materialistic," etc.; for the association of the Inquisition with the "Whore of Babylon," see García Valdecasas's study of *Las academias morales de las Musas*, where the idea recurs. There are grounds here, however, for thinking that the poet has in mind not just the Inquisition but Christianity at large.

39–42 The amatory image is exploited later, ll. 341 ff.

47 *tú*. The victim addresses the crowd (grammatically singular, see *vulgo*, l. 31 and *-le*, l. 44) or his accusers, in particular the Inquisitor General, referred to as *Sabio de Babel* (l. 51); interestingly, the rubric of the partial MS (Leghorn) presents the poem as the declaration of Lope de Vera to the Inquisitor General, while our sources refer to him as having being persuaded to make a written statement after refusing to speak to the inquisitors.

56 *peregrino*. "Strange" or "wonderful" would be possible translations but in view of the special Marrano conotations of the word, "wandering" may be more appropriate.

66 *idumeo*. "Idumean": the Idumeans or Edomites were traditional enemies of Israel, being the descendants of Esau (see Genesis 25:30).

75–76 The reference is to David and Psalms 19:7 "The law of the Lord is perfect."

84–85 The poet may have in mind a biblical source such as Isaiah 44:6 (see l. 166 below) or more probably verse four of the Jewish hymn *Yigdal* "He was the first with no beginning of his own." A Latin translation of the hymn appears in Génébrard's *Chronographia Hebraeorum*.

101 *luminaria*. Jesus, seen as a rival heavenly body in relation to God the sun.

115 *"La Ley fue santa."* "The Law was holy": "but is no more" is implied.

119–30 An element of Neoplatonic cosmology is introduced here: if the macrocosm (which is the order of the universe, l. 120) obeys God, then so too should Man, the microcosm (l. 127).

126 "I am the Lord thy God" (Exodus 20:2): so frequently is the First Commandment bracketed with the Second that the argument naturally turns to the theme of the Oneness of God ("Thou shalt have no other gods before me").

130–31 Isaiah 45:5 "I am the Lord, and there is none else"; Isaiah 42:8 "I am the Lord: that is my name: and my glory I will not give to another."

153 *dividida en dos*. "Divided into two" as in the Old and New Testaments.

166 Isaiah 44:6 "I am the first, and I am the last."

167 *tres dioses*. As in the Trinity.

186 I.e., "graven images."

192–93 *dulía, perdulía*, and *latría* are the three categories of Catholic worship, respectively the veneration of saints, that of the Virgin, and worship due to God alone.

196 *madero* (cf. *piedra*, l. 201). The wood from which statues of saints and Virgin are made.

200 *hierro*. Play on the identically sounding words *hierro*, "iron" and *yerro*, "error" or "sin."

207   An echo of Ecclesiastes 1:2 "Vanity of vanities: all is vanity."

213   *un hombre*, I.e., Jesus.

215–24   The argument is lent weight through reference to the most important Old Testament authorities: Moses the Law-giver, Isaiah the Prophet, and David the Psalmist.

215–18   Deuteronomy 9:15–21; *alguna parte*, 1. 217, appears to reflect the Rabbinic view that the episode of the Golden Calf left its taint on subsequent generations (Babylonian Talmud, *Taanith*, 68 c).

219–22   Isaiah 44:21–22 "Remember these, O Jacob and Israel; for thou art my servant. . . . (22) I have blotted out, as a thick cloud, thy trangressions."

223–24   Psalm 77:15 "Thou hast with thine arm redeemed thy people, the sons of Jacob and Joseph."

226   *muerte*. "Death," an allusion to the Crucifixion.

230   *el muerto*. "The dead man": one would expect *la muerte* ("death") to balance *la vida* ("life") but a double meaning is intended: (1) the dead in general; (2) one particular "dead man," i.e., Jesus.

258   *que antes de morir tuvieron*. A curiously elliptical phrase, alluding to the Christian concept that the death of Jesus granted Man the possibility of eternal life; a suggested reading is *que antes [cuando] tuvieron de morir* "than before, when they had to die."

267   The return to the Maccabean analogy of the beginning of the poem (1. 14) prepares for the conclusion of the first part of the poem.

272   *por nacimiento*. A reference to the fact that Lope de Vera was a convert: he vows to be as one who was born a Jew (note the use of *peregrino*, 1. 271, to suggest true Jewishness).

275   *Cual otro Sansón*.   An interesting comparison in view of the subject of Enríquez Gómez's contemporaneous epic, *Sansón Nazareno*.

280   *los tres mancebos*. The Three Children in the furnace of Daniel 3:12.

285–86   Elijah's ascent to heaven in a chariot of fire, 2 King 2:11.

314   *Mongibelo*. Volcano, often identified with Etna.

319–22   Isaiah's vision of God, Isaiah 6:1 ff.

323–34   There are parallels between this passage and the first two sections of the *Amidah*, one of the central prayers of Jewish liturgy: in addition to the invocation of the Patriarchs, there are the common themes of the powers of God and of God as the Giver of life after death. The *Amidah*'s reference to a promised Redeemer links up with the poem's developing Messianic theme, while the general progress of the prayer to the climax of the *Kedushah* ("Holy, holy, holy is the Lord God of hosts") is reflected in the allusion at the beginning of the second speech to Isaiah 6, from which the *Kedushah* is drawn. Some of the phrases used in the poem recall too the language of the *Amidah* as it occurs in the Ferrara vernacular editions of the liturgy (1553 and later editions).

333–36   Psalms 51:17 "The sacrifices of God are a broken spirit: a broken and a contrite heart, O God, thou wilt not despise." The idea that this is the "perfect sacrifice" is the poet's own; indeed he frequently misquotes the source with the addition: "Corazón contrito y humillado es *perfecto* sacrificio."

338   *conceto*. Both "concept" and "conceit."

341 ff.   The amatory image developed here (as the true marriage of the soul) recalls both biblical tradition, especially Song of Songs, and that of Christian mystical poetry in the Golden Age.

354   The physical presentation of the Loved One is a mixture of Renaissance (here) and Song of Songs (357); cf. *En diálogo de Adán y Eva,* above.

358   *pero no negros.* "But not black" as are those of the dove, l. 357, alluding to Song 4:1 "tus ojos, de paloma."

359–60   Song 4:5 "tus dos tetas, como dos cabritos mellizos de gama."

364   *ministerio.* The priestly line from Aaron onward as guardians of the Law (see Exodus 28). The other complete manuscript reads *hemisferio* "hemisphere" or "world," making it an allusion to Creation.

372   Psalms 25:1 "Unto thee, O Lord, do I lift up my soul."

385   *el libro sagrado.* The "sacred book" is that of Daniel, the most popular of Messianic sources and the basis for this section to the end of the poem: ll. 393–440 evoke the upheavals of Daniel 11, while Daniel 7, 9, and 10–12 are used for subsequent passages (lines 441–78, 479–508, and 509–50 respectively).

393   *La América.* The analogy is clearly with the threat of Rome to Egypt in Daniel 11:30, but the designation of America as the source of the forces of revenge is not self-explanatory: perhaps the poet had in mind the threat posed by the Dutch in Brazil to the Catholic powers of Portugal and (indirectly) Spain.

394   *el año noveno.* "The ninth year": the chronology of the passage is initially based on the Jubilee period 1640–90, which, following the *Zohar,* was regarded as a whole as a period of redemption and into which fell the year predicted for the Resurrection of the Dead (in the Messianic Age)—"408," that is to say 5408 Anno Mundi, or 1648. The "ninth year" may allude to the idea, also from the *Zohar,* that the redemption of the Jews would take place forty years before the Coming.

398–400   Daniel 11:18 "After this shall he turn his face unto the isles, and shall take many." The poet appears to look to a second Columbus (whose *converso* origin is still a matter of academic dispute) to avenge the Jews.

401–2   The reference is almost certainly to the events of the Fronde which took place in 1648–49 and which the poet himself witnessed—he even dedicated his *Sansón Nazareno* to Condé, the leading rebel against Mazarin and the French Crown. The cryptic manner of expressing the date ("before forty-nine") is due simply to the fact of the poet writing his work in 1648 while the events were going on.

403–4   Civil disturbances were a feature of the first stage of the Fronde.

405   The "water-dwellers" may be America again, the new threat to Christianity combined in dissembling alliance with the old, the Turks and Moors (*sitas y agarenos,* l. 406); alternatively, they may be the Venetians, subjugated to the other powers. The parallel is with the fusion through conquest of Persian, Median, and Babylonian empires in Daniel 11:2.

409   *Tres lustros.* Fifteen years, a lustrum being a period of five years (we now reach 1664 according to the poem's chronology).

410–12   Daniel 11:2 speaks of wars between Persians ("Orientals") and Greeks (those who dwell on the "Olympian element" or Mount Olympus). A contemporary reference would be to the incursions of the Turks into eastern parts of Europe in the sixteenth and seventeenth centuries.

415   *el hambre.* "Hunger," one of the many privations traditionally associated with the period prior to the Coming; see Isaiah 8:21 and cf. Daniel 9:25 ("troublous times").

417-24   The two prophets have no parallel in the Book of Daniel; the poet probably has in mind representatives of Christianity and Islam. Note that in the sixteenth century Isaac Abravanel saw the Crusades as bringing about the demise of both these religions.

426   *catorce templos*. The significance of the number fourteen is not readily apparent, but the cryptic use of numbers is typical of this type of prophecy. On the destruction of temples and idols, compare Nostradamus's prophecy of the Fall of Rome (*Centuries* 9:65 in the Rouen edition of 1649).

429   False prophets are a frequent subject of warning in the Bible, as in Daniel 11:14; also Jeremiah, Ezekiel, etc. The obvious allusion from the period, to Sabbetai Zevi and his "prophet" Nathan of Gaza, can be ruled out as being too late for our poet (they did not come to prominence until the 1660s); David Reubeni and Shlomo Molho, who appeared in the previous century, are more likely candidates (Molho at least died in the "square in Babylon" [l. 437], by the hand of the Inquisition of Badajoz in 1538).

441   This phrase is repeated in line 475 as the poet's equivalent of Daniel's "time and times and the dividing of time (or a half)" (Daniel 7:25 and 12:7). There is a tradition of Jewish Messianic speculation regarding the calculation of the date of the Coming which sees this phrase as equivalent to the "thousand three hundred and five and thirty days" of Daniel 12:12. However, as Enríquez's "three" is less than half of seven, it is more probable that he has in mind the lesser figure of "a thousand two hundred and ninety days" mentioned in Daniel 12:11: this added to 391 C.E., the year in which Christianity became the official religion of the Roman Empire, produces the year 1681, which fits in with the overall chronology of the passage. There is in fact no precedent for this precise use of the source, nor does the poet seem well versed in the mysteries of the Kabbalah, but there is a strong sense of the desire to imitate the manner of Kabbalistic speculation.

442   Nimrod, king of Babylon, is the biblical symbol of pride and rebellion against God; for the assocations in Enríquez's poetry of "Babel," see note to l. 34 above.

444   *treinta reinos*. The total disintegration of Christendom is indicated by its division into thirty kingdoms; the poet may have in mind the breaking up of the Holy Roman Empire in the wake of the Thirty Years' War (1618-48), while the biblical reference is to the destruction of the Fourth Kingdom (Daniel 7:19 ff. and 11), symbolized below (ll. 447-56) by the Fourth Beast of Daniel 7:7-11.

449   Since the eighth month approximates to that of *Ab* in the Hebrew calendar, there may be a reference to the solemn fast of the Ninth of Ab and to the tradition which suggests that the month which saw the saddest events which it commemorates—the destruction of the First and Second Temples— will also see the happiest in the form of the Messianic Coming.

453-54   Daniel 11:4 "his kingdom shall be broken, and shall be divided toward the four winds of heaven."

457-59   The "verse" in question is Daniel 12:1 "at that time thy people shall be delivered."

461   *Tubal*. Signifies Spain: the descendants of Tubal, son of Japhet (Genesis 10:2), lived south of the Black Sea whence they were said to have gone to Spain. Note that the chief prince of Tubal (and Meshech) was Gog (Ezekiel 38:3) whose name is coupled with that of Magog in tradition to designate the forces of turmoil forming part of the so-called birth pangs of the Messianic era

(these are reflected in the last forty lines of the poem). The division of Tubal between two 'princes' reflects the secession of Portugal in 1640.

465   The Ingathering of the Exiles is a staple element of Messianic prophecy: note that, in the first instance (cf. below, ll. 473–74), this involves a Return of the *peregrinos* or Marranos to Spain, in keeping with a Sephardi tradition which goes back at least to the twelfth century (see Abraham Ibn Daud's *Sefer ha-Kabbalah);* cf. Pinto, *Alabanza,* 1. 96.

466   *el año sexto.* 'The sixth year'—i.e., of the ninth decade (1686).

467–68   All religions, whether worthy or otherwise, are seen as being overturned prior to the new Messianic order; possibly it reflects the downfall of the "saints" (Daniel 7:21) and that of their oppressors subsequently (Daniel 7:27).

469–72   The reference is to the Jews as the descendants of the surviving Tribes of Israel (Judah and Benjamin), in contrast to the so-called Lost Tribes *(los nueve y medio,* Enríquez's usual designation for the Ten Tribes; lit. 'the nine and a half'). The implication of *fuera* ("besides") is that these too will be acknowledged or rediscovered, in itself an important "sign" of the Coming and made much of by Menasseh ben Israel in his Messianic treatise, *Esperanza de Israel* ("The Hope of Israel"), Amsterdam, 1650.

473–74   The vision is one of the Orient as the place of assembly for both Jews born there *(naturales)* and those from elsewhere in the world *(extranjeros),* completing the process of 1. 465 (q.v. and note).

475   *siete y tres.* See note to 1. 441.

479–84   The vision of harmony is inspired by Isaiah 11:6 "The wolf shall dwell with the lamb, and the leopard shall lie down with the kid; and the calf and the young lion and the fatling together." Since the poet introduces other animals of his own, it may be that they are intended to represent countries or states after the manner of Nostradamus *(Centuries,* 1:93): the eagle might represent the Holy Roman Empire, the (crescent) moon the Turks.

483–84   Presumably we are now in the first stages of the new era, though *tiempos* may take us back to the period of the "times" mentioned in lines 441 and 476: a logical time pattern is not always a feature of this type of "prophecy"!

488   *los príncipes pequeños.* Menasseh ben Israel in his *Esperanza de Israel* refers to the rulers of Ferrara and Leghorn who have dealt justly with Jews as meriting reward in the Messianic Age.

491   *Un rey.* A figure like Cyrus (cf. Daniel 9:24) who released the Jews from Babylon and whose empire comprised the three provinces of Media, Lydia, and Babylon.

493   *noventa.* "Ninety": this completes the Jubilee period of 1640–90 and we now move on to the completion of the prophecy at a point relatively more distant in time.

495   Cyrus extended his empire to the Indus, while the Spanish took theirs to the West Indies: the new empire will extend to include both "Indies."

497–503   This most complex passage is based on the prophecy of the "seventy weeks" *(las setenta [semanas],* 1. 503) found in Daniel 9:24–25, which provides a timetable for the coming of an "anointed one" whom Christian tradition takes to be Jesus and Jewish tradition Cyrus. Enríquez Gómez draws on both in applying the source to a Jewish Messiah. Each week is to be counted as one Jubilee on the basis of the phrase *descanso seteno* ("seventh [day of] rest," 1. 502): just as each week ends in the Sabbath, so each cycle of seven sabbatical years ends in the "rest" of the Jubilee. The figure arrived at thereby is 3,500 years, which when added to a popular *terminus a quo*, the date of Exodus—2448 A.M. in the chronology provided in the Ferrara Bible—produces the year 5948 A.M. This in turn is approximately one Jubilee before the end of the sixth millennium, which is the time the Talmud gives for the duration of the world (Tractate *Sanhedrin*, 97 a–b); further, another view recorded in the same tractate places the Coming in the *last* of eighty-five Jubilees. The poet's method of calculation using Jubilees is justified both by this second Talmudic reference and by the fact that the Zoharitic date of "408" (see note 1. 394) derives in part from an interpretation of Leviticus 25:13 concerning the Jubilee: "In this year of Jubilee you shall return every man to his possession." Enríquez Gómez's acquaintance with the Talmud came through Génébrard's *Chronographia Hebraeorum*, which reproduces the Rabbinic discussion on the Messiah in Latin translation.

509   Daniel 10:15 refers to an emissary who foretells the wars which will lead to the end of the empire of tyranny (as related in Daniel 11). In this poem he seems to replace Elijah or the Messiah ben Joseph (according to varying traditions) as the precursor of the Messiah, son of David.

515–16   Zechariah 8:23 "In those days it shall come to pass, that ten men shall take hold out of all languages of the nations, even shall take hold of the skirt of him that is a Jew, saying, We will go with you: for we have heard that God is with you." This is the acknowledgment by other nations of the new order led by Israel.

517   The analogy between the Messianic liberation and that of the Exodus features largely in the speculative tradition.

519   *dos querubines*. The two "cherubim" are Michael and Gabriel (Daniel 10:13 and 10:5), the guardian angels of Israel.

523   With a circularity typical of the genre, the prophecy appears to return to its starting point in Daniel 11 with its reference to wars and armies of revenge (cf. 1. 381ff.), only this time they are the actual "birth pangs" of the Messiah.

536–37   Numbers 24:17 "there shall come a star out of Jacob, and a sceptre shall rise out of Israel." Note that the use of this and the following quotation, which have very Christian overtones, is justified by their discussion by Elijah ben Asher in his *Sefer Methurgeman* and Maimonides in the chapter *Hilchot melachim* in his *Mishneh Torah*, extracts of which are included in Génébrard's compendium. It nonetheless reflects the poet's Christian culture.

538   Isaish 9:6 "The Prince of Peace."

539–40   Psalms 110:2 "The Lord shall send the rod of thy strength out of Zion: rule thou in the midst of thine enemies."

540   Numbers 24:18 "And Edom shall be a possession."

543   Isaiah 2:3 "for out of Zion shall go forth the law and the word of the Lord from Jerusalem."

Miguel de Barrios

Miguel de Barrios was born in Montilla, near Córdoba, in 1635. Little is known of his life until 1650, when on the arrest of a relative by the Inquisition the family decided to leave Spain for North Africa. Miguel himself made for Leghorn, where once inside the Jewish community there he had himself circumcised. It was there also that he later married Deborah Vaez, who, however, was to die shortly afterwards in Tobago during an ill-starred voyage in search of a new life. The poet returned to Europe, this time to the Low Countries, and for the next twelve years was to divide his time between Brussels and Amsterdam in an extraordinary double existence. In Brussels he was a captain of horse in the Spanish Army and outwardly a conforming Christian, enjoying the patronage of people in high places, such as the Count of Monterey, the Governor of the Spanish Netherlands, while he made his name in his literary career. It was in Brussels that he published his first collections of poetry, *Flor de Apolo* (1665) and *Coro de las Musas* (1672), in which his Jewish persona is but obliquely perceived. At the same time, in Amsterdam Barrios was an integrated member of the Jewish community, calling himself Daniel Levi de Barrios, and a family man once more, with a second wife, Abigail de Pina, and three children. Eventually, in about 1672, he resigned his army commission and settled permanently in Amsterdam. His decision may well have arisen out of disappointment with his literary career in Brussels or possibly out of an intense belief in the imminent coming of the Messiah (Barrios remained a firm supporter of Sabbatai Zevi even after his apostasy). In Amsterdam Barrios became a leading figure in the literary life of the community, being a founder-member of the *Academia de los sitibundos* in 1676 and of the *Academia de los floridos* in 1685 (see Introduction, p. 27). On the other hand, his life was not entirely happy

Allegorical portrait of Miguel de Barrios from *Imperio de Dios en la Harmonía del Mundo* (Amsterdam, 1700?)

there: he came into conflict with the Jewish authorities over some of his writings and his continued Sabbatianism, which also brought him mental disorder. He was constantly beset by poverty and frequently forced to seek alms. In 1686 the death of his wife dealt him a sad blow. He himself died on 2 March 1701.

Barrios is by far the most "baroque" of our three poets: writing in the latter half of the century, he seems to have absorbed all the influences of the *culto* and *conceptista* styles. Much of his poetry is of an ephemeral nature—panegyrics, occasional verse, burlesques, and the like, which are of some historical and social interest but which cannot be considered in general great poetry. At the same time, one can see his burlesque style, for instance, used to good effect in *Alabanza jocosa a la Ley*. Indeed, at his best, Barrios is able to turn all the various devices and motifs of the baroque to good advantage, whether in the expression of Jewish themes, as in the example just quoted, or in treating of the more conventional themes of personal tragedy (as in the "Double sonnets" on the death of his wife) or disillusionment with the world—the *desengaño* theme much explored by Quevedo. The comparison is not too invidious to Barrios. However, it is in the purely Jewish poems that Barrios comes into his own, in poems which combine a restrained but elegant style with an intense penitential fervor, as in the *Días penitenciales* of 1684.

A la muerte de Raquel

Llora Jacob de su Raquel querida
la hermosura marchita en fin temprano
que cortó poderosa y fuerte mano
del árbol engañoso de la vida.
5   Ve la purpúrea rosa convertida
de cárdeno color en polvo vano
y la gala del cuerpo más lozano
postrada a tierra, a tierra reducida.
     ¡Ay, dice, gozo incierto! ¡gloria vana!
10   ¡mentido gusto! ¡estado nunca fijo!
¿Quién fía en tu verdor, vida inconstante?
     Pues cuando más robusta y más lozana,
un bien que me costó tiempo prolijo
me lo quitó la muerte en un instante.

A la segura confianza

Piensa vencer gigante el filisteo:
vence David y su cerviz quebranta;
en el lago Daniel mil himnos canta:
mueren en él cuantos le juran reo.
5   Promulga el fallo contra Mardoqueo
soberbio Amán : patíbulo levanta
y permite el Criador que en su garganta
se ejecute tan bárbaro deseo.
     Todo humano poder es sombra vana:
10   la más incontrastable monarquía
se ve sujeta a la traición villana.
     ¡O infinita de Dios soberanía!
pues sin haber seguridad humana,
vive seguro aquel que en ti confía.

On the death of Rachel

Jacob laments his beloved Rachel's
beauty, now withered in an early end,
and which a powerful and mighty hand
cut down from the illusive tree of life.
5   He beholds the deep crimson rose transformed
from ruddy hue to insubstantial dust
and the splendor of its luxuriant form
brought prostrate to the earth, to earth reduced.
    Woe, he says, inconstant joy! vain glory!
10   deceiving pleasure! never-firm estate!
Who trusts in your green vigor, fickle life?
    For when most robust and most luxuriant
this prize which took me such a time to win
is in an instant torn by death from me.

On well-founded faith

The giant Philistine thinks to conquer:
David conquers and breaks his neck in two;
Daniel in the den sings a thousand hymns:
all those die who swear he is a criminal.
5   Proud Haman promulgates the death sentence
against Mordecai: gallows he erects
and thus allows the Creator on *his* neck
to execute such barbarous intent.
    All human power is but a vain shadow:
10   the most invincible of monarchies
is subject to villainous betrayal.
    Oh, how infinite is God's sovereignty!
for, though human affairs are insecure,
he lives secure who puts his trust in you.

Real consideración del hombre

Yo, ¿para qué nací? Para salvarme.
¿Qué tengo de morir? Es infalible.
¿Dejar de ver a Dios y condenarme?
Triste cosa será, pero posible.
5   *Posible, ¿y duermo y río y quiero holgarme?*
Posible, ¿y tengo amor a lo visible?
¿Qué hago? ¿En qué me ocupo? ¿En qué me encanto?
Loco debo de ser, pues no soy santo.

Glosa

¿Quién soy yo? No lo sé. ¡Gran desacierto
10   es el no conocerse uno a sí mismo!
¿Cómo sabré quién soy? Cuando despierto
de mí me sueño el más confuso abismo.
De mí propio saldré: apenas acierto.
¿Quién lo impide? Un alegre parasismo.
15   Si he de morir, ¿qué sirve deleitarme?
Yo, ¿para qué nací? Para salvarme.

¿Qué miro? Las mudanzas de la vida.
¿Qué escucho? Los avisos de la muerte
¡O, qué pena es pensar en la caída!
20   ¡O, qué horror esperar el golpe fuerte!
¿Adónde iré que escape de la herida?
De qué la he de sentir todo me advierte.
¿Que ha de llegar el mal? ¡Lance terrible!
¿Qué tengo de morir? Es infalible.

25   Es la muerte forzosa y heredada.
Mas si es ley y quietud, ¿qué me atormenta?
La memoria en deleites ocupada,
el saber que he de dar de todo cuenta.
¿Qué podrá darme vida? La enmendada.
30   ¿Dónde voy, cielos, si me representa
el bien la reducción y el no enmendarme
dejar de ver a Dios y condenarme?

The true concern of Man

For what purpose was I born? To seek salvation.
Must I perish? It is inevitable.
That I fail to see God and be condemned?
A sad thing it would be and yet possible.
5 *Possible, yet I sleep, laugh and seek pleasure?*
Possible, yet I love what eyes can see?
What my deed, what my concern, what my delight?
I must be a fool, since I am not a saint.

Gloss

      Who am I? I do not know. What gross error
10   it is not to have knowledge of oneself.
      How shall I know who I am? When awakened
      from myself, I dream of the direst abyss.
      I shall depart myself: scarce do I succeed.
      What prevents me? A happy state of being.
15   If I must die, what use my seeking pleasure?
      For what purpose was I born? To seek salvation.

      What do I behold? The changefulness of life.
      What do I hear? The warning signs of death.
      Oh, how the thought of that decline afflicts me!
20   Oh, the horror of awaiting that harsh blow!
      Where shall I go that I may escape the wound?
      All things warn me that I am bound to feel it.
      That hurt is bound to come? What a fearsome fate!
      Must I perish? It is inevitable.

25   Death is our necessary inheritance.
      But if peace it is decreed, why am I vexed?
      My memory, troubled by my pleasures past,
      the knowledge that I must give account of all.
      What can grant me life? A life that is reformed.
30   Where do I go, heavens, if in changing seems
      to lie my profit and by not reforming
      that I shall fail to see God and be condemned?

Mal podré hallar su luz, si la del suelo
ocupa mi atención: ¡o, cuánto yerra
35   el que imagina penetrar al cielo,
andando con los ojos por la tierra!
La justa acción, el penitente anhelo
guían a inmortal paz en mortal guerra.
Si desto me arrebata lo irascible,
40   *triste cosa será, pero posible.*

Posible, ¿y en el golfo de tan larga
tormenta el alma que de errar no cesa,
temiendo hundirse con la grave carga,
no echa del corazón lo que le pesa?
45   Posible, ¿y el deseo no me embarga
de sequir la razón con cuanta priesa
pueda alcanzar el punto de salvarme?
Posible, ¿y duermo y río y quiero holgarme?

Posible, ¿y de mi propio no procuro
50   huir de modo que de mí triunfante
entre en la corte del celeste muro
con arco de oro y palma de diamante?
Posible, ¿y con dolor y llanto puro
suspender no pretendo cada instante
55   el del supremo Juez amago horrible?
Posible, ¿y tengo amor a lo visible?

¡Piedad, inmenso Dios! que los ardores
intento yo apagar de tus enojos,
andando el mar que alteran mis clamores,
60   aun más que por el cielo, por mis ojos.
Mas ¿qué engaños, qué objetos, qué rigores
empañan el cristal de mis antojos?
Ansias, ¿adónde el corazón levanto?
¿Qué hago? ¿En qué me ocupo? ¿En qué me encanto?

65   Si sólo es rey quien reina en sus pasiones
y esclavo el rey si le dominan ellas,
¿cómo al poder no acudo? ¿con qué acciones?
¿cómo al bien no me inclino? ¿con qué estrellas?

Scarcely shall I find his light, if that of earth
holds my attention: oh, how greatly errs
35   he who imagines that he can reach heaven
by walking with his eyes fixed upon the ground!
Just action, yearning for repentance are what
guide one to immortal peace in mortal war.
Should impetuosity snatch it from me . . .
40   *a sad thing it would be and yet possible.*

Possible, yet in the gulf of such long
torment the soul, which does not cease to wander,
fearing to sink beneath the heavy burden,
does not throw from the heart that which weighs it down?
45   Possible, yet desire does not prevent
my following after reason with sufficient haste
that I may reach the point of my salvation?
Possible, yet I sleep, laugh and seek pleasure?

Possible, and yet I do not try to flee
50   from myself, so that, triumphing over myself,
I may enter the celestial city's fold,
bearing bow of gold and palm of diamond?
Possible, and yet with anguish and pure tears
I do not seek at each moment to avert
55   the dreadsome threat of the supreme of Judges?
Possible, yet I love what eyes can see?

Have pity on me, boundless God! for the heat
of your wrath I endeavor to extinguish
by traveling the sea my cry unsettles,
60   much more than by heaven's deed, through my own eyes.
But what illusions, what figments, what forces
are these that cloud the glasses of my fancies?
Anxieties, wherefore do I stir my heart?
What my deed, what my concern, what my delight?

65   If only he is king who rules his passion
and a slave the king, if these rule over him,
how can I not find the power? By what means?
How can I not incline to good? By what fate?

Si en el arbitrio están las elecciones,
70   ¿cómo la injusta, o celo, no atropellas?
Temo la llama, ¿y no me anego en llanto?
Loco debo de ser, pues no soy santo.

La memoria renueva el dolor
(Sonetos dobles fúnebres)

Cayó en tierra mi amable y dulce esposa,
y en su caída al cielo se levanta;
lloro su triste ausencia, cuando canta
la eterna aurora su quietud gloriosa.
5   De un mundo a otro sube victoriosa,
dejándome su amor con gloria tanta
que mientras vela a sombra de azul planta
me da la firme luz de que reposa.
Del amor levantamos más el vuelo,
10   yo en sustentarlo en mí con su memoria,
ella en darle alas por volar al cielo.
Tanto me vence su ideal victoria,
que, solo en mi gran pena, hallo el consuelo
de conocer que aun es mayor su gloria.
15   ¿Ya te partiste, o cuerda esposa amada,
de esta vida inconstante y trabajosa,
en alma pura a la ciudad gloriosa
y en bulto blanco a funeral morada?
¡Qué señoril, qué afable, que amorosa
20   gobernabas mi casa! ¡Y qué amorosa
tristezas me alivió tu vista hermosa!
y hoy me las llegas más, de mí apartada.
Limpio amor nos tuvimos, no amor ciego
de atender a las cosas de la tierra,
25   sino a las que tu alma dan sosiego.
Anhelo a la quietud que en sí te encierra
porque con humos de tu amor soy fuego
y cuando estás en paz, yo estoy en guerra.

Tres prendas de ti tuve: una contigo
30   está en la luz y en sombras dos conmigo,
porque cuando en el cielo hallas al día
a mí se me hace noche el alegría.

If it lies within my power to make choices
70 why, O faith, do you not blot out the wrong one?
I fear the flame, yet do not drown myself in tears?
I must be a fool, since I am not a saint.

Memory renews pain
(Double sonnets of mourning)

She fell to earth, my sweet and lovely wife,
and having fallen rises up to heaven;
I weep for her sad absence, when eternal
dawn sings of her glorious tranquillity.
5   She mounts victorious to another world,
leaving to me her love with such a splendor
that, whilst watching over with a blue plant's shade,
it sheds me the steady light in which she rests.
We set our love upon a loftier flight,
10   I, through her memory, sustaining it in me,
she, by giving it wings to fly to heaven.
Her ideal victory overwhelms me so,
that, alone in my great grief, I find comfort
in knowing that her glory is the greater.
15   Have you now gone, O wife, discreet and loved,
from this life of inconstancy and travail,
as a pure soul to the glorious city
and in white form to funereal abode?
How like a queen, how kindly, how modestly
20   you ordered my household and how lovingly
your pretty sight dispelled my troubled moments!
Today, since far from me, you bring them closer.
A spotless love we had, not love made blind
through attendance on the matters of the earth,
25   rather upon those which grant your soul its peace.
I long for that quietude which encloses you,
for with the smoke rising from your love I burn
and while you are at peace, I am in midst of war.

I had three pledges from you: one is with you
30   in the light and two with me in the shadows,
because, while you in the heavens find the day,
for me all joyousness is turned into night.

Alabanza jocosa a la Ley santísima en la fábrica de la sinagoga

Gran casa tiene la Ley,
¡oqué enamorados halla!
¿quién duda que son ilustres,
pues entran en tan gran casa?

5   Hasta los jueces del pueblo
han dado en galantearla,
mostrándose muy celosos,
viendo que con todos anda.

Timbre y no mancha le es esto,
10   pues por recóndita causa
cuando más galanes tiene
entonces es más honrada.

Dios en su primer carrera
de la vida la hizo planta,
15   para que en carrera tal
fuese del mundo alcanzada.

Luchando la echó en el suelo
la Justicia, por la gracia
que en el cielo está mirando
20   cómo en la tierra la tratan.

Much afligen a Israel
los pueblos que a la Ley hallan
tan fuerte de condición,
que él solo puede llevarla.

25   Fúndanse en la Ley las leyes
que pisa Israel, y aclama
a la que compra con sangre
por no querer-la de gracia.

Del contagio inmundo hizo
30   cuarentena el que del agua
fue sacado, por mostrarse
hombre de Ley y palabra.

•   •   •   •   •

In lighthearted praise of the holy Law in the foundation of the Synagogue

The Law has such a great house—
oh, look what suitors she does have!
Who can doubt they are illustrious,
since on such a grand house they call?

5   Even the judges of the people
have engaged in wooing her,
showing themselves very jealous
at seeing her go to everyone.

This brings her credit not dishonor,
10   since for a close-hidden reason
the more gallants that she possesses
the more greatly is she honored.

God in his first creative act
made her the plant of life,
15   so that by means of her pursuit
it would be gained by all the world.

With a struggle, Justice felled her
by a graceful stroke of fortune,
for he in heaven is watching
20   to see how on earth they treat her.

Israel is sorely afflicted
by the peoples who find the Law
to be so strong of character
that Israel alone can take her.

25   On the Law are founded the laws
in which Israel walks and they praise
the Law they freely buy with blood,
for not loving the grace-ful one.

He who was drawn from the water
30   set up a ''quarantine'' against
the foul contagion, to show himself
a man of Law and of his word.

•   •   •   •   •

Leche la llama Esaías
porque aun la ciencia más cana
35   con ella es niña de teta
y a pechos toma enseñarla.

Agua la nombra el profeta
citado por lo que apaga
la encendida culpa en cuantos
40   se ve clara como el agua.

Arbol de vidas, trae copa
de salvación al que la alza,
por ser de tan buena cepa
que su vino en la Ley saca.

45   Es desleído el que dice
''no leí en la Ley santa,''
ni sabe cuántos son cinco
el que sus libros no alcanza.

Confiésala a ojos cerrados
50   en la *Semah* el que la exalta,
en la *Amidah* a pies juntillas
y en la *Teba* a voz alzada.

Vivica al que la honra
y al que la desprecia mata,
55   muy por la hoja de Ley
y muy por la Ley de Espada.

•   •   •   •   •

Mucho se ha dado a la vida
con resolución tan rara
que a cuantos mueren por ella
60   al punto con Dios los manda.

Atrévese al que la escribe
a zurrarle la badana,
y al que la guarda en la vida
Dios lo agradece en el alma.

Isaiah calls her the "milk"
because even most learned age
35   is with her as a child at breast
and takes it to heart to teach her.

The prophet calls her the "water,"
so-called by the way she douses
the burning sin in those in whom
40   one may see as clear as water.

Tree of life, she brings salvation's
branchy bowl to those who raise her,
because they are of such good stock
they draw their vintage from the Law.

45   It is an ill-read man who says:
"I have not read the holy Law";
nor does he know how many books
make five who does not grasp her books.

He acknowledges her with blind faith
50   who exalts her in the *Shema,*
holding ground in the *Amidah,*
and with voice raised in the *Teba.*

She grants life to him who honors
and death to him who scorns her,
55   deadly is the blade of the Law—
deadly for the Law of the Blade.

•   •   •   •   •

To life she is so devoted
with such rare determination
that everyone who dies for her
60   at once she sends to dwell with God.

He who copies out the Law dares
to lay his hand upon her skin
and he who in life maintains her
God keeps his soul with gratitude.

65   La letra que entra con sangre
en la divina enseñanza
saca Israel con tal sello
que de Dios es aceptada.

      Es hermosa como el sol
70   por las líneas en que aclara
los ojos a letra vista
que Dios en el cielo paga.

      David, Pinhas, Mosseh, Aaron
son con los tres patriarcas
75   sus planetas, y sus signos
los doce pueblos de marca.

      Miren si se da a temer,
por Dios que es beldad del alma
pues nadie prueba su fuerza
80   que señalado no salga.

      Esto aun las piedras lo saben
desde que por cierta causa
todos los diez mandamientos
le pusieron en la cara.

85   Al vario son de los tiempos
que sus maravillas cantan,
si no es el pueblo de Dios,
los demás hacen mudanzas.

      Anda por toda la tierra
90   tan valentona de fama,
que solamente con sello
deja a la gente cortada.

      No duda el hacer milagros
cn la gente que la alaba,
95   porque el fuego de Dios
sacó los humos de santa.

65   The letters which at cost of blood
become inscribed in holy teaching
Israel transcribes with such true print
that by God they are accepted.

She is beautiful as the sun
70   in the lines through which she lights up
the eyes with open letters,
which God in heaven later pays.

David, Phinehas, Moses, Aaron,
jointly with the three Patriarchs,
75   are all her planets, and her signs
the twelve tribes of distinguished *marque*.

See whether she gives cause to fear
because of God, the soul's beauty,
for none that dare to test his strength
80   come unmarked from the encounter.

Even the stones know this is true,
since for a certain reason
all of the Ten Commandments
thrust themselves into their face.

85   To the varied song of the seasons
that sing her wonders' praises,
if this is not God's own people,
all else performs a changing dance.

She wanders the wide world over,
90   so boastful of her honor that
she only puts her seal upon
the people that is fitly cut.

She doubts not she can do wonders
through the people that praises her,
95   because the fire of God has drawn
the smoke from a holy nation.

A nadie pareció fácil
aunque a todos hace cara,
y por esto cada día
100   tienen con ella palabras.

Bien lo conoció Moisén
pues porque fuese guardada
ordena en su testamento
la pusiesen en el arca.

105   Es con sabios entendida,
con políticos urbana,
y del mundo tan señora
como el Señor criada.

Es mujer de letras tales,
110   que los que anhelan su patria
andan en puntos con ella
por ser gente de esperanza.

Tan enigma de Dios viene
115   que sólo Israel la alcanza,
vestida de sempiterna,
y no de tela pasada.

Con la escala de Jacob
en luz del divino alcázar,
su azul puerta da la llave
120   de los que tiene por guardias.

Son maravillas de Ley
los siete que en Carpentania
mueren de su amor en fuego
por dar luz de su constancia.

125   La Inquisición, de diez cuernos
bestia, al pueblo santo ultraja
con cuernos siete en Hesperia
y con tres en Lusitania.

To no one she appears easy,
although she turns her face to all,
and it is for this reason that
100   every day they speak with her.

Moses was familiar with this,
for, so that she should be kept well,
he ordered in his testament
that they should put her in the ark.

105   With wise men she is learned,
with wordly men urbane,
and she is as much a mistress
of the world as handmaid of God.

She is such a lettered lady
110   that those who desire her kingdom
struggle with her point by point,
since they are the hopeful people.

So much is she God's mystery
that only Israel can reach her,
115   being clothed in everlasting
and not in cloth whose prime is past.

By means of Jacob's ladder,
lit by the heavenly fortress,
her blue door opens to the key
120   of those she regards her keepers.

The seven of Carpentania
are wondrous emblems of the Law;
for love of her they died in fire
to blaze abroad their constancy.

125   The Inquisition, the ten-horned
beast, offends the holy people
with seven horns in Hesperia
and three in Lusitania.

Los dos mancebos de Osuna
130   la Ley envía a las brasas,
porque en palma como Fénix
de sus cenizas renazcan.

Los tres que Lisboa quema
vivos no temen las brasas,
135   porque ara de Ley su amor
a Dios con el fuego llama.

Inquisidores desmiente
aunque disculparlos traza
por tan niños de doctrina
140   que se destetan con Papas.

A los ídolos deshace
y a la gente que los labra
con tan falsos testimonios
que aun a Dios se los levanta.

145   Dio fía su casa a quien
con hacienda de Ley se halla
tan parecido a la orden
celeste que nunca acaba.

Tres veces de Pascua al año
150   en su templo a todos llama,
por ser tal que a Dios se da
el que viene a festejarla.

De rigurosas tormentas
al pueblo saca en dos tablas,
155   y a Pinhas el sacerdocio
ganar hace por su lanza.

Mucho en *Sebuot* se huelgan
los que la ven de Dios dada,
porque entonces los recibe
160   con una cara de Pascua.

The Law sent to the brazier
130   the two youths of Osuna
so in victory like the Phoenix
they would be reborn from ashes

The three that Lisbon burned alive
did not fear the glowing brazier
135   because the altar of the Law
calls them to sacrifice to God.

She gives inquisitors the lie,
though she contrives to excuse them
as being so childish in doctrine
140   that they are weaned on "paps."

She wreaks destruction on idols
And on the people that fashion them,
bearing such false witness that they
even raise them up to gods.

145   God trusts his house to those
that are so rich in Law that they
are close to the celestial
order that never will be ended.

On three pilgrim days in the year,
150   she calls all Jews to her temple,
since he who comes to court her is
as one who gives himself to God.

The people from harshest torments
she rescues on two rafts of stone,
155   and through the lance of Phinehas
she bestows on him the priesthood.

At *Shavuot* they much rejoice
to see her given them by God,
because she then receives them all
160   with a face wreathed in "Paschal" smiles.

Con balanza en *Kipur* viene,
con *Pesah* sus triunfos canta,
por una a trompa tañida
y por otra a mano alzada.

165   Siempre la traen entre ojos
y en bocas los que declaran
que Dios porque la conozcan
con el dedo la señala.

Anduvo muy de caída
170   el día que fue quebrada,
y por eso grita el pueblo
cuando alguno la levanta.

Aunque no es muy entendida,
se precia de bien mirada
175   y de hablar siempre verdad,
con tener setenta caras.

Enseñándose al que espera,
por esmerarlo en su gracia,
es su boca de rubíes
180   y sus ojos de esmeralda.

•   •   •   •   •

Vestida a las maravillas
por el amor que la exalta,
a sus amantes recibe
con una cara de Pascua.

185   Por escritura da fe
de Dios en las líneas sacras,
donde por estar bien vista,
es de todos ojeada.

Cañas es cuando se pone
190   en las puertas de las casas,
porque en un *Semá Israel*
le digan de Dios palabras.

On *Yom Kippur* she brings the scales,
sings at *Pesach* of her triumphs;
the first marked with the trumpet's blast,
the second with a hand held high.

165   They carry her between the eyes
and on the lips those that declare her,
for so that they shall know her well,
God points her out with a finger.

She fell helter-skelter downward
170   on the day when she was broken,
and thus the people shout out loud
when any person lifts her up.

Though she is not well understood,
she boasts she is well looked upon
175   and that she always tells the truth
since she has seventy faces.

Showing herself to him that waits,
hoping to shine in her favors,
her mouth of rubies is composed
180   and her eyes of emeralds.

•   •   •   •   •

Bedecked in marvelous attire
by those that through love exalt her
she receives her would-be husbands
with a face wreathed in "Paschal" smiles.

185   In writing she pledges her word,
given by God in holy lines,
for which being so good to behold,
she is looked up and down by all.

Encased she is when she is placed
190   on the doorposts of their houses,
so that in *Shema Israel*
they shall declare the words of God.

Buenos desposados tiene
en los himnos de Cabañas
195 donde haciéndole gran fiesta,
todos la traen en las palmas.

Cuando los llaman a *sefre*
a fe que les cuesta cara,
porque ella se paga sólo
200 de los que della se pagan.

Nadie quiere que la enmiende:
demos a los jueces gracias,
que la saben ministrar,
con ser ella la que manda.

Providencia particular de Dios sobre Israel

Proposición

Dos favores al pueblo más sublime
hace la Omnipotencia sin segunda:
con piedad uno cuando lo redime,
con justicia otro cuando a Egipto inunda.
5 La competencia de ambos no se exime
de echar a los juicios su coyunda
para inquirir cuál de los dos favores
del sumo Protector de más fulgores.

Respuesta

Con ardiente columna el Señor guía
10 al israelita y al egipcio ciega,
tanto que el roto mar con saña fría
al uno paso da y al otro anega:
pune al agua la injusta tiranía
que mucho niño hebreo al Nilo entrega,
15 y premia el fuego gente que a Dios clama,
porque no adora a la balante llama.

She has a happy wedding day
praised in hymns at Tabernacles,
195 when, making a great feast for her,
they all with their palms acclaim her.

When they are called up to the *sifre*,
it for certain costs them dearly,
because she is repaid only
200 by those who pay love's dues to her.

Nobody she wants to change her:
let us give thanks to the judges
for knowing how she should be served,
for she is the one who rules us.

God's special providence towards Israel

Proposition:

The Omnipotence who has no rival grants
two favors to his high-exalted people:
the one of mercy when he redeems them,
the other of justice when he drowns Egypt.
5 The fittingness of each does not exempt us
from harnessing our powers of judgment
to ascertain which of these of the supreme
Protector's favors is the more resplendent.

Response:

With a burning column the Lord guides both
10 the Israelite and the blind Egyptian,
so that the parted sea with a cold anger
gives way to the one and destroys the other:
water punishes the unjust tyranny
that casts to the Nile many a Hebrew child,
15 and fire rewards the people who call on God,
because they will not adore the bleating flame.

Mayor es la piedad del Rey eterno
cuando salva que su justicia cuando
castiga, porque nunca tiene interno
20   odio al que está sus fueros quebrantando:
peca Adán y el Señor le muestra externo
rigor, por el jardín que paseando
viene, para que tenga espacio el hombre
de que el pecar más que el morir le asombre.

25   En Egipto empezó la idolatría
y en ella peligró el hebreo tanto,
que fue piedad de la soberanía
de Dios librarle del egipcio encanto,
y la justicia punir la alevosía
30   del cocodrilo egipcio que con planto
tierno, llamando al dócil pasajero,
lo aparta del camino verdadero.

Así parece que favor más puro
hace al hebreo el Padre soberano
35   en punir el dragón de Egipto impuro
que en redimirlo de enlazante mano;
porque no es tanto el cautiverio duro
como negar a Dios el egipciano.
pues la prisión del cuerpo es triste calma
40   y el ídolo es oscuro mal del alma.

Pero sin duda que favor más raro
hace el Señor a la elegida gente
en redimirlo del egipcio avaro
que en vengarlo del bárbaro inclemente;
45   puesto que el Señor Dios es sol y amparo
del que le implora y del que penitente
ve que gloria mayor el pueblo alcanza
con la soltura que con la venganza.

Enseña la rabínica doctrina
50   que Micael, de la piedad glorioso
ángel, delante del Señor camina
más que el de la justicia presuroso:

Greater is the mercy of the eternal
King when he saves than his justice when he
punishes, because he never holds within
20 rancor towards him who breaks his statutes:
Adam sins and the Lord shows him external
harshness through the garden where he walking
comes, so that man might have the time and space
to go more in fear of sinning than of death.

25 It was in Egypt idolatry began
and in it the Hebrew wandered, so much so
that it was mercy on the part of God
to release him from the Egyptian spell,
and justice to chastise the perfidiousness
30 of the Egyptian crocodile, who with tears
that touch the heart lures the innocent traveler
and leads him aside from his true pathway.

Thus it appears that the sovereign Father
bestows a truer favor on the Hebrew
35 by punishing the foul Egyptian dragon
than by redeeming him from the binding hand;
because harsh captivity is not as bad
as the Egyptian's denial of God,
for the body's bondage is a woeful calm
40 but idols a dark affliction of the soul.

But without doubt the Lord grants a favor
of greater worth to his elected people
in redeeming them from the mean Egyptian
than in avenging them of the cruel heathen;
45 since the Lord God is a sun and shelter
to him who entreats him and who, penitent,
sees that the people gain a greater blessing
through their release than through their being avenged.

The discourses of the Rabbis teach us
50 that Michael, the angel of most glorious
mercy, walks before the presence of the Lord,
and not he who executes swift justice:

porque aquél con dos alas encamina
al pueblo, en claro día nebuloso
55   pilar; éste a Daniel vuela con una,
de mar oscuro fúlgida columna.

Y la piedad de Dios es dos piedades
como de Micael son dos las alas,
una librando de penalidades
60   al pueblo y otra de inmundicias malas:
dale así dos gloriosas libertades
el sumo Rey de las celestes salas,
una del cuerpo con su mano interna,
otra del alma con su Ley eterna.

65   Además de volar Gabriel tan poco
con un ala, su vuelo y voz detiene
cuando va contra algún dominio loco,
cuando a dar de otros las señales viene:
no gusta de hacer daño, ni tampoco
70   Micael, que oprimido Judá pene,
porque entonces con brío soberano
defendiendo a Judá, mata al tirano.

Por industria de Amán el peregrino
pueblo acabara en el sangriento plazo,
75   si por medio de Ester el Rey divino
no lo librara del violento brazo:
esta clemencia en auxiliar camino
supera a la justicia que echó el lazo
al de Amalec, pues sube al azul velo
80   y la misericordia sobre el cielo.

Muchos cien miles libra en el sagrado
pueblo el Señor de fúnebres martirios
al matar por su orden nuncio alado
ciento y ochenta y cinco mil asirios:
85   pues el número excede del librado
reino judaico al de los muertos sirios,
más gran favor del alto Rey alcanza
en librar Israel que en la venganza.

because the first with two wings guides the people
on their way, a cloudy pillar in bright day's
55   midst; the second flies with one to Daniel,
a resplendent column from the dim dark sea.

And the mercy of God is yet two mercies,
as the wings of Michael are in number two,
one freeing the people from calamities,
60   and the other one from vile uncleanness:
thus the supreme King of the celestial halls
bestows upon them two glorious freedoms,
one of the body with his internal hand,
and one of the soul with his eternal Law.

65   Besides the fact that Gabriel cannot fly far
with one wing, he holds in check his flight and voice
when he goes forth against some mad dominion
or when he comes to give warnings of others:
Nor does Michael delight to cause the slightest
70   hurt, for when Judah is oppressed he suffers,
because in defending Judah with supreme
valor, he then is forced to kill the tyrant.

Through Haman's scheming labors the wandering
people would have ended on that bloody date,
75   if by the means of Esther the divine King
had not freed them from that arm of violence:
this clemency is a better means of help
than the act of justice which threw the noose
round that son of Amalek, since it ascends
80   the veil of blue and mercy reigns in heaven.

Many hundred thousands in the sacred town
the Lord frees from lamentable martyrdom,
when a winged envoy kills by his command
one hundred, four score and five thousand Syrians:
85   since the number of the Jewish kingdom's saved
exceeds that of the Assyrian dead,
the highmost King grants her a greater favor
by freeing Israel than by his vengeance.

       De la verdad es ángel saludable
90   Rafael en la mano omnipotente
     que Uriel, de la paz ángel estable,
     examina a su luz el obediente:
     allí cura, aquí une el admirable
     Autor; y es a Israel más conveniente
95   favor sanar y unir los corazones
     que el de anegar egipcios escuadrones.

       Conserva la justicia por temida
     lo que la paz aumenta por amada,
     y así désta la ayuda es más crecida
100 cuando de aquélla más feroz la espada.
     Con el arco de paz a la afligida
     familiar alivia la piedad sagrada
     y con la Ley de la verdad alumbra
     al que, si a Dios se humilla, a Dios se encumbra.

105   Si su misericordia más no fuera
     que su justo rigor, no amonestara
     al pueblo que huya de la culpa fiera
     porque el arrepentido siempre ampara.
     Luego si a la justicia así supera
110 la clemencia, merced es más preclara
     redimir que vengar al que no es fuerte,
     porque lo uno da vida y lo otro muerte.

       Brilla Gabriel en noche tenebrosa
     y al campo faraónico deslumbra
115 del Mar Rojo columna luminsoa
     con que el Señor al pueblo suyo alumbra:
     y esta merced aunque es tan prodigiosa
     ante de la verdad más se le encumbra
     el favor que on nube al pueblo salva
120 en el margen que a verlo sale el alba.

       El templo Amstelodamo se parece
     al de Jerusalén en la hermosura
     y en la grandeza, donde resplandece
     con luces de oraciones la Ley pura;

Angel of truth, bringer of salvation is
90   Raphael who stands at the all-powerful hand,
while Uriel, of peace the constant angel,
examines by his light all those who serve him:
there healing, here uniting the admirable
Author moves, and it is a far more fitting
96   favor to Israel to heal and unite hearts
than to engulf all the Egyptian squadrons.

Justice keeps and preserves by being feared
that which peace, through being loved, increases,
and thus this second's aid is the more increased
100   when the sword of the first is more ferocious.
With the bow of peace the sacred mercy
alleviates the suffering family
and with the Law of truth it enlightens those
whom, if once bowed to God, it will raise up to him.

105   If his lovingkindness were no greater than
the rigor of his justice, he would not warn
his people that they should flee from vile sin,
for he always aids them that have repented.
Therefore, if clemency is thus superior
110   to justice, it is a more signal mercy
to redeem the weak than to avenge their wrong,
because the one grants life and the other death.

Gabriel shines brightly in the gloomy night
and Pharaoh's camp is left in dazed confusion
115   by a luminous column on the Red Sea,
through which the Lord illumines his own people:
and though this mercy is a prodigious wonder,
it is more uplifted in the scale of truth
by the favor of the cloud which saves the people
120   at the brink, for then comes the dawn to view it.

The temple that stands in Amsterdam resembles
that which stood in Jerusalem in beauty
and in grandeur, and in it brightly shines
the pure Law lit up by the lights of prayers;

125 comenzó cuando al holandés ofrece
horrores del francés la guerra dura,
y al *Kahal Kadós* que por piedad sagrada
se libra al fin de la francesa espada.

Al pueblo de Israel es mayor gloria
130 vivir seguro entre hórridos contrarios
con templo celestial y Ley notoria,
que con el exterminio de adversarios:
de lo libre sale la victoria
que espantó a los egipcios temerarios,
135 luciendo a vista de enemigos duros
que tienen de su luz males oscuros.

Pregón harmónico del Día del Juicio

No busco a la pompa humana,
sí a la divina grandeza,
que en el teatro del tiempo
hace al mundo su apariencia.

5 Los Días Penitenciales
le dedico, porque puedan
hacer noche a los pecados
con luz de la penitencia.

¿Quién no tiembla cuando Dios
10 en su tribunal se asienta,
llamando a juicio el mundo
para que el mundo lo tenga?

En todas sus obras bueno,
justo en todas sus carreras,
15 metiendo en un puño al cielo,
con el pie manda a la tierra.

Toma en Libra su balanza
donde aún lo más leve pesa:
¿quién vendrá a pesar de culpas
20 que a pesar de culpas venga?

125   it was begun when the Dutch were suffering
the horrors of harsh war at the Frenchman's hand
and the *Kahal Kadosh* too, who through divine
mercy were freed at last from the sword of France.

       For Israel's people it is a greater boon
130   to live secure amid cruel hostility
with a heavenly temple and well-known Law
than to have all her enemies extinguished;
for out of freedom comes forth the victory
that caused the brazen Egyptian to quake,
135   shining in the full face of harsh enemies
who suffer hidden woes through its dazzling light.

A rhythmical prayer for Judgment Day

       I do not seek the pomp of men,
rather the grandeur which is God's,
for he appears before the world
on the eternal stage of time.

5   It is to him I dedicate
these Penitential Days, so that
they, by the light of penitence,
may into darkness cast my sins.

       Who does not tremble when the Lord
10   sits upon his tribunal seat
and calls all the world to judgment,
so judgment they might learn to have.

       Good is the Lord in all his works
and just in all his proceedings;
15   holding the heavens in his grasp,
he commands the earth at his feet.

       Like Libra he holds his balance,
in which the lightest sins are weighed:
who will come to have his sins weighed,
20   despite the sins that weigh him down?

Quien juzga el castigo acaso
se juzga sabio y es bestia,
pues de sí dice ignorancias,
cuando de sí, Dios, sentencias.

25   En junta de ángeles brilla
y entre jueces trae diadema,
¿en qué cuenta no caerá
el que corre por su cuenta?

Quién en el coche del tiempo
30   puede atrás volver sus ruedas,
cuando el mundo es todo espacio
y toda la vida es priesa?

De fuerzas se arman las gentes
por defender lo que observan:
35   ¿quién fuera del pueblo santo
a no juzgar Dios de fuera?

Al que sin verdad lo invoca
responde en su fortaleza
con dos piedras en la mano
40   por ser de Ley las dos piedras.

Da de justicia castigo
y perdona de clemencia:
¿quién le va apenas con llanto
que le va con llanto a penas?

45   ¿Quién huirá de su justicia
cuando todo cine y media,
cerca Dios del que lo llama
por verse de todo cerca?

Los penitentes le llevo
50   por la primicia más cierta,
de materia que habla en forma,
de forma que habla en materia.

He who thinks to judge God's justice
is not a wise man but a fool,
for he reveals his ignorance,
while from God comes only wisdom.

25   He shines amid the angel host
and among judges wears the crown;
who can fail to meet his reckoning
by reckoning to flee from it?

Who can turn back the wheels of time
30   that bear his carriage ever on,
when all the world is vain delight
and all of life is frantic haste?

The nations arm themselves with might
to defend what they believe in:
35   what would happen to God's people,
were he not out there to judge them?

From his citadel he replies
to him who calls his Name in vain
with two stones given by his hand,
40   for Tablets of the Law are they.

His punishment is justly dealt
and with clemency he pardons:
who comes to him with scarce a tear?—
with tears he meets his punishment.

45   Who will try to flee his justice,
when all things he girds and measures?
For God is near to him who calls,
since he is near to all that is.

I guide the penitents to him,
50   as the truest first-fruit offering,
of matter heard in ritual form,
of form that through base matter speaks.

¡Nobles jueces! pues sois ojos
del sumo Rey, ved la ofrenda:
55   ardará en las siete luces
que tiene Dios a su mesa.

¡Oyela, pueblo prudente!
así te oiga y defienda
Dios, con la espada de Ley
60   que la Ley de Espada quiebra.

No se vio hierro en la obra
del Templo santo y no es buena
la obra del que con yerros
en el sacro templo entra.

65   Tan sin fruto y con dolor
espira el que vive a ciegas,
que quien lo venda no halla
cuando halla quien lo venda.

Buscar a Dios es hallarlo,
70   huir de culpas, vencerlas,
y la nueva desta vida
es entrar en vida nueva.

Acto sexto de contrición

Dios nuestro y Dios de nuestros padres puro,
nuestra oración delante de ti venga;
no te encubras de nuestra rogativa,
porque no con audacia ni con duro
5   pecho, de la disculpa nos valemos
para que tu clemencia nos reciba
y a tu vista arrogantes pronunciemos
que somos justos y que no pecamos;
mas todos, nuestros yerros confesamos,
10   afligidos, postrados, temerosos,
humillados, contritos y llorosos.

Noble judges, the eyes of the
Supreme King, look at the offering!
55 It will burn in the seven lamps
that illuminate God's table.

Listen to her, prudent people!
So may God hear you and defend
you with the sword of the Law,
60 which crushes the Law of the Sword.

They used no iron when they wrought
the Temple, and it is not right
that he who has wrought evil deeds
should enter the sacred temple.

65 So profitless and painful is
the death of him who blindly lives
that, eyes bound, he will not find God,
when he finds him who binds his eyes.

To search for God is to find him,
70 to flee from sin to conquer it,
and the good news that this life brings
is that we can start life anew.

Sixth act of contrition

Our God and God of our fathers, perfect,
permit our prayers to come before you;
do not hide yourself from our beseeching,
because we do not in brazenness nor
5 with hardened heart assume forgiveness,
so that you in clemency receive us
and that we in your sight arrogantly
say that we are righteous and have not sinned;
rather do we confess we all have sinned,
10 afflicted, prostrated, in awesome dread,
humbled, contrite, in tears of affliction.

Cometimos pecados diferentes
a imitación de nuestros ascendientes;
robamos, delinquimos fraudelentos,
15   deshonramos lascivos y violentos,
hicimos atorcer, maleficiamos,
aconsejamos mal, prevaricamos,
fuimos soberbios, falsos, mentirosos,
inobedientes, cautos y dañosos;
20   al bueno y al sapiente aborrecimos,
al devoto y al recto escarnecimos,
con cerviz dura al débil angustiamos,
de tus sendas al simple desviamos,
ciegos erramos y pecar hicimos,
25   abominamos y rebeldes fuimos.

Confesámoslo todo en los tormentos
del cautiverio horrible y dilatado;
perdona al pueblo aflito a ti postrado:
ve que lloramos cuantos maleficios
30   nos hicieron quitar de tus juicios,
que nada nos guió el aviso santo
hasta sentir la pena en el quebranto.

Sobre los que nos juzgan eres justo
y anduvimos nosotros en lo injusto:
35   ¿qué diremos delante de ti, ansiosos,
sino que fuimos torpes y alevosos?
¡Da, o Morador de célicas alturas,
la maná del perdón a tus criaturas!
Tú lo encubierto y descubierto sabes,
40   en tu mano del mundo están las llaves,
todo lo abarcas sabio y poderoso:
perdona al pueblo misericordioso,
líbranos de pecados y prisiones,
por pedirte contritos nos perdones.

We have committed many divers sins
in imitation of our ancestors;
we have robbed, we have deceitfully transgressed,
15   we have shamefully and grossly defamed,
we have led astray, we have corrupted,
we have counseled evil and defaulted,
we have been proud, dishonest, deceitful,
disobedient, reluctant and hurtful;
20   the good and the wise we have abhorred,
the devout and the righteous we have mocked,
we have, stiff-necked, caused the weak affliction,
we have led the simple from your pathways,
we have blindly erred and made to sin,
25   we have hated and have been rebellious.

We confess all this amid the torments
of our dreadful, too-long captivity;
forgive the afflicted race before you bowed:
see how we lament the many evils
30   that made us turn away from your judgments,
for in no way did holy counsel guide us,
until we in our undoing felt the pain.

Above all who judge us you are most just
and we who have walked in unrighteousness:
35   what shall we, uneasy, say before you
but that we have been foolish and deceived?
Grant, O you who dwell in celestial heights,
the manna of pardon to your creatures.
You know both the hidden and the revealed,
40   in your hand you hold the keys of the world,
wise and powerful, you embrace it all:
pardon compassionately your people,
free us from our sins and our enslavements,
since we humbly beg that you forgive us.

Acto séptimo de contrición

En que se dan las causas de ser agradable a Dios las lágrimas del
penitente y de que cometiendo diferentes culpas las diferentes
partes del cuerpo, solamente la de los ojos paga por todas con
lágrimas.

> ¡Señor del mundo! mundo soy pequeño,
> de ti criado para obedecerte:
> soñéme sol y tierra ya me sueño,
> con ríos que visible cumbre vierte;
> 5   en las culpas lucí y ya en mi despeño
> lo que evaporo en nube se convierte,
> porque cuando las culpas tienen nube
> el llanto entonces a tu gracia sube.

> Considero las causas venturosas
> 10   de agradarte las lágrimas de cuantas
> ánimas, de ofenderte pesarosas,
> flores de perdón buscan en tus plantas;
> el decirlas con ansias lacrimosas
> es pedirte perdón de culpas tantas,
> 15   que a no excederlas tu clemencia pura
> no tuvieran mis lágrimas ventura.

> Sobre el agua de que cubriste al mundo
> se movía tu espíritu sagrado:
> mundo me hiciste vivo y me hice inmundo,
> 20   cubierto con las sombras del pecado:
> ya de lágrimas altas mar profundo,
> gimo a ti, porque oyendo al congojado,
> sólo en las aguas que la vista llueve
> tu purísimo espíritu se mueve.

> 25   En dos partes las aguas dividiste,
> unas sobre los cielos superiores,
> en la cóncava tierra otras pusiste
> para apagar sus hórridos ardores:
> el alma para el cielo en que la hiciste
> 30   tiene baño de aguas interiores,
> y aguas externas lloro en lo contrito
> por apagar las llamas del delito.

Seventh act of contrition

In which it is explained why the tears of the penitent are pleasing to God and why, while different parts of the body commit different sins, it is only the eyes that pay for all of them through tears.

    Lord of the world, a little world am I,
created by you in order to obey you:
I dreamt that I was sun, now that I am earth,
with rivers that the clear-viewed peak pours down;
5   I outshone in sins and now in my downfall
that which I distill is transformed into clouds,
because when sins are as a cloud in number,
then mounts the flood of tears to reach your grace.

    I meditate upon the happy causes
10   that make you take pleasure in the tears of such
souls that, repenting having sinned against you,
seek the flowers of forgiveness at your feet;
to speak of them with tearsome words of anguish
is to ask you for forgiveness for such sins
15   that, were your pure mercy not greater than they,
my tears would not gain their happy fortune.

    Upon the waters with which you covered
the earth your sacred spirit moved about:
you made me a living world and it soils me,
20   enshrouding me in the shadows of sin;
already now become a deep sea of tears,
I cry to you, since, hearing the afflicted,
your purest spirit is only moved to move
upon the waters that the eyes rain down.

25   In two parts you divided the waters,
some to reside in the upper heavens,
the rest you placed in the hollow of the earth
to extinguish the fearsome fires it holds:
the soul, regarding heaven where you made it,
30   has internal waters by which it is bathed,
and in remorse I weep external waters
to extinguish the flames of my transgression.

Gratas te son las lágrimas, por cuanto
el agua simboliza tu clemencia,
35   y manchas lava de la culpa el llanto
en fuente de la justa penitencia:
sólo en la agua tiene húmedo quebranto
el rayo que deshace a la eminencia:
sólo a lavarme en lágrimas me obligo,
40   por detener al rayo del castigo.

Descubriste aguas a la tierra,
y que tienes memoria (David canta)
de que es el hombre polvo, si se encierra
en mar de llanto que al infierno espanta;
45   ya con foso de llanto a infernal guerra,
muro terreno en tu memoria santa,
descubro que tu agrado he conseguido
en ser polvo, de aguas defendido.

Con lágrimas vocíferas del alma
50   a ti vuelvo contrite, ¡o Rey glorioso!
en vela el corazón, la vida en calma,
navego al puerto de perdón dichoso:
si es huir de la culpa triunfal palma
del que busca tu gracia lagrimoso,
55   ya por ir mar veloz a tu amor santo
me arrojo a la corriente de mi llanto.

Vi hermosuras, vi haciendas, vi manjares
que mi carne y demonio y mundo fueron;
vi que por ver mi lengua dio pesares,
60   que mis manos insultos cometieron,
que hice mis brazos de furiosos mares,
que mis pies a pecar siempre corrieron,
y todos por el ver, de tales modos,
que mis lágrimas hoy pagan por todos.

65   Si mis manos entrego a la memoria,
no palpo si no es áspides de horrores,
en sus palmas las líneas de mi historia
con letras que acepté de los errores:

To you tears are pleasing, in as much as
water is symbolic of your clemency,
35   and weeping washes away the stains of sin
in the fountain of a just repentance;
only towards water does the lightning ray
that destroys the peak show watery compassion:
only am I forced to wash myself in tears,
40   so to stop the lightning ray of punishment.

You uncovered the land amongst the waters
and you, so David sings, remember still
that man is as dust, if he covers himself
in a sea of weeping that keeps hell at bay;
45   now with moat of weeping against hell's onslaught,
an earthly dike set in your sacred memory,
I discover that I have gained your pleasure
by being dust, by waters stout defended.

With tears loud uttered from my soul, I return
50   to you in penitence, O glorious King,
my heart on watch aloft, my life becalmed,
I voyage to the port of happy pardon:
if to flee from sinning means the victor's palm
for him who, shedding tears, beseeks your grace,
55   to swiftly scud the sea to your holy love
I now launch into the current of my tears.

I saw beauty, I saw wealth, I saw repasts
that were my flesh, my demon and my world;
I saw that, through seeing, my tongue brought troubles,
60   that my hands committed acts of insult,
that I made great show of deeds like raging sea,
that my feet ran ever headlong after sin,
and all this I did through seeing, in such a way
that today my tears do pay for all of them.

65   If I offer up my hands to memory,
I feel nothing with them but asps of horror,
in their palms the lines of my history, written
with letters of the sins that I accepted:

pagarlas temo y a tu ejecutoria
70   las confieso en tormento de temores;
de tu justicia apelo a tu amor santo
en confesión amarga, en dulce llanto.

Apresuré los pies a la delicia
que me dio la manzana del pecado
75   y al gustarla encontré con la justicia
que me arrojó del Edén de tu agrado:
condénasme a sudar por la caricia
que te hace el ser mi Médico sagrado
y ya aunque amor ve mucho, tiene antojos
80   de que con tu calor sudan mis ojos.

Flamas de culpas en soplante fragua
mi lengua echa si pido que me asista,
y en su defensa el llanto es lengua de agua,
raudal el alma al margen de la vista;
85   si te agrada el llorar cuando lo fragua
la contrición que tu piedad conquista,
no oigas a mi fiscal, porque a tu agrado
con voz del alma el llanto es mi abogado.

No tengo parte en mí que me socorra
90   sino el río que sale por la puente
de los ojos, porque en sus aguas corra
el nido de mi acto penitente;
la infanta egipcia no el trabajo ahorra
de sacar a Moisén de la corriente:
95   porque saques mi alma de quebranto
la llevo en la corriente de mi llanto.

Los ojos postas son que están de vela
en el cuerpo de guardia, con la vista
que para el alma va de centinela
100   y para el apetito de conquista;
mi vida es posta que al error recela
y a tu clemencia pido que me asista,
y para que oyas su terrible espanto,
te dispara el mosquete de mi llanto.

I fear to pay them—in your execution
70 I confess them in torments of fear and dread;
in your court I appeal to your sacred love,
in bitter confession, in sweet lamenting.

I hastened on my feet towards vain pleasures
which placed into my hand the apple of sin,
75 and on tasting it I found, the sentence passed,
that I was cast from the Eden of your grace:
you make me sweat for the tenderness
which is what makes you my holy Physician
and now, though love sees much, it has blind fancies
80 which owing to your heat cause my eyes to sweat.

Flames of past crimes in a bellowing forge
my tongue pours out, if I call on you for help,
and for its defense, tears are tongues of water,
the soul a torrent on the vision's edge;
85 if weeping gratifies you, when contrition,
which achieves your mercy, shapes it on the forge,
be deaf to my accuser, since weeping is
my counsel who with the soul's voice seeks your grace.

There is no part of me that can give me aid,
90 save the river that emerges from the bridge
of my two eyes, so that on its waters rides
the nest that cradles my act of penitence;
the Egyptian princess spares no effort
in rescuing Moses from the current:
95 so that you may rescue my soul from breaking,
I bear it upon the current of my tears.

My eyes are posted sentries who stand on watch
in the body's guard, together with the sight
which sallies forth as sentinel for the soul
100 and the conqueror of raiding appetite;
my life is a guard who fears to make mistake
and I beg assistance of your clemency;
and so you may hearken to its awful dread,
it fires off the musket of my weeping.

105   Agrádate oír la voz llorosa
y piadoso socorres al contrito
porque nunca la víctima olorosa
atiendes como al corazón aflito;
por humillarse a tu piedad gloriosa
110 alcanza Achab perdón de su delito:
ya me humillo con lágrimas, por cuanto
la humildad hace que te agrade el llanto.

    Es propiedad de nobles generales
defender sus soldados delincuentes
115 de los duros ministros criminales
que a su castigo anhelan diligentes:
los ojos por ser guardas principales
del cuerpo, con las armas de dos fuentes,
lo libran de tus iras justicieras
120 en las marchas que siguen tus carreras.

    ¡Ya las sigo, o Señor! suspende enojos,
que por ver a mi lengua, pies y manos
cómplices, solicito con los ojos
librarlos de suplicios inhumanos;
125 el que lleva coléricos arrojos
les da en verse al espejo temples sanos:
porque serenes el airado seno,
un espejo de lágrimas te enseño.

    Das, juzgando entre jueces, el derecho
130 al que toca, y mis ojos, de sí jueces,
a llorar se condenan porque han hecho
pecar la lengua y manos tantas veces;
contemplarte benigno y satisfecho
de tu obra enternece candices:
135 y por esto te agrada el tierno llanto
que de amor nace en fuentes de quebranto.

105   It pleases you to hear the voice of weeping
        and, merciful, you succor the repentant,
        for you never pay the fragrant sacrifice
        as much heed as you do the afflicted heart;
        by humbling himself before your glorious
110   mercy, Ahab gained the pardon for this crime:
        now I humble myself with tears for as much
        as humbleness makes tears acceptable to you.

        It is a fitting thing for noble generals
        to protect their soldiers that have done wrong
115   from the harsh enforcers of the laws of crime
        who diligently pursue their punishment;
        the eyes, since they are the chief among the guards
        of the body, armed with two springs of water,
        deliver it from your justice-wreaking wrath
120   in troop movements that follow down your highroads.

        Those I follow now, O Lord! Stay your anger,
        for, having seen my tongue, my feet and my hands
        act as accomplices, I seek through my eyes
        to set them free from inhuman punishments;
125   he who is prone to angry outbursts wisely
        tempers them on seeing himself in a mirror:
        so that you will pacify your wrathful breast,
        I hold up to you a mirror of tears.

        Judging above all judges, you give judgment
130   on whom it falls, and my eyes, their own judges,
        condemn themselves to weep, because they have caused
        my tongue and my hands so many times to sin;
        guileless souls are moved to pity to behold
        you benign and well contented with your works,
135   and thus you are pleased by the tender weeping
        which from love is born in compassion's fountains.

Imperio de Dios en el teatro universal

Día primero

Resulta el primer día en el rotante
teatro universal con el gobierno
del mundo que jamás tiene un semblante,
sacando los que Dios mira *ab eterno,*
5   Van de la suspensión a lo inconstante
adonde del juicio juez interno,
el concepto de Dios, siempre de un modo,
nunca se altera aunque se altera todo.

Antes de lo criado no hubo antes,
10   sólo hubo Dios, en quien no cabe el hubo,
mirando cuantas cosas emanentes
tendrían el principio que él no tuvo:
en su eterna atención siempre constantes
sin tiempo hasta su tiempo las retuvo,
15   haciéndoles de nada cuando quiso,
prototipo de todas indiviso.

Da luce de su imperio sin segundo
nao o templo de velas bien vestido,
amante el alto del más bajo mundo,
20   en muchas partes junto y dividido.

Por la vuelta del círculo rotundo
contínuamente el día es repetido,
mas a Dios todo como desandado
y lo futuro como lo pasado.

25   Ninguna cosa en nada se resuelve,
pues desde cuando el Ser que en todo luce
hace de nada cuanto en sí se envuelve,
no hay algo que de nada se produce:
con la mudanza sólo a trocar vuelve
30   la forma que a otras formas se reduce;
sólo Dios permanece en un estado
porque siempre es Señor, nunca cridado.

•   •   •   •   •

God's dominion over the theater of the universe

Day one

The first day upon the revolving stage
of the universe ends with the government
of the world, which never shows to us its face,
presenting those whom God from all time has seen.
5   They move from suspended to inconstant state,
one to which the internal judge of judgment—
the concept of God whose nature stays the same—
never, changing, falls, although all things do change.

Before creation came, there was no before,
10   there was only God, in whom there is no "was,"
contemplating how many emergent things
would have the beginning that he did not have:
ever constant under his eternal gaze,
without time until his time retained them,
15   fashioned by him from nothing when he willed it,
he the undivided prototype of all.

His matchless kingdom is endowed with lights
by nave or temple richly decked with candles,
the upper world loving well the lower one,
20   in many zones united and divided.

Through the turning of the round-formed circle
the day is continually repeated,
but for God all is as if it were undone
and what is to be is as what has yet been.

25   No thing can be transmuted into nothing,
since from the time when the Being who shines in all
made from nothing all that is embodied,
there is no thing that is produced from nothing:
with change form only comes to be exchanged
30   and to be reduced to other forms of being;
God alone remains in one state, since he is
ever Lord, never having been created.

•   •   •   •   •

¿Qué más prueba, qué erario más sublime
se halla de ser el mundo comenzado?
35   La "vision deleitable" dar no exime
ejemplo en quien no ve cómo es formado.
Mejor el ángel a Esdrás se lo exprime
porque en el mudo vientre el engendrado
da voz de estar el mundo así suspenso
40   hasta que a luz lo saca el Rey inmenso.

Aristóteles calla, cierra el labio
Platón cuando del mundo da el origen
cuanta dicta razón el amor sabio,
cuantos al alma sacros textos rigen.
45   Son el hombre y el mundo desagravio
de su Autor si estas voces le dirigen
enseñando uno su principio donde
otro por más antiguo el suyo esconde.

Quien por el sueño causa otras figuras
50   suele verlas después como ha soñado,
ejemplo de que el Rey de las alturas
primero ve lo que ha de ser formado
en las del tiempo imágenes futuras,
de suerte lo tenía todo obrado,
55   que con no ser el mundo entonces, era
delante del gran Dios como si fuera.

Monta la voz *teom* pasmo y abismo,
capaz de suspender cuanto le sonda
hasta que el Rey inmenso por sí mismo
60   desata al luminar que al cielo ronda;
clara prueba, constante silogismo
de ser hecha la máquina redonda
por el poder que como en sueño tiene
todo lo que después a formar viene.

65   Así *ab eterno* el sumo Rey ignoto
ve de los elementos que el constante
se mete por el frígido alboroto
en medio de la fábrica rotante;

What greater proof, what treasure more sublime
is to be found than that the world was begun?
35   The "vision of delight" scarce lets us give
example that does not show how it was formed.
The angel explained it best to Esdras,
for in the silent womb the unborn child
proclaims that the world was thus in suspense
40   until the boundless King brought it to the light.

Aristotle is silent, Plato his lips
keeps sealed when the origin of the world is shown
by as much reason as learned love dictates,
by as many holy texts as rule the soul.
45   Man and the world are the vindication
of their Author, if these voices guide him,
each one showing his principle to lie where
another being more ancient hides his own.

He who in dreams creates the forms of others
50   is wont to see them after he has dreamed them,
a living proof that the Lord of the heavens
sees first of all what is to be created
in future images of time to come,
so that he had it all beforetimes wrought;
55   for though the world was not then made, it was
in the great God's mind as if it had been done.

The word *tehom* means convulsion and abyss,
with power to astound all that plumb its depths,
until the boundless God by his own doing
60   unbinds the luminary that roams the heavens;
a clear proof, a perfect syllogism
to demonstrate the round machine was made
by the power who as in a dream retains
all that which he later comes to fashion.

65   Thus *ab eterno* the supreme, unknown King
watches the elements, for the constant One,
striking through the chill confusion sets himself
in the midst of the revolving fabric;

de la universal nave gran piloto,
70   pone al timón espíritu vagante,
las alas del amor, velas cogidas
en el muelle suspenso de las vidas.

Así la general mistión revuelta
que a la presciente eternidad resulta,
75   entre mantillas de cristal envuelta,
con la cobija del pavor se oculta.
Así la Ley que varias dudas suelta
eleva al mundo en impresión adulta,
influyéndole sueño turbulento,
80   cuna la oscuridad y arrullo el viento.

Así las *sefirot* y sus mansiones
se elevan por el Ser independiente,
las esferas así, así las regiones
elementales pasman juntamente.
85   Así es todo confusas suspensiones
hasta que dice Dios omnipotente
"sea luz" y luz es, mas es de modo
que en el principio da criado todo.

Saca del hondo caos el detenido
90   litigio y el Artífice increado
queda en sí mar inmenso recogido,
siempre tranquilo y nunca apasionado:
todo lo exhala y no es disminuido,
todo lo ciñe y no es acrecentado,
95   con ondas de eficientes resplandores,
glorias sus aguas, vidas sus vapores.

Con los rayos del sol las gracias bellas,
partes del año y de su carro alientos,
las sabias horas entre las estrellas,
100   la harmonía de cielos y elementos,
la gentil Hebe echando sus centellas,
la jovial Venus que une pensamientos
a Dios alaban, por el son facundo
que juntas hacen el sarao del mundo.

great pilot of the ship of the universe,
70   he sets at the helm a wandering spirit,
hoists stunsails of love, furling the mainsails
in the harbor where our lives suspended lie.

Thus the general restless embryonic form
which proceeds from the eternal foreknowledge,
75   wrapped around in swaddling bands of crystal,
conceals itself behind a cloak of terror.
Thus the Law which several doubts untangles
raises up the world stamped in an adult mold,
a tumultuous dream its inspiration,
80   darkness its cradle, the wind its lullaby.

Thus the *sefirot* and all their mansions
through the independent Being rise and exult,
thus the spheres and thus the elemental
regions in conjunction stand in wonderment.
85   Thus all is nothing but confused suspension,
until God the omnipotent one utters:
"Let there be light" and light is, but such it is
that "in the beginning" all stands created.

From the deep chaos he removes the long-drawn
90   conflict and the increate Artificer
remains in himself a vast, secluded sea,
ever tranquil, never given to passion:
he exhales all and is not diminished,
he encompasses all and is not increased,
95   with waves of effectual resplendences,
his waters being glories, his vapors lives.

With the rays of the sun, the beautiful graces,
offspring of the year and living breaths that move
its chariot, the learned hours amongst the stars,
100   the harmony of heavens and elements,
graceful Hebe casting round her fiery sparks,
merry-hearted Venus who thoughts unites as one,
all give praise to God with flowing melody
by which they create the whole terrestrial dance.

105 Con voz fragante la encendida rosa,
Arión de hojas en delfín de espinas,
sonora la ave en rama generosa
al dulce son de cuerdas cristalinas,
cuanto puebla con vida presurosa
110 golfos amenos, selvas neptuninas
son de Dios ecos, por tan raros modos
que sin salir de sí, resuena en todos.

La luminosa máquina incesable,
el orden natural maravilloso,
115 el ñudo de elementos agradable,
la obediencia del piélago espumoso,
la variedad del mixto generable,
la hermosura del campo deleitoso,
todo que hay Dios en todo considera,
120 que dentro de sí existe y obra fuera.

 • • • • •

¿Quién sino Dios pudiera componerlo
¿quién sino Dios llegara a publicarlo?
¿quién sino Dios hubiera de proveerlo?
¿quién sino Dios mostrara conservarlo?
125 ¿quién sino Dios supiera comprehenderlo?
¿quién sino Dios bastara a gobernarlo?
y en fin, ¿quién sino Dios desta manera,
no haciendo nada en sí, todo lo hiciera?

Distinguiendo en lo grave y en lo leve
130 del vasto caos la concepción soluble,
el Padre universal que todo mueve
lo llama a junta en lazo indisoluble:
pone medida a cuanto el ser le debe,
pero sin peso al ámbito voluble,
135 prorrumpiendo en su planta y en su mano
el tiempo niño y el amor anciano.

La madre universal naturaleza
y el tiempo sacan la mistión en brazos,
toda manos y ojos su cabeza,
140 toda solturas y su boca lazos;

105   With fragrant voice, the flaming rose, Arion
      of petals riding on a dolphin of thorns,
      the sonorous bird on overflowing branch
      with sweet sound of chords of crystal clarity,
      all that which with urging life inhabits
110   delightful bays and forest-scapes of Neptune
      are echoes of God, in ways so wondrous that he,
      without passing from himself, resounds in all.

      The luminous machine that knows no ceasing,
      the miraculous order of nature,
115   the gratifying union of elements,
      the obedience of the foamy ocean,
      the variety of generated things,
      the beauty of the delightful countryside
      all consider that God exists in all things,
120   for he within himself exists and acts beyond.

      •   •   •   •   •

      Who but God could be able to devise it?
      who but God could manage to publish it?
      who but God could be the one to fit it out?
      who but God could show he would preserve it?
125   who but God could know how to understand it?
      who but God could suffice to govern it?
      and finally, who but God could in this way,
      making nothing in itself, make everything?

      In light and weighty aspects of the vast chaos
130   discerning the conception that could be unleashed,
      the universal Father who all things moves
      bids all convene in indissoluble bond:
      he gives measure to all that owes him being,
      but not weight to the inconstant bounds beyond,
135   and from his stem and from his hand issue forth
      the infant time and love of ancient vintage.

      The universal mother, Nature, and Time
      bring forth the lively bundle in their arms,
      all arms and legs, it seems, its head all eyes,
140   all unleashed motion, its mouth ensnaring charms;

apuntados de incógnita grandeza,
no yerran su papel dándose abrazos,
representando en órdenes veloces
la gran comedia del ''Secreto a voces.''

145   De camino la vida apresurada,
racional planta del vergel rotundo,
en cada hoja tiene una jornada
y en cada paso un entablado mundo.
De capa el cielo y el querube de espada
150   la hacen hasta que Dios, Rey sin segundo,
el enredo deshace del engaño,
la Ley su empeño y su papel el año.

Hablan el Cielo de ángeles vestido,
el Movimiento en varias distinciones,
155   las Virtudes en tálamo lucido,
el Género y Lugar con mutaciones,
el Amor y el Objeto sin vestido,
la Disención y Paz con prevenciones,
el Hado y el Suceso con antojos,
160   con pies la Acción y la pasión sin ojos.

Acto primero: el Ser que todo encierra
sobre cuanto querube vuela lozano
en el cielo se abaja y en la tierra
para ver lo que sale de su mano:
165   de la sabiduría nunca cierra
las puertas al amor que soberano
la galantea sobre el accidente,
luz de su vista, sombra de su mente.

La paz que por tirarles áurea punta
170   carcaj toma en brillante vestuario,
con el arco celeste les apunta
que edificio sostiene extraordinario;
no hay apagarse su amorosa junta
fuego activo, por ser en modo vario
175   para tan grande ardor el mar pequeño
y menor la gran fábrica que el Dueño.

prompted by a greatness that is hidden,
they do not muff their lines, embracing each other,
performing with swift successive changes
the great play "The Secret Told for All to Hear."

145   Traveling on its way, ever-hurried life,
that rational seedling in the spheric garden,
in every "leaf" contains a daylong "act"
and in every step a world set on the stage.
Heaven with cloak and cherub with dagger
150   play it out till God, King without peer,
unties the knot of the play's entanglement,
the Law being his purpose, the year his role.

In it speak: Heaven adorned with angels,
the (spheres') Movement in all its diversity,
155   the Virtues in their shining bridal chamber,
Place and Kind in their various changing garb,
Love and Love's Object without adornment,
Dissension and Peace with their dispositions,
Fate and Events with their capricious whims,
160   Action fleet of foot and Passion blind of eye.

Act One: the Being who all encompasses
upon whatever cherub nimbly flies
lowers himself to heaven and to earth
to see that which has issued from his hand;
165   he never closes the doors of wisdom
to the love with which in his sovereign manner
he favors all accidental nature,
the light of his eyes, the shadow of his mind.

With celestial bow (arch that sustains
170   the whole rare edifice) he aims at them
the kiss of peace, which to fire its golden tip
borrows a quiver from a brilliant wardrobe;
there is no putting out this loving union's
living fire, for in its variable way
175   the sea is too small to match such great ardor,
still less the great construction than its Master.

Córrese el velo de la niebla fría,
canta la luz en coros permanentes
que hace Dios toda con sabiduría,
180   fin de los fines, ente de los entes;
salen la Variedad y Alegría
a su loa por partes diferentes
y en la nube del alta presidencia
descienden la justicia y la clemencia.

185   El Discurso a sus pechos y el Juicio
enseñan engendrados del Gobierno
que las manos les da del ejercicio,
motor de entrambas como amante eterno;
en hombros del Favor y del Auspicio
190   pasan por el Elisio y el Averno,
a verle a sus ventanas van los casos,
porque ninguno salga de sus pasos.

De las dudas que pasan a evidencias
sonoras se descuelgan los conceptos
195   por las cuerdas que son sus contingencias,
cítara de los célicos preceptos:
perspectiva de raras inherencias,
al auditorio de ánimas aceptos,
con ser continua da admiración tanta,
200   que el más enmudecido más la canta.

La materia parece blanda cera
que no se trueca en cuanta forma admite
y Dios el chanciller de tal manera
que un sello no le da sin que otro quite.
205   Sin menguar ni crecer, quedando entera,
a nuevas impresiones se permite,
dócil camaleón, teatro instable
y solamente firme en lo mudable.

Viento de alteractiones la Discordia
210   con tal divide al mundo repugnancia
que besa a la Justicia la Concordia
porque pone concierto en su distancia;

The veil of chilly mist is drawn aside,
the light in everlasting choirs sings
that God creates all things in wisdom,
180 he the end of ends, the being of beings;
out step Variety and Merriment
from different sides to sing his praises
and on a cloud from the lofty royal box,
descend to stage Justice and Clemency.

185 Engendered by the Power that governs all,
Discourse, nurtured by him, and Judgment show
that he grants them the skills of their profession,
moving their hands with love's eternal strings;
on the shoulders of Patronage and Favor,
190 they pass through Elysium and Avernus,
"cases" come to see Judgment from their windows,
so no one shall stray from their accustomed line.

From doubts that are resolved into resounding
proofs, slip gently down the concepts
195 along the c(h)ords that are their contingencies,
a cittern of the celestial precepts:
a "perspective" of rare propensities
for the audience of acceptable souls,
it so amazes in its continuity
200 that the most dumb yet sings its praises loudest.

Matter appears as if made of pliant wax
which yet does not turn to any form it wills,
and God is such a Chancellor that he does not
make one seal without removing another.
205 Not diminishing, not growing, staying whole,
it allows new impressions to be made,
a tractable chameleon, a fickle
stage, constant only in its changefulness.

The wind of violent changes, Discord,
210 divides the world with such contrariety
that Concord speeds to the embrace of Justice,
for Justice reconciles their differences:

mayor que el cielo la Misericordia
lo cubre y trae sonora consonancia
215   con las alas que Dios le da ligeras,
bueno en sus obras, justo en sus carreras.

Manto de gloria el cielo ángeles cubre
y no tapa los ojos penetrantes
con que el supremo Rey siempre descubre
220   las cosas más ocultas y distantes.
Jamás del poder suyo el rastro encubre
en las estampas de sus pies brillantes,
tan dueño de la máquina formada,
que se ve en toda sin mirarse en nada.

225   De cielo, fuego y aire, de agua y tierra
consta el teatro en donde con voz santa
la paz discorde de concorde guerra
del infinito Autor las glorias canta:
responde al cielo que su amor encierra
230   y el cielo al elemento en que levanta
el menor mundo al Rey divino el vuelo
de tierra, de agua, de aire, fuego y cielo.

De su poder da fúlgida evidencia
con la oculta beldad que al hombre llama,
235   todo voces el aire de su ciencia,
todo luces el coro de su fama.
Excede a la mayor circunferencia
y al más distante corazón inflama,
encendiendo a la vida que es su esposa,
240   fuego entre zarzas y entre espinas rosa.

De la luz se divide la tiniebla
y al paso que una baja otra se encumbra:
de asombros ésta un hemisferio puebla
por Dios y aquélla otro hemisferio alumbra.
245   Llama día a la luz, noche a la niebla
y a desposorio tal las acostumbra
que con distancia en lazo de alegría
fue la tarde y mañana sólo un día.

greater than the heavens, lovingkindness
covers the world and brings sweet-sounding harmony
215   on the nimble wings that God bestows on it,
good in his deeds and just in his proceedings.

Mantle of glory, heaven hides the angels
but does not bind the penetrating eyes
with which the supreme King always perceives
220   the things that are most hidden and remote.
He never conceals the traces of his power
in the track left by his shining feet—so much
is he the master of the machine he made
that, evident in all, nowhere is he seen.

225   Of heaven, fire and air, of water and earth
consists the theater where with holy voice
the discordant peace of concordant war
sings the glory of the infinite Author:
he replies to heaven which his love enfolds
230   and heaven to the element through which
the lesser world is raised to the divine King
by flight of earth, water, air, fire and heaven.

Resplendent evidence of his power he gives
with the hidden beauty that calls to man,
235   the air of his knowledge all filled with voices,
the chorus of his fame all suffused with light.
He moves beyond the greatest circumference
and inflames the most distant heart of man,
setting alight the life that is his bride,
240   a flame amid the bush, amid thorns a rose.

From the light the darkness is divided
and as one descends the other rises up:
one hemisphere the second fills with terrors
by God's word and the first lights up the other.
245   He calls the light "day," "night" the misty darkness
and so accustoms them to their betrothal
that, linked through distant by a bond of joy,
the evening and the morning are but one day.

Notes

In the following notes, as in the preparation of the texts themselves, reference has been made to the edition (with introduction) of K. R. Scholberg, *La poesía religosa de Miguel de Barrios*, (Columbus: Ohio State University Press, 1963).

A la muerte de Raquel

In this poem, sonnet 7 in *Flor de Apolo* ([Brussels, 1665], p. 199), Barrios traverses the whole gamut of baroque pessimism, relating to the theme of death. Even though it may have been inspired by the death of his first wife, it seems more of an *exercice de style* and less sincere than the *Sonetos dobles fúnebres* (see below). The interest of the poem lies in the successful combination of baroque themes with the biblical motif.

7 *gala.* "Splendor," "finery," usually applied to clothes, hence the showy outward form.

9 *gloria vana.* A mild wordplay on *vana gloria*, "vainglory."

13 An allusion to the years Jacob served Laban in order to gain Rachel, Genesis 29.

A la segura confianza

Biblical examples are used here to relate the *engaño* or "tricking" of would-be persecutors of Israel with the theme of *desengaño*, the worthlessness of life in this world, for which faith in God is the only cure. (Sonnet 8 in *Flor de Apolo*, p. 200.)

1–8 Three examples from 1 Samuel 17, Daniel 6, and Esther illustrate the idea of historic irony where the would-be persecutor falls victim to poetic justice (a concept which is the mainspring of Golden Age drama).

Real consideración del hombre

This poem, from the collection *Libre albedrío* 'Free will' ([Brussels, 1680], pp. 36–38), shows Barrios writing in the complete Golden Age mold, trying his hand at a favorite gloss of the period on a poem written, according to Lope de Vega, by Pedro de los Reyes. This is the poem which appears immediately after the title. For Christian versions, one may point to an example by Quevedo. The concern with repentance before death and divine judgment, with its overtones of Original Sin, is markedly Christian; however, Barrios skillfully turns this theme into a powerful and sincere expression of his own sense of guilt for past inadequacies of faith and conduct, which one may surmise is the same "Marrano guilt" expressed by the other two poets.

10–11 *conocerse . . ./. . . sabré.* The contrast between these two verbs meaning "to know" is as in French *connaître* and *savoir*, "to be acquainted with" and "to know a fact."

30 *¿Dónde?* = *¿Adónde?* ("whither") shortened for the meter.

38 *immortal . . . en mortal.* An aural wordplay which would have had more effect in the seventeenth century, when orthography hesitated between *i* and *e*.

41–44   The poet may have in mind the burden which baptism (the "water" which is in the gulf, l. 41) represents for the enforced Christian.

59–60   The image is of the poet's entreaties disturbing the sea of his tears, like rain, an interesting variation on the obvious tears/rain analogy.

62   *antojos*. "Desires" or "fancies"; there is a play also on *anteojos*, "spectacles." The illusions, etc., which cloud his vision may be the delusions of his past Christianity.

70   *la injusta* = *la injusta* [*elección*], "the wrong choice."

La memoria renueva el dolor

This extract is the first of the three "Double sonnets of mourning" (from *Estrella de Jacob* [Amsterdam, 1686], pp. 29–32), which make up the poem that Barrios wrote on the death of his second wife.

Title. For the theme of memory as a stimulus of pain, cf. Enríquez Gómez's *Cuando contemplo mi pasada gloria*, l. 16ff.

7–8   Heaven (where the loved one is) is depicted as a blue tree which even as it casts its shadow or provides shade (*sombra* suggests both), sheds the light of their love upon him. The ellipsis is typical of Barrios's *conceptismo*.

27   A familiar metaphor of "burning love" is fused here with the image of the funeral pyre (*humos*, "smoke").

28   *en guerra*. Metaphorically "in turmoil," but also literally "at war": if death is "peace," then life is logically "war."

29–32   This four-line *estribillo* or "coda" provides the themes for the other double sonnets, namely the contrast between the poet's sorrow and his wife's heaven-found joy and the joys and sorrows concerning their three children (the three "pledges" of l. 29).

Alabanza jocosa a la Ley santísima en la fábrica de la sinagoga

Alabanza jocosa is given here according to the version which appears in *Triumpho del Govierno Popular* (Amsterdam, 1683, section *Luces de la Ley*, pp. 9–15, British Library exemplar pp. [589–95]). In it Barrios elaborates the traditional analogy of the Law with a beautiful woman (enshrined in the *chatanim* of the festival of *Simchat Torah*, see below, ll. 181–84) in a virtuoso display of conceits and wordplays. Wit and humor combine with a deep respect on the poet's part for the Law, which is his topic.

1   *casa*. "House," the usual word for the Temple in the vernacular liturgy, hence "synagogue" (cf. Pinto Delgado, *Lamentaciones 1:12*, l. 38).

13–14   A reference to the Rabbinic tradition that the Torah was created before the Creation as the "blueprint" for Creation itself. *Carrera* "career" or "race" (ll. 13, 15) combines with *planta*, "sole of the foot" as well as "plant," to provide an image of running and pursuit, reinforcing the echo of the passage from the liturgy that the Torah is "the Tree of Life to those that seize her."

17–20   Justice (i.e., God as Giver of Justice) has sent the Law to earth for the benefit of Man and now watches, in order to dispense reward or punishment, to see how well he adheres to it.

18   *gracia*. (1) "joke" or "clever stroke," alluding to the irony that what

appears to be misfortune (the struggle of l. 17, with its sexual overtones) turns out to be for the best; (2) "grace," benefit bestowed by God.

22 *los pueblos.* Christianity (and Islam?) which claims to have inherited Israel's role and finds it hard to accept her persistent faith in the Law.

24 *llevar.* (1) "bear," "support" regarding the burdens of being the people of the Law; (2) "prevail," again with sexual overtones.

28 Wordplay depending on different distributions of the words in the phrase; (1) *por no quererla de gracia,* "by not loving it for free": Israel's adherence to the Law brings its cost in suffering; (2) *por no querer la de gracia,* "through not loving that [law] of grace," i.e., Christianity. Note that with this stanza the theme of Israel's martyrs is introduced.

30–31 Exodus 2:10; Moses led the Children of Israel forty years in the wilderness—*cuarentena,* "quarantine," literally a period of forty (days).

33 The reference seems to be to Isaiah 28:9 "Whom shall he teach knowledge? and whom shall he make to understand doctrine? them that are weaned from the milk, and drawn from the breasts."

36 *a pechos toma.* "Takes to heart"; *pechos* = breasts, cf. *niña de teta,* "suckling."

37 Isaiah 44:3 "For I shall pour water upon him that is thirsty."

41 *copa.* (1) The ensemble of leaf and branches of a tree, relating to the idea of the Law as the "Tree of Life" (cf. note l. 14); (2) "bowl" or "cup."

42 *alza.* "Raises" as with a cup or the lifting up of the scrolls of the Law in the service of the synagogue; also "praises."

43–44 Through the association of *copa* (l. 41) with the *kiddush* cup (for the blessing over wine) the image changes to that of the Law as a vine which provides a good vintage for the Jew who through his devoutness proves himself to be of "good stock."

45 *desleído.* "Weak," "diluted," but here used in the sense of the opposite of "well-read" (*leer,* "to read"); this begins a whole series of plays on the idea of letters, printing, and like images.

47 *Saber cuantos son cinco* is the Spanish equivalent of "to know how many beans make five"; an allusion to the five Books of Moses.

48 *alcanza.* (1) "to reach out for"; (2) "to understand."

50 *Semah.* The transcription of Hebrew words here and below follows the poet's own.

51 *a pies juntillas.* "Tenaciously"; literally with feet together, alluding to the fact that the *Amidah* is said standing.

52 *Teba.* The Ark of the Law; the curious change here, compared with *Semah* and *Amidah,* which are both prayers, may be explained by taking *alzada* ("raised" referring to the voice) as applying to *Teba* and meaning "locked up": the sense would then be of shouts of acclamation raised by the worshipers as the scrolls are returned to the ark, which may have been a practice of the period (cf. ll. 171–72).

56 *la Ley de Espada.* "The Law of the Sword," i.e., Christianity.

62 The original sense of *zurrar la badana,* "to flog," was of dressing a sheepskin, suggesting here the parchment used for the scrolls of the Law. Copying out the Law is traditionally the obligation of the pious Jew.

65–66 Israel's suffering for the sake of adhering to the Law becomes part of the lesson of the Law itself; *letra,* "letter" or "hand."

71 *a letra vista.* (1) "openly," "clearly"; (2) by analogy with *letra abierta,*

an open letter of credit.

73–75   These four biblical figures with the Patriarchs make up the seven "planets" which surround the "sun," which is the Law; the "signs," of course, are those of the zodiac.

76   *de marca*. (1) "excellent of its kind," "of good class"; (2) "marked" by circumcision.

79–80   The "mark" becomes now the imprint of God's wrath upon the presumptuous or rebellious.

84   *Poner en la cara* = "to thrust something in someone's face."

85–88   The relationship of God and Israel is a stable and enduring truth compared with the changefulness of nature.

88   *mudanzas*. (1) "changes"; (2) figures performed in dance.

92   *cortada*. (1) "cut to fit," "in proper fashion"; (2) "cut," another reference to circumcision.

96   *humos*. (1) "smoke," cf. image of fire, l. 95; (2) "vanity," "pretension."

santa = santa gente, see l. 94, i.e., Israel, the people of God, who has often curbed their "pretensions" (see previous note).

100   *tienen . . . palabras*. "Converse," a reference to daily prayers.

102   *guardada*. (1) "protected"; (2) "kept," "adhered to."

106   *criada*. (1) "maid"; (2) "made," "created."

109–12   The reference is to the interpreting of the words of the Torah by cryptic means, such as *gematria,* in order to predict the Messianic Coming. Note that the images of letters coalesce here with that of the Law as woman, reintroduced in l. 97.

114   *alcanza*. See note to l. 48.

116   Barrios counters the claim that Judaism is "a creed outworn"; cf. note l. 22.

117–20   Two images are at play here: the struggle of the individual to reach God in heaven (cf. Jacob) and the steps of the *bimah,* or dais, by which one ascends to the Ark of the Law.

121   The theme of martyrdom already seen now centers on a contemporary event, the *auto de fe* held in Madrid, 30 June 1680; a note by Barrios in the *Triumpho* edition of the poem explains the reference.

122   *Carpentania*. Ancient name for the central province in which Madrid lies.

125   *diez cuernos*. The "ten horns" are the various tribunals of the Inquisition; the figure is correct for Portugal (*Lusitania,* l. 128), but fifteen would be more accurate for Spain (*Hesperia,* l. 127).

129   Nothing more is known concerning these two youths.

133   This *auto* took place in Lisbon on 10 May 1682.

140   *Papas*. (1) "Popes"; (2) "paps."

145   Through the transition of martyrs and idolaters we come back to the function of the Law in the practice of the synagogue towards the poem's conclusion.

152   Observance of the Law is equated with the self-sacrifice of martyrs.

154   *tablas*. As well as the Tables of the Decalogue, "planks" or "boards" of a ship used to save one from drowning.

155   Numbers 25: Phinehas, the priest, averted the plague on Israel by slaying Zimri and Cozbi.

157   *Shavuot*, Pentecost, celebrates the giving of the Law to Moses.

160   *Pascua*. Passover, being the festival of freedom, is synonymous with joy.

161   *Kipur*. The Day of Atonement as the day on which Israel is judged for her sins; it ends with the blowing of the *shofar* or ram's horn trumpet (l. 163).

164   *a mano alzada*. Probably a reference to the four cups of wine raised up in the course of the Passover meal.

165   The phylacteries, one of which is worn on the forehead, contain portions of the Law.

166   *en bocas*. The *Amidah* begins "O Lord, open thou my lips that my mouth shall declare thy praise."

168   *el dedo*. The "finger" is that on the "hand" (Hebrew *yad*) which is used for pointing out the text during the reading of the Law (to avoid touching the scroll).

170   Exodus 32:19; *Quebrada*, "broken" in both senses: the physical breaking of the tablets by Moses and the transgression of the Israelites against the Law.

172   *cuando alguno la levanta*. "When anyone lifts her up," i.e., in the course of the synagogue service.

176   An allusion to the Rabbinic expression concerning the many ways in which the Torah can be interpreted.

179   The conventional descriptive terms for a beautiful woman in Golden Age poetry are cleverly applied to the rich adornments found on the covers round the scrolls of the Law.

184   The repetition of l. 160 brings the poem back to the principal festivals with that of *Simchat Torah*, which marks the end and the renewal of the weekly cycle of Pentateuchal readings. *Amantes* (l. 183) refers to the titles *chatan Torah* ("bridegroom of the Law") and *chatan be-reshit* ("bridegroom of the Beginning") given to the men who read the last and first portions of the Law, respectively.

187   *bien vista*. (1) "good to behold"; (2) "well regarded."

188   *ojeada*. "Viewed," "stare at," a humorous analogy for the reading of the Law.

189   *cañas*. "Reeds" or "bones" suggest the casing of the *mezuzah*, containing a portion of the *Shema* and fixed to the doorpost of a Jewish home; *caña* is also a measure of wine, suggesting the celebration which accompanies its fixing.

196   *palmas*. "Palms" as of hand and the palm leaf, which together with certain other plants forms the *lulav* which is waved during the festival of Tabernacles.

197-200   A reference to the custom that those who are called up to the reading of the Law are expected to give a sum of money to charity for the privilege.

204   Barrios carries through the betrothal image to its comic conclusion: it is the Law, as it were, that will "wear the trousers" in this marriage.

Providencia particular de Dios sobre Israel

This poem, from *Estrella de Jacob* (pp. 79–82), takes the form of a disputation on the question of whether God's special regard for Israel is best manifested by his acts of mercy toward her or by his punishment of her enemies. The basic analogy is that of the Exodus.

9   The pillar of fire, Exodus 13:21.

13 ff.   The concept of poetic justice recurs as in *A la segura confianza* (see note to ll. 1–8).

14   Pharaoh's decree against male children of the Israelites, Exodus 1:22.

15   *clama.* (1) "cry out in anguish," i.e., suffering on account of refusing to idolatrize (l. 16); (2) = *llama,* "call," appealing to God (poetic).

16   *llama.* "Flame" but also paronym of verb "to call." (See previous note, (2).

20   *fueros.* In origin, the contractual bonds between individuals in the feudal system of hierarchy, thus appropriate for the relationship of God and Israel.

22   *por.* (1) "by means of": by depriving Adam of the Garden of Eden he was punished; (2) "through," "in," a reference to God's "walking in the garden" (Genesis 3:8).

49–51   Wherever the angel Michael appears, so too is the presence of God, the *Shechinah,* to be found, according to Midrash *Exodus Rabbah* (2:5).

52   *el de la justicia.* The "angel of justice" is Gabriel; for instance, the Rabbis (Talmud Tractate *Shabbath* 55a) identified him as the angel of Ezekiel 9:3–4 who marked the foreheads of those in Jerusalem who were to be spared.

53–55   According to the Post-Talmudic commentator Rashbam, an angel accompanied the pillar of cloud of Exodus 13:21 ff., here assumed to be Michael, as he was the guardian angel of Israel.

55   *Daniel.* Gabriel is referred to by name as the angel who informs Daniel (Dan. 9:21 ff.) of the prophecy of the "seventy weeks," which has Messianic connections (see Enríquez Gómez, *Romance,* ll. 497–503 and note).

74   *plazo.* "Due date" or "term set for the repayment of debt, etc." Cf. Haman's decree, Esther 3:13; according to the Talmud, Esther was enabled to become queen by Gabriel preventing Vashti from appearing at the king's command and thus falling into disfavor.

79   *Al de Amalec.* I.e., Haman, who as an Agagite (see Esther 3:1) was a descendant of Agag, king of Amalek and enemy of Saul in 1 Samuel 15.

83   The destruction of the Assyrian army under Sennacherib, 2 Kings 19:35; Midrash *Exodus Rabbah* (18:5) names Michael as the angel in question.

89   *saludable.* Literally "health-giving," an allusion to the Hebrew meaning of Raphael; similarly Uriel, "light of God," is alluded to in l. 91 *(a su luz).* Barrios thus includes reference to all of the four archangels.

101–2   *la afligida/familia.* The family of Noah: the rainbow (Genesis 9:12 ff.) was the token of the covenant between God and Noah, while the principles the covenant established, the so-called Noachide laws, were a prototype of the Law of Moses.

113   Gabriel is associated here with the pillar of fire, as was Michael with the pillar of cloud (ll. 53–55).

114   *deslumbra* "Dazzles," but also a play on the root word *lumbre,* "light," exploited for its metaphorical associations: the Egyptians are confounded even if they do not actually see the pillar of fire, by virtue of its consequence, which is the safe passage of the Israelites and the drowning of the Egyptians; the causal link is underlined by *del,* literally "of," in the following line.

121   A contemporary reference to the Jewish community of Amsterdam (the *Kahal Kadosh* of l. 127) brings the theme of the poem up to date; the new

synagogue was dedicated in 1675 (see Plate 1, p. 25).

126   The war in question was the Franco-Dutch War of 1672-78, during which William of Orange ordered the opening of the dikes to repel the enemy.

129-36   The poet's conclusion is that God's mercy outweights his vengeance, both materially and spiritually—Israel is granted peace and freedom from tyranny, while her moral security is assured through the Law and the promise of heavenly reward. This is underlined by the play on *celestial*, l. 131, alluding to both the beauty of the Amsterdam synagogue and heavenly reward.

135-36   The idea that Israel's enemies, if their lives are preserved, become witnesses to God's mercy has been present throughout and is now made explicit.

Pregón harmónico del Día del Juicio

Pregón harmónico is the first of a series of poems which Barrios wrote, under the general heading of *Días penitenciales* (in *Estrella de Jacob*, pp. 37–64), for the period of the High Holy Days of the New Year and Day of Atonement which reflect the mood of reflection and repentance. Some of them are actually versions of the liturgy (see below).

Title.   *Día del Juicio* ("Day of Judgment") translates Hebrew *Yom ha-din*, another name for *Yom Kippur*.

5   Cf. title of the collection (see above) to which this poem serves as an introduction.

9-11   Barrios provides notes in the margin, giving biblical references: these will be quoted where relevant and not simply designed to impress. Here: Isaiah 41:1 "let the people renew their strength: let them come near; then let them speak: let us come near together to judgment."

13 Psalms 145:9 "The Lord is good to all; and his mercies are over all his works."

19-20   *a pesar.* (1) "to weigh"; (2) "in spite of."

21   Jeremiah 10:14 "Every man is brutish in his knowledge."

22   *se juzga.* Literally, "judges himself to be." Barrios makes much use in this poem of parallelism, contrasting the two senses of words rather than elaborating conceits out of a single reference.

24   *sentencias.* (1) "judgment" or "sentence" as in law; (2) "wise saying" or "maxim."

27-28   *Caer en cuenta* = "to be brought to account"; cf. *por su cuenta*, "on his account" or "for his own sake."

31   *espacio.* (1) "space"; cf. "time," l. 29; (2) "procrastination," "putting off the evil day;" (3) "diversion," "amusement" (17th century).

35-36   *fuera.* (1) "would be," imperfect subjunctive of *ser*, "to be"; (2) "outside."

38   *fortaleza.* "Fortress," with a suggestion of the abstract noun "strength," "fortitude"; cf. weakness of Man.

39   *piedras.* "stones," hence Tablets of the Law.

43-44   *apenas.* "scarcely," cf. *a penas*, "to pain or punishment." Note also chiasmus of these words with *con llanto*.

46-47   Psalms 145:18 "The Lord is nigh unto all them that call upon him."

51-52   *materia.* (1) "matter under discussion"; (2) "matter" as opposed to "spirit" or "form" (cf. the following).

forma. (1) "form," "ritual" or "established practice"; (2) "form," i.e., the essential modification of matter by which it has existence, as defined in Scholastic philosophy. By means of the ritual of prayer, the essential being of the individual's soul is expressed, from within the confines of his lowly body.

55–56 Barrios combines, perhaps unconsciously, the Jewish symbol of the seven-branched candelabrum with the Christian idea of the church altar as "God's table."

60 *la Ley de Espada*. I.e., Christianity, as in *Alabanza jocosa*, 1. 56.

61–62 1 Kings 6:7; *hierro*, "iron" and *yerro*, "error," "sin," have the same pronunciation.

68 *quien lo venda*. Death is the "binder of eyes" referred to here.

Acto sexto de contrición

Also taken from *Días penitenciales (ed. cit.*, pp. 58–60), this is one of seven "Acts of Contrition" to be found there and is based on a central prayer of the Yom Kippur service, the *Viddui* (short form). Barrios follows the vernacular prayer book as his source, and the corresponding passages will be quoted in the edition *Orden de Ros Asanah y Kypur* of Efraim Bueno and Jona Abravanel (Amsterdam, 1652), pp. 365–66.

1–11 Cf. *Viddui*, first section *Tavo lefanecha:* "Nuestro Dio y Dio de nuestros padres, venga delante ti nuestra rogativa, que no nos desvergonçados de fazes, y duros de ceruiz para dezir delante ti. A. [Adonai] nuestro Dio, y Dios de nuestros padres, justos nos y no pecamos. Empero pecamos, nos, y nuestros padres."

5 *pecho*. Literally, "breast": the Spanish word has connotations of "courage," "boldness"; cf. *audacia* in the previous line.

12–25 Cf. *Viddui*, section *Ashamnu:* "Culpamos, falsamos, robamos, hablamos fealdad, hizimos atorcer y hizimos enmalecer, soberviamos, violamos, ajuntamos falsedad, aconsejamos consejos malos, mentimos, escarnecimos, desobedecimos, aborrecimos, prevaricamos, desviamos, rebelamos, angustiamos, endurecimos cerviz, enmalecimos, dañamos, erramos, abominamos, y hizimos errar."

13 This harks back to the last phrase of the previous section: "pecamos, nos, y nuestros padres."

20 Note how Barrios varies the pattern of the confession by relating the sins to the people whom they affect.

30–32 Cf. *Ashamnu* (cont.): "y apartamos de tus mandamientos, y de tus juyzios los buenos, y no aprovechó a nos."

32 *quebranto*. (1) "breaking" as in contravening God's Law; (2) "breaking" or "being broken," the downfall which results from (1).

33–34 Cf. *Ashamnu* (final part): "y tu justo sobre todo el vinien sobre nos, que verdad hiziste, y nos enmalecimos."

35–44 Cf. section *Atta yodea:* "Que diremos delante ti, morador de alturas, y qué recontaremos delante ti, morador de cielos? de cierto las [cosas] encubiertas, y las descubiertas tu sabes. Tu sabes secretos de mundo, y ocultas de encubrimientos de todo bivo. . . . Sea voluntad delante ti .A. nuestro Dio, y Dio de nuestros padres que perdones a nos (a) todos nuestros pecados, y perdones a nos (a) todos nuestros delitos, y perdones, y quites todos nuestros rebellos."

Acto séptimo de contrición

In the last of the "Acts of Contrition" *(ed. cit.,* pp. 61–64) Barrios treats the theme of repentance with some of the resources of theological disputation on a theme which, according to Scholberg (ibid., p. 348, note 78), was debated in the *Academia de los Floridos.* Baroque subtlety and conceit combine here with a mood of sincere repentance that is rather more than mere playing with words.

3   *tierra.* "Earth," cf. *sol* "Sun"; also in the sense of "dust."

12   *plantas.* "Plants" but also "soles of feet"; cf. *Alabanza,* ll. 13–14 and note.

17–18   Genesis 1:2: "And the Spirit the God moved upon the face of the waters."

19   *mundo . . . inmundo.* "World" and "unclean": the words are visual opposites.

21   *altas.* Strictly goes with *lágrimas* "tears": great in number, they make a deep sea of tears. The sense of "lofty," "nobly inspired" may also be intended.

33 ff.   The assocation of water with "cleansing sin" may be a conscious or unconscious echo of Christian baptism; cf. *Real consideración,* note 1. 41–44.

42–43   Psalms 103:14 "He remembereth that we are dust."

51   *en vela.* "On watch;" possibly with simultaneous idea of "with sails hoisted," from *vela,* "sail."

en calma. (1) "becalmed," hence "at ease," comforted by the idea of forgiveness, (2) "becalmed" in nautical sense, "deprived of wind," suggesting the difficulty of the soul's voyaging.

61   Cf. *hacer un brazo al mar* = "to do something with great pomp and show."

68   *letras.* (1) "letters," cf. images of writing l. 67; (2) "letters of credit," cf. images of payment l. 69.

69   *ejecutoria.* "Writ of execution" or "judgment."

70   *en tormento.* "Torment" or "torture": the memory of the Inquisition and its practices is never far from the surface of the Marrano poet's mind, making it an obvious image to exploit.

79   *antojos.* (1) "fancies," "desires"; (2) = *anteojos,* "spectacles," cf. *Real consideración,* l. 62.

81   *Flamas = Llamas,* "flames" (poetic).

82   *si pido que me asista.* "If I call on you for help": a marginal note by Barrios says "En tarde de *Kipur"* ("On the afternoon of *Yom Kippur").*

92–94   Exodus 2:3 ff.

97–104   The military metaphor no doubt recalls the poet's days as a captain of horse in the Spanish army (also ll. 113–20).

98   *en el cuerpo de guardia.* (1) "in the body [which is] on guard" *(de guardia);* (2) "in the corps of guard."

107–8   Psalms 51:16–17 "For thou desirest not sacrifice; else I would give it: thou delightest not in burnt offering. (17) The sacrifices of God are the broken spirit: a broken and a contrite heart, O God, thou wilt not despise." (Also quoted by Pinto Delgado, *Lamentaciones 2:7,* l. 12, and Enríquez Gómez, *Romance,* ll. 331–36.)

109–10   1 Kings 21:27–29.

115   *ministros.* Civilian officers of the law who would seek to pursue soldiers for civil offenses.

Imperio de Dios en el teatro universal

In this poem, dating from about 1673 (according to Scholberg, *ed. cit.*, p. 102), Barrios presents in verse the story of Creation and discusses its significance with the help of both Jewish sources and classical philosophy. The basic metaphor is that of the stage, God being the Author who presents his work of creation upon the stage of the universe. The extracts are representative passages from a poem which in full is some 125 stanzas *(octavas)* in length.

Title.   The title is that of the fuller second edition (Amsterdam? 1700?) which is followed here; the poet adds a subtitle: "Don Miguel de Barrios draws aside the curtain."

Día primero.   Cf. *jornada* = "act" (of play), which in origin suggests the period of one day. The subtitle suggests other "days" to follow: according to Scholberg, Barrios's intention was to produce a whole *Torah* in verse but encountered opposition from leading members of the Jewish community who considered the idea a profanity.

1–8   This first stanza does not appear in the first edition but it provides a necessary introduction to the setting and principal image of the poem.

(First section: Amsterdam edition, stanzas 1–3)

25   A marginal note by Barrios (of which there are many, mainly of a "cosmetic" nature) reminds us of the existence of another poem on the Creation theme, *La Semaine, ou Création du Monde* by Guillaume Du Bartas (Paris, 1578), which enjoyed a reputation in its day.

29   A note to this line refers the reader to Manasseh ben Israel's popularizing work *Conciliador* (Question 30, Genesis). Barrios draws on the same source for a Talmudic analysis of the first sentence of the Hebrew text of Genesis (stanzas 49–51). Though an interesting curio, it has not been reproduced in this edition, since it amounts to a mere versification of the source and is of no great poetic value.

(Second section: Amst. ed., stanzas 81–91)

33   *prueba.* "Proof," "sign," i.e., of God's hand in the working of the universe: the poem now turns to describing the actual nature of the creative act.

35   *La vision deleitable de la filosofía y artes liberales* was the title of a compendium of medieval sciences written by the fifteenth-century Spaniard Alonso de la Torre.

37–38   The analogy of the full womb is seen in Apocryphal 2 Esdras 4:40–42, where, however, the context is that of the origin of evil; the angel is Uriel, the angel of enlightenment (cf. *Providencia particular*, l. 91).

40   *a luz lo saca.* (1) "Brings it to the light," i.e., gives light to it; (2) cf. *dar a luz*, "to give birth to." The metaphor of birth is taken up at various points later.

41–44   The poet argues that even the greatest of Greek philosophers were unable to explain the origin of the world in terms of the "logical truth" which is the One God.

47   *principio.* "Principle" in the sense of (1) fundamental origin, and (2) guide to conduct, etc.

57   *teom.* The sense of this Hebrew word is explained by the following words in the line. Barrios indicates his source to be Ruth 1:19 "all the city was moved [*tehom*, "astir"] about them."

71   *alas*. Normally "wings" (a cliché in combination with "love"), here "stunsails" or "studding sails."

73   *mistión*. "Mixture": the suggestion of childbirth, however, is evident from the rest of the stanza.

77   The Law is seen as created "in the beginning"; cf. *Alabanza jocosa*, ll. 13–14 and note.

81   *sefirot*. An allusion to Kabbalistic ideas which deeply interested the poet; it could be said that his very treating of the theme of Creation reflects a Kabbalistic concern.

82   *se elevan*. (1) "are raised"; (2) "exult," "are elated." The image is of the *sefirot* or spheres being created as it were to form an audience for God's "play."

97–120   A passage of pure lyricism rare in Barrios's poetry, beautifully achieved.

104   *sarao*. "An informal evening dance" (Portuguese *sarão*).

105   *Arión*. The name of Arion, the Greek poet who was saved from drowning by a dolphin, is synonymous with harmony.

(Third section: Amst. ed., stanzas 110–125)

122   *publicar*. "Publish" in the original sense of "make public."

128   *nada en sí*. "Nothing in itself": while being the ultimate Creator, God does not preside over every act of coming into being.

129–30   God is seen as weighing everything in the chaos in order to assess its potential before "building"; God the "Artificer," an image seen elsewhere in the poem (stanza 104: not reproduced), becomes almost at once that of God the "Father" (ll. 131, 136).

135   *planta*. Also "sole of foot"; cf. *mano*, "hand."

138   *mistión*. See note l. 73: the image of Creation as childbirth fuses into that of writing a play as childbirth. The metaphor of God as playwright is now fully developed to the end of the poem.

141   *apuntados*. "Prompted" in theatrical sense.

142   *dándose abrazos*. "Embracing each other"; also possibly = *dándose a brazos*, "coming to grips," as in the conflict developed by the plot.

144   *El secreto a voces* is the title of a play by Calderón de la Barca, dating from 1642 when Barrios was still in Spain: that he expected his readers to pick up the reference attests to the continuous flow of literary contact between Spain and Amsterdam. The point of the title is of course that God, though hidden, is revealed in his creation.

145   ff. Nature replaces childbirth as the second element in the continuing double metaphor.

147   *jornada*. "Act" (see note above on subtitle of poem).

148   *entablado*. "Put on stage" from *tabla*, "stage."

149–51   The standard form of drama in the period was the *comedia de capa y espada* ("cloak and dagger"), plays of honor, in which complicated plots (*enredo*, l. 151) develop as a result of some *malentendu* (*engaño*, l. 151). Frequently (cf. l. 150) an appeal to the king is resorted to in order to resolve such complications—unless the reference is to God as the ultimate *deus ex machina*.

161   ff. The type of theater pictured here is that of the later Golden Age, in which much use was made of stage machinery such as descending tableaux or

chariots lowered from gallery to stage; see N. D. Shergold, *A History of the Spanish Stage* (Oxford, 1967), p. 372 ff.

165–66   An allusion to the use of a multiplicity of doors for surprise entrances.

169–72   Wordplay on the idea of *arco*, "bow" or "arch" (l. 171), by way of *arco iris*, "rainbow," God's sign to Noah, through to *paz*, "peace" or "kiss of peace" (l. 169).

185   *a sus pechos.* From *pechos*, "breasts," hence "nurtured"; possibly also a reference to the chest as source of the voice, the use of which is an important element of the actor's craft.

187   *manos.* "Hands," hence "skills," "dexterity."

188   *motor.* A word taken from philosophy denoting God as the Prime Mover.

  amante. (1) "lover"; (2) "ropes guiding a ship's sails."

190   *Elisio . . . Averno.* Representations of heaven and hell on the stage, or possibly a reference to the success or failure of a play.

191   *casos.* (1) "cases" as in a court of law; (2) = *casos de honra*, the "questions of honor" which form the substance of the play's plot. The first idea is taken up by the reference to God's judgment in *-le* (l. 191) which looks back to *Juicio* (l. 185).

192   *ninguno.* (1) "no one"; (2) "neither one" referring back to *Discurso* and *Juicio* in l. 185: neither Man's "discourse" nor his "judgment" (the word does double duty, cf. previous note) should err if he is to be favorably judged by God. *salga de sus pasos.* Cf. *salir de su paso*, "to vary one's behavior or normal way of acting," from *paso* = "step"; *paso* also suggests the movement of actors on stage, as well as being a "sketch" or "curtain raiser" or "passage of writing" as in a play.

195   *cuerdas.* (1) "cord," "rope" used for the descent of an actor to stage (cf. ll. 146–51 and note); (2) "string" as of musical instrument, cf. *cítara*, l. 196. Note the way in which images from philosophy are drawn into the stage metaphor to ring the changes.

197   *perspectiva.* "Perspective" as in a stage set.

227   This is the resolution of the conflicting elements of Chaos into a harmony which is nonetheless disparate and divergent.

230   *elemento.* "Element," i.e., the soul. The reference to the ascent of the soul to heaven may again reflect Kabbalistic mystical notions or those of the Spanish mystical poets such as Luis de León (the two are not without their interrelation).

239   *esposa.* "Bride": the image of the soul as the "bride of Christ" is extensively exploited, by San Juan de la Cruz in particular, among the Christian mystics. Note that for the Kabbalists the *Shechinah* was also the "bride of God."

Bibliography of Principal Works Consulted

General

Alonso, Martín. *Enciclopedia del idioma*. Madrid: Aguilar, 1958.

Alonso García, Damián. *Literatura oral del ladino entre los sefardíes de oriente a través del romancero*. Madrid: World Sephardi Federation, 1970.

Babylonian Talmud. Edited by I. Epstein. London: Soncino Press, 1935.

Beinart, H. "The *Converso* Community in 15th Century Spain" and "The *Converso* Community in 16th and 17th Century Spain." In *The Sephardi Heritage*, edited by R. D. Barnett, pp. 425–78. London: Vallentine, Mitchell, 1971.

Benardete, M. *The Hispanic Culture of the Sephardic Jew*. New York: Hispanic Institute in the United States, 1953.

La Biblia, que es, los sacros libros del Viejo y Nueuo Testamento. Trasladada en Español. [Translated by Cassiodoro de Reyna.] [Basle], 1569.

Blondheim, D. S. *Les Parlers Judéo-Romans et la vetus latina*. Paris, 1925.

Caro Baroja, J. *Los judíos en la España moderna y contemporánea*. 3 vols. Madrid: Ediciones Arion, 1961–62.

———. "El proceso de Bartolomé Febos o Febo." In *Homenaje a don Ramón Carande*, vol. 2, pp. 59–92. Madrid: Sociedad de Estudios y Publicaciones.

Castro, Americo. *La realidad histórica de España*. Buenos Aires: Biblioteca Porrúa, no. 4, 1954; English edition, *The Structure of Spanish History*, translated by E. L. King. Princeton, N.J.: Princeton University Press, 1954.

Jones, R. O. *A Literary History of Spain. The Golden Age: Prose and Poetry*. London: Benn, 1971.

Lea, H. C. *A History of the Inquisition in Spain*. 4 vols. New York: Macmillan Co., 1906.

292

Menéndez y Pelayo, M. *Historia de los heterodoxos españoles*. 2d ed. Madrid: Consejo Superior de Investigaciones Científicas, 1965.

Orden de Ros Asanah y Kypur, traduzido en Español, y de nuevo enmendado y añadido el Keter Malchut y otras cosas. Amsterdam: Ephraim Bueno & Jona Abravanel, 5412 [1652].

The Oxford Book of Spanish Verse. 2d ed. Edited by J. B. Trend. Oxford: Clarendon Press, 1940.

Quevedo y Villegas, Francisco Gómez de. *Las lágrimas de Hieremías castellanas*. Edited by J. M. Blecua and E. M. Wilson. Madrid, 1953 (*Revista de filólogia española*, Anejo 55).

Révah, I.-S. "Histoires des parlers judéo-espagnoles." *Annuaire du Collège de France*, 1970, pp. 553–62.

———. "Les Marranes." *Revue des études juives* 118 (1960): 29–77.

———. "Les Marranes portugais et l'Inquisition au XVIᵉ siècle." In *The Sephardi Heritage*, edited by R. D. Barnett, pp. 479–526. London: Vallentine, Mitchell, 1971.

———. *Spinoza et le Dr. Juan de Prado*. Etudes juives, vol. 1. Paris, 1959.

Rose, C. H. *Alonso Núñez de Reinoso: The Lament of a Sixteenth-Century Exile*. Rutherford, N.J.: Fairleigh Dickinson University Press, 1971.

Roth, Cecil. "Le chant du cygne de Don Lope de Vera." *Revue des études juives* 97 (1934): 97–113.

———. *A History of the Marranos*. London, 1932; new ed., New York: Jewish Publication Society of America, 1966.

———. *A Life of Manasseh ben Israel*. Philadelphia, 1934.

———. "Les Marranes à Rouen." *Revue des études juives* 88 (1929): 113–37.

———. "The Religion of the Marranos." *Jewish Quarterly Review*, n.s. 2 (1931–32): 1–33.

———. "The Rôle of Spanish in the Marrano Diaspora." In *Studies in Honour of I. González Llubera*, edited by F. Pierce, pp. 299–308. Oxford: Dolphin Book Co., 1959

Shergold, N.D. *A History of the Spanish Stage from Medieval Times until the End of the Nineteenth Century*. Oxford: Clarendon Press, 1967.

Sicroff, A. *Les controverses des statuts de "pureté de sang" en Espagne du XVᵉ au XVIIᵉ siècle*. Etudes de littérature étrangère et comparée, no. 39. Paris: Didier, 1960.

Silver, A. H. *A History of Messianic Speculation in Israel from the*

First through the Seventeenth Century. 2d ed. Boston: Macmillan, 1959.

Van Praag, J. A. "Almas en litigio." *Clavileño* 1 (1950): 14–26.

Wagner, M. L. *Caracteres generales del judeo-español de Oriente.* Madrid, 1930 (*Revista de filológica española,* Anejo 12).

Yerushalmi, Y. H. *From Spanish Court to Italian Ghetto—Isaac Cardoso: A Study in Seventeenth Century Marranism and Jewish Apologetics.* New York: Columbia University Press, 1970.

Individual Poets: Works and Studies

João Pinto Delgado

Delgado, João Pinto. "Dialogos contra a cristiandade" [title given by later bibliographer for Pinto Delgado's "Autobiography"; see Révah, below]. Portugees Israelitisch Seminarium *Etz Haim,* Amsterdam, MS 48 D 39.

———. *Poema de la Reyna Ester. Lamentaciones del Propheta Ieremias. Historia de Rut, y varias Poesías.* Rouen: David du Petit Val, 1627. Facsimile edition, with introduction by I. S. Révah, Lisbon: Institut Français au Portugal, 1954.

Fishlock, A. D. H. "The *Lamentaciones* of João Pinto Delgado." *Atlante* 3 (1955): 47–61.

———. "Lope de Vega's *La hermosa Ester* and Pinto Delgado's *Poema de la Reyna Ester:* A Comparative Study." *Bulletin of Hispanic Studies* 32 (1955): 81–97.

———. "The Poems of João Pinto Delgado." Ph.D. diss., University of London, 1952.

———. "The Rabbinic Material in the *Ester* of Pinto Delgado." *Journal of Jewish Studies* 2 (1950–51): 37–50.

Révah, I. S. "Autobiographie d'un Marrane, édition partielle d'un manuscrit de João (Moseh) Pinto Delgado." *Revue des études juives* 119 (1960): 41–130.

Wilson, E. M. "The Poetry of João Pinto Delgado." *Journal of Jewish Studies* 1 (1948–49): 131–43.

Antonio Enríquez Gómez

Gómez, Antonio Enríquez. *Academias morales de las Musas.* Bordeaux: Pedro de la Court, 1642.

————. *La culpa del primer peregrino*. Rouen: Laurent Maurry, 1644.

————. "Romance al diuin Martir Juda Creyente martirizado em valledolosid [*sic*] por la Inquisision." Bodleian Library, MS Opp. Add. 4° 150 (Neubauer Catalogue no. 2481), fols. 46v–50r.

————. "Romance que se hizo a Bien Abenturado Juda Creiente que fue quemado Biuo por la Unidad de Dios, y obseruante de la Ley de Mosseh dada por Dios a Israel, siendo de Rasa de gentil, siendo preso por el Tirano tribunal de la Inquisicion." Portugees Israelitisch Seminarium *Etz Haim*, Amsterdam, MS 48 A 23 (second manuscript of preceding). See also Roth, "Le chant du cygne," *Revue des études juives* 97 (1934) in general bibliography.

————. *Sansón Nazareno*. Rouen: Laurent Maurry, 1656.

García Valdecasas, J. G. *Las "Academias morales" de Antonio Enríquez Gómez (Críticas sociales y jurídicas en los versos herméticos de un "judío" español en el exilio)*. Seville: Publicaciones de la Universidad de Sevilla, Serie Derecho no. 9, 1970.

Oelman, T. "Antonio Enríquez Gómez's 'Romance al divín mártir, Judá Creyente': Edited Text with Introduction." *Journal of Jewish Studies* 26 (1975): 113–31.

————. "Two Poems of Antonio Enríquez Gómez: *Romance al divín mártir, Judá Creyente* and *Sansón Nazareno* (edited texts with introduction and notes)." Ph.D. diss., University of London, 1976.

Révah, I. S. "Antonio Enríquez Gómez" [lecture synopsis]. *Ecole pratique des Hautes Etudes, IVᵉ Section Sciences historiques et philologiques, Annuaire*, 1966, pp. 338–41.

————. "Un Pamphlet contre l'Inquisition d'Antonio Enríquez Gómez: La Seconde Partie de la 'Politica Angelica' (Rouen, 1647)." *Revue des études juives* 121 (1962): 82–168 (for authoritative biography of Enríquez Gomez).

Rose, C. H. "Antonio Enríquez Gómez and the Literature of Exile." *Romanische Forschungen* 85 (1973): 63–77.

Miguel de Barrios

Barrios, Miguel de. *Estrella de Jacob sobre Flores de Lis*. Amsterdam, 1686.

————. *Flor de Apolo*. Brussels: Baltazar Vivien, 1665.

————. *Imperio de Dios en la Harmonía del Mundo*. [Amsterdam?], [1700?].

————. *Triumpho del Govierno Popular y de la Antiquedad Holandesa*. Amsterdam, 5443 [1683].

Scholberg, K. R. *La Poesía Religiosa de Miguel de Barrios*. Columbus: Ohio State University Press, 1963.

————. "Miguel de Barrios and the Amsterdam Sephardic Community." *Jewish Quarterly Review* 53 (1962–63): 120–59.

See also the following reviews of Scholberg, *Le poesía religiosa:* Pring-Mill, R. D. F., *Romantisches Jahrbuch* 15 (1963): 370–72; and Wilson, E. M., *Bulletin of Hispanic Studies* 40 (1963): 178–80.

Printed and bound by CPI Group (UK) Ltd, Croydon, CR0 4YY

13/04/2025